J.K. LASSER PRO™

GUIDE TO TAX AND FINANCIAL ISSUES IN DIVORCE

Bruce L. Richman,
CPA/ABV, CVA, CDP

John Wiley & Sons, Inc.

Library of Congress Cataloging-in-Publication Data:

Richman, Bruce L.
    J.K Lasser pro guide to tax and financial issues in divorce / Bruce L. Richman.
        p. cm. — (J.K. Lasser pro series)
    Includes index.
        ISBN 0-471-09888-4 (cloth : acid-free paper)
        1. Divorce settlements—Taxation—United States. 2. Close corporations—Valuation—United States. 3. Equitable distribution of marital property—United States. I. Title: Guide to tax and financial issues in divorce. II. Title. III. Series.
    KF6333 .R53 2002
    343.7305'2'08653—dc21

                                                        2001007528

Printed in the United States of America.

10 9 8 7 6 5 4 3 2 1

Contents

iv Contents

Preface

Going through divorce can be one of the most traumatic things we do. The uncertainty, despair, financial burdens, and the loss of someone we really loved and cared about at one time. In many cases a loss of a good friend. A commitment that has gone bad.

But divorce is also a new start, the next phase in one's life. A learning experience and growth in the process of life. Experience. As someone once said to me, if you are over 30 and do not have any baggage, then you have not experienced life.

I hope that this book will give the guidance and the knowledge to help you through the process and get you set for the next phase of your life.

Having gone through the process, I miss my last relationship and the friendship that I had. She is truly my friend.

My children are always special to me, and I wish them the best in life and will always be there for them. Joshua, Talia, and Noah are the joy of my life and they are always in my heart and on my mind. I love each of them.

Acknowledgments

Putting together this book was based on knowledge and experience that I have gathered over many years working in the area of divorce. I have been blessed to have worked with some of the finest matrimonial attorneys, from whom I have learned a great deal. I also thank the fine family law organizations at which I have had the opportunity to speak, and whose members I have met and learned so much from: the American Academy of Matrimonial Lawyers, the Family Law section of the American Bar Association, and the Family Law section of the Illinois State Bar Association, to name a few.

I would also like to give a special thanks to Gunnar Gitlin, who was instrumental in giving me guidance with this book and who provided me with great assistance and encouragement. I have been honored and privileged to have worked with Gunnar and coauthored other material with him in the past. A true professional.

Gunnar J. Gitlin is a partner in the matrimonial law firm of Gitlin & Gitlin in Woodstock, Illinois (located approximately 50 miles northwest of Chicago). He is a Fellow of the American Academy of Matrimonial Lawyers (AAML). Mr. Gitlin has frequently lectured on family law topics to organizations, including the Law Education Institute (1999, 2001), Illinois Institute for Continuing Legal Education, the AAML, the Illinois State Bar Association, and various local bar associations.

Mr. Gitlin is the author of numerous articles published in the *Illinois Bar Journal* including an article published in August 2000 on final and appealable orders in divorce cases. He is the coauthor of the Business Valuation Chapter of the

Illinois Institute for Continuing Legal Education's Illinois *Family Law Handbook* (2000 edition). He is also the author of "Business Valuation in Divorce—What is Double-Dipping and How is it Quantified?" published in the *American Journal of Family Law* and cited in the bibliography of *Valuing Small Businesses & Professional Practices,* 3rd Edition, 1998, and *Valuing a Business,* 4th Edition, 2000.

Gunnar J. Gitlin has created a CD-ROM database, "Gitlin on Divorce Computer Research System." It contains a report of every significant Illinois family law case since January, 1987. Mr. Gitlin is a member of the Board of Governors of the Illinois Chapter of the AAML and is a member of various committees of the AAML. In June 2001 he was co-chair of the American Academy of Matrimonial Lawyer's Institute for Family Law Associates (1999–2000, 2000–2001). He is also coeditor of the American Bar Association Family Law Section's Fax News Update Service (1999–2001).

SECTION

I

FINANCIAL ASPECTS OF DIVORCE

CHAPTER

1

Introduction

The devastating truth hits one Monday afternoon when you are served with divorce papers. Whether it comes as a surprise or not, the reality that you are about to go through a divorce has now hit. We now rush to defend. The feelings of anger, hurt, getting even, and winning begin to go through one's mind. The problem is we begin to think from the heart and not the head. It is not uncommon to feel lost, scared, empty, and uncertain. What will the future bring? What will this cost me? How can I survive? What is my attorney doing? These are all feelings and questions that both men and women have. Many battles would not need to be fought if we only knew the financial consequences.

Knowledge Is Power

The question "Is my attorney really being creative and understanding of my financial consequences?" is often met with a blank stare. The key to a successful divorce and the ability to negotiate on an equal footing with your spouse is knowledge. Knowledge is power. The reason most cases can not be mediated is the lack of knowledge by one party or both. The more knowledge the parties have, the more likely a case is to be settled and the easier they will feel with the final settlement. This book will provide that knowledge in the area of tax and financial matters that affect divorce. Various areas of divorce will be covered with the use of checklists and easy to read discussions of the topics, laid out in a direct format. The book is broken down into three sections: Section I—Financial Aspects of

3

Divorce, Section II—The Tax Side of Divorce, and Section III—The Valuation Process.

The book is designed not only as a technical resource but as a guide to assist you in raising the issues or questions to ask your attorney or soon to be ex-spouse. It is also designed for those who have not filed for divorce but wish to familiarize themselves with the multitude of issues that will need to be addressed and in effect do some pre-divorce planning. Interestingly enough, for many, this will be the first time that they get a true understanding of their personal financial situation. I have had many clients, married for 20, 25, and 35 years, who never even knew what their total family assets, or even their living expenses, were. In many cases, neither spouse really know what the other spouse earned. There is often a false understanding of what life should be and what it really is. Again, this may be the first time that both parties get a true picture of their expenses and earnings. Though, at times I refer specifically to men or maybe women, my comments are truly gender neutral. I have had many sophisticated clients who did not have any true idea of the details of their spending and the makeup of their assets. For those who do not have major estates and huge incomes, the simple knowledge of the basic tax and financial issues can lead the parties to accept the reality and work out a proper settlement. Knowing, understanding, and accepting what you have as a marital estate can take you a long way from what you think you deserve, which may be totally warranted, to what is equitable based on the marital estate.

Finding and Selecting the Right Divorce Attorney

Putting a professional team together to complete your divorce in a successful and cost efficient manner is an important first step. Many people will run out to hire a big name attorney in an effort to scare their spouse. Wrong! Again, it goes back to using one's head and not heart when interviewing lawyers and understanding their strengths and weaknesses and the type of cases that they deal with. It is very important to find out how much work they do in divorce. I believe that the practice of matrimonial law is one of the most difficult areas because the divorce lawyer not only needs to understand the law, but play psychologist, understand tax issues and financial matters, have a business acumen, ability to negotiate, and understand real estate and business valuations. Thus, finding a lawyer who practices in this area full time is a critical element in the selection process. Figure 1.1 provides a checklist to use when interviewing a prospective attorney. Using the checklist in your discussions will enable you to compare the candidates and make an informed decision.

It is also important to understand the type of case that you have: Is child custody an issue? Do you have a significant estate? Do you have sophisticated invest-

FIGURE 1.1   Checklist for Selecting an Attorney

Question to ask or information to obtain	Response
Do you charge a consultation fee for an initial consultation?	
Do you provide a written memorandum on the consultation and the advice given?	
What is the complete name of the law firm?	
What is the name of the lead attorney assigned to your case?	
Is he or she a partner in the firm?	
Who is the associate to be assigned to your case, if any?	
How much time will the associate be assigned to your case as opposed to your lead attorney?	
For each attorney obtain their resume and ask about their experience.	
How many years has the attorney been practicing as a divorce attorney?	
Does the attorney handle divorces on a full time basis?	
What are their strengths? Do they specialize in litigation, child custody matters, financial matters, etc.?	
What is the name of any paralegal that would be assigned to your case? (Remember, that the use of paralegals in a simple asset and income case can lead to significant savings).	

(continued)

FIGURE 1.1   Continued

Question to ask or information to obtain	Response
What is the name of the lawyer's secretary or administrative assistant?	
What is the fee arrangement that the lawyer will charge and how does he or she charge?	
What is the amount of the retainer?	
How will the attorney get paid and when? Will you be required to pay monthly or will the attorney wait until the case is settled to get paid?	
What is the lawyer's policy on returning phone calls? When should you expect to have your phone calls returned?	
Does the attorney believe in and support mediation as a form of settling a case?	
Is the lawyer(s) who will be on your case a member of the American Academy of Matrimonial Lawyers?	
Is the attorney listed in the book, Best Lawyers in America? (This book lists the top lawyers in the nation in their various fields of specialization.)	
Who do you think are the best matrimonial lawyers and how do you compare to them?	

ments?, etc. It is important for you to ask yourself these questions honestly so that you can select the right attorney for your case. Each attorney may have a particular expertise or strength in a specific area, such as child custody or financial matters.

The first question I hear is always, where do I start in finding the right lawyer? If you already have located a good certified divorce planner or financial expert, that person should be able to assist you in your search. Some people find a divorce lawyer through recommendations from professionals such as clergy, therapists, and marriage counselors. Other lawyers that you may know are often also a good referral source for a divorce lawyer. With any referral source, you can always ask "Would you send your brother, mother, or sister to them?"

The local Bar Association can also provide you with names of experienced matrimonial lawyers. In this case, always ask for a couple of names so you will have a few to interview. Calling the local chapter of the American Academy of Matrimonial Lawyers is also a good source of qualified matrimonial attorneys. If you go to the library you can probably look in the Martindale-Hubbell Law Directory or The Best Lawyers in America. Given today's technology, the Internet is another source to begin your search. Lastly, if all else fails, you can always turn to the yellow pages. Many states do not allow lawyers to state a specialty, however, they usually will allow them to state that their practice is "concentrated in" or "limited to" an area of law, such as matrimonial.

In the end, one of the most important factors to consider when selecting an attorney is their reputation. Ask other matrimonial lawyers what they think of a particular attorney. The responses may shock you.

During your initial interview, besides just asking the questions in Figure 1.1, start to get a feel for whether or not you and the lawyer will be compatible. Remember you will be spending a lot of time with this attorney and your future financial well-being may be tied to his or her performance as well as personal needs and desires from the case. Make sure that you can share your most confidential matters with the lawyer without you feeling that the lawyer is being condescending or judgmental. It is very important that there is good chemistry between the lawyer and yourself. The problem with this area is that most of it will be based on your gut feeling and how you feel when you come away from the interview. Remember to write down your feelings so you can go back to your notes later on in the selection process.

A number of people going through divorce, especially when there are not a lot of assets involved and the people are civil, will ask whether the lawyer they find can represent both parties in an effort to save costs. Since attorneys are advocates for their clients, this is a difficult situation for an attorney. I do not know many that would handle it and I would not recommend it. If you have an issue or a question that may be advantageous to you, it will probably be disadvantageous to your spouse. In essence, both you and your spouse should have your own representation. Having said this, this does not stop you from representing yourself. Representing yourself in court without the assistance of an attorney is called *pro se*. But remember the old saying, "A person who represents himself, has a fool for a lawyer".

Gathering of the Assets

The first step is to gather and understand what the marital estate is. Many couples live like kings with very few assets to show for it. They may be living a million-dollar lifestyle only to find out they are in debt with very few real assets. So where can I turn to find out what my assets are? First pull together the obvious assets that you are aware of:

- *The personal residence.* Pull the insurance policy. There may be a rider attached detailing personal property and jewelry and its appraised value. Obtain a copy of any recent appraisals that you may have. (If you recently refinanced your mortgage, there would have been an appraisal. Go to your local real estate agents and ask them to pull the recent sales from the multiple listings to get an idea of the current fair market value. Then you can go on the Internet to find a preliminary value of your house. Take pictures of your house.

- *Obtain a copy of the most recent mortgage statement.* If you know who is servicing your mortgage, you can call and get a history of the payments made and the current balance outstanding and if there is an escrow account maintained. Many times real estate taxes are escrowed and paid by the mortgage company. Any excess escrow amount would be an asset of the marital estate.

- *Listing of all bank accounts.* Include those that are checking, savings, and money market accounts. A simple review of schedule B of your joint federal individual income tax return will assist you.

- *Investment accounts.* This includes all brokerage accounts, mutual funds, and CDs. Even if you and your spouse trade on-line, there will be an account and a listing of investments. This should also include stock options from your employer including those that are vested and non-vested. Given the environment of the dot.com companies, a large portion of management and even staff's compensation may be in some form of a stock option. What a stock option is, how it is valued, taxed, and handled for purposes of the divorce is important. The issue of stock options in divorce and how to handle them is still developing and a basic overview of this subject is summarized in Appendix A.

■ *Retirement Accounts.* This will include not only both spouses' individual retirement accounts (IRAs) but also all employer-sponsored plans: Defined Contribution Plans (profit sharing and 401(k) plans); Defined Benefit Plans (pension plans); Nonqualified plans (Stock Appreciation Rights); and Employee Stock Option Plans (ESOPs). Defined Contribution and Defined Benefit plans are discussed in Chapter 6. Normally, employer-sponsored plans will have a handbook describing the plan and its benefits. It is also not uncommon for the employer to provide a summary of benefits.

■ *Business Interests.* This would include all closely held businesses that you or your spouse owns. These can be ones that you are active in, such as a business which you own and work at or investments made from a passive investment perspective such as an investment in a real estate limited partnership. The key here will be the determination of the fair market value of these business interests. In Section III we provide a straightforward overview of this process and basic terminology used by appraisers. Again, a review of one's federal tax return can provide information on one's pass-through investments.

■ *Life Insurance.* When listing the various life insurance policies, it is important not only to know the amount of coverage, but also the cash surrender value. Obtain details such as: policy number; beneficiary; insured; cash value; policy holder loans; and owner of the policy.

■ *List of personal property.* Don't be afraid to photograph or video tape the contents of your residence. You can also hire an expert to inventory and value your personal property.

■ *Automobiles.* List the make, model, and year of each vehicle. Make a distinction between those that are owned and leased. The values can be determined easily through the Internet from one of the auto sites that price out used vehicles.

■ *Other miscellaneous items.* Include items such as boats, artwork, jewelry, coin or stamp collections, and airline mileage. (This becomes tricky as most airlines will not allow the transfer of miles, thus forcing one spouse to cash in tickets to be used over the next year.)

- *Liabilities.* Don't forget to list all of the liabilities such as: credit cards, personal loans, and judgments. It is important that any loans between family members be documented to show intent as a loan as opposed to a gift.

These items can be put into a marital balance sheet which will summarize the assets and liabilities. Additionally, the spreadsheet can be used to allocate assets and determine the overall allocation of the marital estate. Figure 1.2 provides an example of a marital balance sheet worksheet. You will notice that the worksheet not only lists the individual assets but also categorizes them between marital and non-marital and provides an area to show how the allocation of the assets for settlement may be structured. For those states that are not community property states, usually the assets are allocated on an equitable basis. It is important to note that equitable does not necessarily mean equal. This concept is further discussed later in this section. However, the beauty of this worksheet prepared in Excel, is that it provides a complete picture of the parties' assets and how their allocation will provide each on an individual basis and as a percentage of the total marital estate. A worksheet such as this one gives a good picture of the proposed or negotiated settlement. The next step would be to use this worksheet to analyze the individual assets allocated and the income that they will generate for purposes of assistance with one's annual cash flow needs. The worksheet can also be used to look at those assets that will grow in the future and use it as a starting point to see how each party's net worth will grow or decrease over time. This can assist in determining whether a proposed allocation is equitable. Obtaining an equitable distribution of the marital estate requires understanding of the business assets, tax implications, pension rules, etc. Thus, the marital balance sheet worksheet is the best place to start in determining what type of discovery will need to be done, what experts will be needed, and what other issues will need to be resolved. Although in Section II we deal with the tax issues of divorce, it is important to mention here that though each state may handle tax implications differently, in general it is important that your attorney understands how the tax issues impact the equality of the assets allocated and get this into evidence. In most states, if your attorney does not get the tax implications into evidence, the judge may not be bound to consider its implications. However, in a few states, the courts will not speculate as to the future impact of the tax that may or may not arise in the future and will only consider situations where the tax is imminent. Remember that not only are you and your spouse interested in the tax impact of your divorce, but so is the IRS. I have seen many a case that has been settled due to the fact that going to trial could generate serious problems with the IRS. There is a saying to remember, even if you are bitter with your soon-to-be ex, "Don't kill the goose that lays the gold eggs."

FIGURE 1.2 Marital Balance Sheet

IN RE MARRIAGE OF BOATMAN
NOAH and DEZ BOATMAN
SUMMARY OF MARITAL ASSETS AND LIABILITIES

Asset No.	Asset Category/ Description		Account Number	Owner	Date Valued	VALUE	MARITAL ASSETS	NON-MARITAL ASSETS	Ref.	ALLOCATION OF MARITAL ASSETS NOAH	DEZ
ASSETS											
I	RESIDENCE										
1	17 Boat Lane, Boatville, MA										
	Current Value		$ 700,000.00		8/31/01				A		
	Less:										
	Mortgage Value—Fleet Mortgage		(187,142.16)		8/31/01				B		
	NET EQUITY					512,857.84	$ 512,857.84				$ 512,857.84
2	Residential Lot in the new Boatville development										
	Current Value—Land		150,000.00		7/15/01				C		
	Less:										
	Mortgage Value		$ (50,000.00)						D		
	NET EQUITY					$ 100,000.00	100,000.00			$ 100,000.00	
	Total Residence					$ 612,857.84	$ 612,857.84	$ -		$ 100,000.00	$ 512,857.84
II	CASH AND CASH EQUIVALENTS										
1	First Bank of Boatville	prime savings	12-245-665	W	7/15/01	$ 55,000.00		$ 55,000.00	E	$ -	
2	First Bank of Boatville	checking	35-5684-558	JT	8/15/01	3,500.00	3,500.00		F		3,500.00
3	First Bank of Boatville	savings	0254-58-9985	JT	8/15/01	25,000.00	25,000.00		G		25,000.00
7	Boatville Savings National Bank	checking	226548	H	8/31/01	36,759.13	36,759.13		H	36,759.13	-
8	Boatville Savings National Bank	Money Market	435895	H	8/31/01	95,534.23	95,534.23		I	25,400.00	70,134.23
14	Cash—held in safe at home by Noah				8/31/01	52,000.00	52,000.00		J	52,000.00	
	Total Cash & Cash Equivalents					$ 267,793.36	$ 212,793.36	$ 55,000.00		$ 114,159.13 #	$ 98,634.23

(continued)

FIGURE 1.2 Continued

Asset No.	Asset Category/Description		Account Number	Owner	Date Valued	VALUE	MARITAL ASSETS	NON-MARITAL ASSETS	Ref.	ALLOCATION OF MARITAL ASSETS	
										NOAH	DEZ
III	INVESTMENT ACCOUNTS										
1	Goldman Sachs	stocks	6589-58-98774	H	8/12/01	$ 625,000.00		$ 625,000.00	K	$ -	$
2	Morgan Stanley	stocks	56-5959842	H	8/31/01	210,000.00	210,000.00		L	210,000.00	
3	Boatville Investments	stocks	652894	H	8/10/01	52,500.00	52,500.00		M	52,500.00	
4	Merrill Lynch	stocks	54H-56481S	H	8/31/01	1,173,500.00	1,173,500.00		N		1,173,500.00
	Total Investment Accounts					$ 2,061,000.00	$ 1,436,000.00	$ 625,000.00		$ 262,500.00	$ 1,173,500.00
IV	RETIREMENT ACCOUNTS										
1	Individual Retirement Accounts (IRA)—Noah Boatville Investments		1369052	H	8/31/01	$ 535,460.00	$ 535,460.00		O	$ 535,460.00	
2	Individual Retirement Accounts (IRA)—Dez Morgan Stanley		5689-56-R	W	8/20/01	123,600.00	123,600.00		P		$ 123,600.00
3	Profit Sharing Plan—Noah's from Boatmake, Inc. Profit Sharing Plan			H	8/31/01	896,425.00	896,425.00		Q	448,212.50	448,212.50
	Total Retirement Accounts					$ 1,555,485.00	$ 1,555,485.00	$ —		$ 983,672.50	$ 571,812.50
V	REAL ESTATE:										
1	15 Boat Street, Boatville, MA Current Value: Less: Mortgage Value:	Rental Property $ 325,000.00 (168,000.00)				$ 157,000.00	$ 157,000.00		R	-	157,000.00
	Total Real Estate					$ 157,000.00	$ 157,000.00	$ -		$ -	$ 157,000.00

12

VI LIFE INSURANCE

1 Empire General Life Assurance Corporation
Policy Number: 00060929
Insured: Noah
Beneficiary: Dez
Total Death Benefit: $ 1,000,000
Policy Value: $ 36,750.00
Existing Debt: 0
Net Cash Surrender Value: $ 36,750.00
Policy Owner: Noah

	$ 36,750.00		36,750.00		S	$ 36,750.00
Total Life Insurance	$ 36,750.00		36,750.00	$	-	$ 36,750.00

VII BUSINESS INTERESTS

Boatmake, Inc.	750 shares (75% ownership) Valued by Valuators are Us, Inc.	H	975,000.00	975,000.00	T	$ 975,000.00
Total Business Interests			$ 975,000.00	975,000.00	$ -	$ 975,000.00

VIII AUTOMOBILES

1 2000 500SE Mercedes		H	65,000.00	65,000.00	U	65,000.00
4 2001 Honda MiniVan		W	26,500.00	26,500.00	V	26,500.00
Total Automobiles			$ 91,500.00	91,500.00	$ -	$ 26,500.00

IX HOUSEHOLD FURNISHINGS

1 Furniture and Fixtures		JT	45,000.00	45,000.00	W	$ 45,000.00
2 Antiques	Dez's personal collection	W	265,000.00	125,000.00	140,000.00 X	125,000.00
Total Household Furnishings			$ 310,000.00	170,000.00	140,000.00	$ 170,000.00

(continued)

13

FIGURE 1.2 Continued

Asset No.	Asset Category/Description	Account Number	Owner	Date Valued	VALUE	MARITAL ASSETS	NON-MARITAL ASSETS	Ref.	ALLOCATION OF MARITAL ASSETS	
									NOAH	DEZ
X	MISCELLANEOUS									
1	Jewelry		W	8/17/01	$ 186,000.00	$ 186,000.00		Y		186,000.00
2	Airline Mileage	1.5 million miles on United	H	8/31/01	18,750.00	18,750.00		Z	18,750.00	-
3	Base Ball Card Collection		H	8/26/01	38,000.00		38,000.00	AA		
4	Doll Collection		W	8/10/01	19,250.00		19,250.00	AB		
	Total Miscellaneous				$ 262,000.00	$ 204,750.00	$ 57,250.00		$ 18,750.00	$ 186,000.00
	TOTAL ASSETS				$ 6,329,386.20	$ 5,452,136.20	$ 877,250.00		$ 2,555,831.63	$ 2,896,304.57
XI	LIABILITIES									
	Credit Cards									
	Master Card	2159-8486-84	W	8/21/01	9,750.00	9,750.00		AC	9,750	
	Visa	254-55895-879541	H	8/31/01	3,750.00	3,750.00		AC	3,750	
	Total Credit Cards				$ 13,500.00	$ 13,500.00	$ -		$ 13,500.00	$ -
XII	Other Debt									
	Taxes due on 2000 Income tax liability					$ 34,500.00	$ 34,500.00			$ 34,500.00
	Note due to the Business—Boatmake, Inc.					132,000.00	132,000.00			132,000.00
	Loan to Mother				6,000.00	6,000.00			6,000.00	
					$ 172,500.00	$ 172,500.00	$ -		$ 172,500.00	$ -
	TOTAL LIABILITIES				$ 186,000.00	$ 186,000.00	$ -		$ 186,000.00	$ -
	NET WORTH				$ 6,143,386.20	$ 5,266,136.20	$ 877,250.00		$ 2,369,831.63	$ 2,896,304.57

	NOAH	DEZ
OVERALL ALLOCATION PERCENTAGE OF MARITAL ESTATE	45.00%	55.00%
OVERALL ALLOCATION PERCENTAGE OF MARITAL ESTATE AND AFTER CONSIDERING EACH PERSON'S NON-MARITAL PROPERTY	39.19%	60.81%
OVERALL ALLOCATION PERCENTAGES		

14

FOOTNOTES:

(A) Owner Abbreviations

JT = Joint Ownership
H = Owned by Husband
W = Owned by Wife

(B) Sources of Value

A Appraisal done by Real Estate Realty Group on as of August 31, 2001
B Mortgage statement dated 8/31/01
C Since this was just purchased on June 30, 2001, the purchase price was used.
D Mortgage taken from Boatville Mortgage Company
E Per monthly statement dated 7/16/01
F Per monthly statement dated 8/15/01
G Per monthly statement dated 8/15/01
H Per monthly statement dated 8/31/01
I Per monthly statement dated 8/31/01
J Per monthly statement dated 8/31/01
K Per printout of statement from online service
L Per faxed statement from Morgan Stanley as of 8/31/01
M Per monthly statement dated 8/10/01
N Per monthly statement dated 8/31/01
O Per monthly statement dated 8/31/01
P Per computer printout from A J. Broker on 8/20/01
Q Monthly brokerage statement for 8/31/01
R Appraisal done by Real Estate Realty Group on as of August 31, 2001 and mortgage statement from Mortgage are Us, Inc.
S Per statement of benefits from Noah's agent from Boatville Insurance Group
T Valuation by The Investigative Valuation Group, LLC as prepared as of August 31, 2001. The IV Group was appointed by the Court as the independent evaluator.
U Kelley Blue Book value as of 8/31/2001, assumed 35,000 miles per year
V Kelley Blue Book value as of 8/31/2001, assumed 15,000 miles per year
W Valued by Mia Johnston, ASA a certified personal property expert with MJ Furniture sellers.
X Valued by Mia Johnston, ASA a certified personal property expert with MJ Furniture sellers.
Y Valued by Mrs. Jane Knowing, a certified gemologist as of 8/31/01
Z Per Noah's monthly mileage statement dated 8/31/01. Assumed 20,000 needed per ticket with an assumed value of $250 per ticket.
AA Appraised by the Baseball Collectors Group from Cooperstown, NY on June 30, 2001. This was originally done for the insurance coverage on the collection.
BB Appraised by an expert from the Insurance company which appraised it for insurance coverage on May 17, 2001
CC Per 8/31/01 monthly credit card statement.

15

Discovery

In order to obtain the complete list of assets, both parties will need to make a full disclosure of the assets that they have. However, just because the assets are not disclosed by one spouse does not necessarily mean that other assets don't exist. This is where the phase of the divorce process called discovery comes in. In this phase research and investigation is important. A proper laid out plan for discovery is key and the participants of the divorce can play a key role in working with their attorney in getting this done, but like anything else there is a cost versus benefit to everything and the discovery phase is no exception. Sitting down and being realistic and having your lawyer be realistic with you is important. I have seen parties spend thousands of dollars in the discovery phase only to find no more in assets than had been previously disclosed, but one spouse was on a mission or witch hunt to satisfy personal feelings and beliefs. Remember the old saying, "I know he has millions hidden away," even though he has worked for a company as a laborer making only $50,000 a year and supporting a family of five for the last ten years. The discovery phase is important but it has to be handled wisely and cost effectively.

In the discovery process, as well as throughout the divorce process, a Certified Divorce Planner or forensic accountant who has a specialty in divorce can be a great asset. By giving advice and working with the attorney, the forensic accountant can be a key member of the divorce team. The earlier the financial expert is involved, the better. It is important that the financial expert meets with the client early as this is an important tool in creating the framework and being able to address the issues specific to the individual. These professionals, who are usually accountants or CPAs by background, are trained to read and interpret financial data. They have the ability to take the information obtained through discovery, analyze it, and organize it into a useful and understandable form. The forensic accountant well-versed in matrimonial matters can: The key is having a financial advisor or forensic accountant who is a specialist in divorce matters. It takes a person who has direct experience to add value to your team. My advice is don't settle for Uncle Joe who is the family CPA.

- Identify the issues of the case at the initial stage of the divorce, provide direction, and avoid being too late at the end.

- Assist the attorney in the discovery process by ensuring that the necessary documents are identified and ultimately requested. Financial experts are trained to locate, read, and interpret financial data and put it in a format that is useful and easy to follow for the attorney and client.

- Show best case and worst case scenarios and add some reality to the decision-making process by giving an independent view of the situation. Remember, a good independent financial expert is an advocate of his or her own opinion, as opposed to the personal feelings of the client.

- Assist in structuring a divorce settlement by clearly showing the financial impact of the various offers that are present and providing creative and alternative settlement ideas.

- Review and address all of the tax consequences of the divorce settlement. So many times this is overlooked in the settlement and the drafting of the settlement agreement and only found when it is too late to correct.

- Provide valuation of the various business interests that the parties may have. Though discussed later, many of the good forensic accountants in divorce are well-trained in the area of business valuations. Again, this goes into reviewing the qualifications of your financial expert and his or her experience in divorce situations.

- Assist in preparation of the attorney for the opposing financial expert's deposition and examination at trial.

- Provide testimony at trial if the case is not settled with regards to the financial matters. The financial expert may also be called to explain difficult and technical matters to both sides to assist in the settling of a case.

As you can see, a good financial expert, well-versed in matrimonial and valuation matters, can be a key asset to any divorce team. However, the seasoned financial expert does not replace the lawyer or the legal skills that the lawyer brings to the table. He or she supplements and enhances the attorney's skills which is why finding the right expert is key. There are many who would like to be in this area of practice as opposed to actually being in this area. Family law has its own unique issues and concepts and it is important to select a financial expert who is adept and knowledgeable of family law and its many concepts in order to avoid the many pitfalls that can occur in this area. Like selecting an attorney, this is a difficult process because it is not something one is involved with every day. The key elements to consider are:

- Look for referrals. Usually this can come from the attorney you are using or interviewing. (The expert you hire can also assist in selecting the right attorney for your case.)

- Ask for a curriculum vitae (CV), which should provide details of the consultant's experience and qualifications.

- Find out what percentage of the consultant's business is in the area of family law because just like in the attorney selection process, you want someone who is well-seasoned in this area, not a part-time practitioner.

- Look on the Internet under divorce.

- Attend seminars where forensic accountants and financial experts in matrimonial matters will be speaking. This gives you a chance to see their skills and technical abilities in understanding the key issues.

- Call the various professional societies, such as the American Institute of Certified Public Accountants (they have a society in every state); American Academy of Matrimonial Attorneys; Society of Certified Divorce Planners; National Association of Certified Valuation Analysts. You can also search the various web sites under divorce and financial advisors.

Additionally, be active in your case. Not only can you be a great source of information, depending on your skills, your involvement may reduce the attorney's and accountant's fees and costs by doing some of the work that may have been done by them. Additionally, being involved keeps you updated on the status of your case and the strategies being implemented.

As previously mentioned, the key to getting infor mation is through the process of discovery. The attorney can obtain information and documents by such source as:

- *A notice to produce.* A formal legal request of specific documents submitted by your attorney to the opposing counsel

- *Subpoena.* A formal legal request directly to the source of the documents, such as a subpoena to the credit card company for copies of the husband's monthly credit card statements for the past five years

- *Written interrogatories.* Formal written legal request to have the other side answer specific questions in writing

- *Deposition.* A formal legal setting where individuals will be asked specific questions by your attorney while they are under oath. The proceedings are recorded by a court reporter who will produce a transcript of the session. As mentioned previously, the financial expert can be of great help in preparing the attorney when deposing other financial experts and developing questions for obtaining financial information.

The information obtained through a notice to produce can be used for many phases of the divorce in addition to determining the assets of the marital estate, such as in developing the couple's lifestyle and the valuation of any closely held business. It is important in today's electronic age that the information you request is all inclusive, consisting of not only originals and hard copies, but to include all information maintained on a computer disk, computer hard drives, back-up disks, and so on. An example of the documents requested in a general notice to produce is shown in Figure 1.3.

FIGURE 1.3   General Financial Document Request—Notice To Produce

---

Unless otherwise stated this document request is for documents covering the period of 1998 through 2001.

A. **Individual Tax Returns:** Federal and state income tax returns (see Figure 1.4, the Request for Copy or Transcript of Tax Form 4506), including all schedules and W-2 statements, for the years 1998 through the present, filed by you, or filed by anyone on your behalf, or filed by another or others holding an interest in the below described property, whether jointly or solely, including any of the entities listed below:

   a. Business entities in which you own or owned during the years stated. This includes sole proprietorships, partnerships, joint ventures, and corporations;

   b. Trusts in which you have or had during the years listed above a beneficial interest.

   c. Trusts in which you act or acted during the years listed above as a trustee.

B. **Documents Supporting Tax Returns:** The following documents relating to all returns produced pursuant to item number 1 above, including:

   1. Amended returns;

   2. Estimated returns and vouchers;

   3. All schedules filed with the return;

   4. All worksheets used in preparing the return, whether the worksheets were prepared by you or by an agent acting on your behalf;

(continued)

FIGURE 1.3   Continued

---

5. All documents used to support any deductions being claimed;

6. All W-2 forms, 1099 forms, and any other verifications of income received;

7. All notices, correspondence, and documents relating to audit or review of your return.

C. **Paycheck Stubs and Documents Reflecting Income:**

1. Your paycheck stubs for the last _____ pay periods prior to the date of this notice.

2. All other documents indicating salaries, commissions, overtime, bonuses, and compensation from _____ to date.

3. All documents reflecting payment for or reimbursement to you for automobile, travel, entertainment, meals, personal living expenses, and all other benefits provided to you by your employer or from any source.

D. **Financial Statements:** Copies of all financial statements and records containing financial information, net worth, or loan statements, which have been submitted by you to a bank or lending institution, or in connection with applications for credit, for the last _____ months.

E. **Employment Contracts, Employee Manuals, etc:** Written employment contracts which you have entered into since _____. Any other documents, letters, manuals, etc. memorializing or otherwise setting forth the terms of your employment, your pay structure, your employee benefits, etc.

F. **Partnership Agreements and Tax Returns:**

1. Any written partnership or joint venture agreements which you have entered into within the past _____ months.

2. Tax returns for any partnership or joint venture in which you have been involved for the past _____ years.

G. **Life Insurance:** All policies of life insurance owned by you, whether on your life, or the life of anyone else, including any such policies which have been canceled, or otherwise terminated for any reason, since _____. Documents shall include: a) statement of beneficiaries and changes of beneficiaries; b) all statements of cash surrender values; and c) all statements indicating loans taken against the cash surrender value and verification of payment of premiums.

FIGURE 1.3   Continued

H. **Health Insurance:** All policies of health insurance (medical/hospital) certificates for such policies and any written materials setting forth the benefits of such policies, which policies are owned by you, or supplied to you by your employer.

I. **Savings, Checking, and Other Accounts:** All bank statements, passbooks, canceled checks, check registers and withdrawal and deposit slips for all checking accounts, savings accounts, NOW accounts, credit union accounts, certificates of deposit, or any other type of bank account or form of deposit, in your name individually, or jointly with any other person or entity, in the name of another individual on your behalf, in your name as trustee, guardian, or custodian. Provide all such documents for any such accounts, whether open or closed from _____, to date. For all such accounts for whose records you keep in any computerized financial accounting or planning program such as Quicken, Money, etc., provide copies of the computer data on disk, together with all printed reports and information identifying the program for the past _____ years.

J. **Monies Owed to You:** All accounts receivable now due to you, or any other documentation of monies now due to you, including, but not limited to, any written contract or agreement by virtue of which money is due to you, mortgages, trust deeds, and promissory notes.

K. **Stock, Mutual Funds, Bonds, etc.:** All documents relating to stocks, securities, mutual funds, bonds, and money market accounts—owned by you, whether jointly or solely, standing in your name as trustee, guardian, or custodian for another or held by a trust in which you were the beneficiary—at any time from _____ to present.

L. **Brokerage Account:** Brokerage account documents shall include:

1. Monthly statements detailing all transactions and balances in accounts including margin accounts;

2. Confirmations, receipts, and cancelled checks for each security transaction;

3. Bills for commissions and receipts or canceled checks indicating such payment.

4. Copies of all brokerage account statements for any brokerage account in which you had an interest for the past _____ months.

(continued)

FIGURE 1.3   Continued

M. **Other:** Stocks or securities acquired by any means other than a brokerage account, the documents shall include:

1. The certificates, bonds or security;

2. Bills, receipts, and cancelled checks showing the purchase or sales of stocks or securities;

3. All documents evidencing acquisition by gift, inheritance, exchange, stock split, or any other means.

N. **Stock Options:** Copies of all savings, stock purchases, and stock option plans in which you participate through your employer or which are available to you through your employer or otherwise. Include all statements indicating amounts being held in such plans for your benefit, all transactions affecting such plans, and any projections regarding future value.

O. **Estate Documents:** All records and documents you have in your possession relating to the estate of _____, deceased. Such documents include the will and any codicils to the will; all inventories and accountings filed with the court, all correspondence with the executor/administrator, the court and other beneficiaries and all pleadings relating to any litigation which involves the estate.

P. **Retirement Benefits and Loan Documents Through Employer:**

1. All documents evidencing any interest you have in deferred income plans, including, but not limited to, pension plans, retirement plans, annuities, employee stock option plans, thrift plans, etc., including the following: the summary plan description (often called the plan booklet), all plan documents, all statements from the plan since _____ to date, and written plan procedures which are used by any plan in order to determine if a domestic relations order is qualified.

2. All documents and statements indicating any loans from your employer or otherwise, whether directly from credit union or taken out using amounts in pension, profit sharing, retirement, savings, stock purchase, or stock options plans as collateral.

3. Written reports or opinions of any expert *(including, but not limited to, actuary, accountant, business consultant)* regarding any profit sharing, pension, retirement, or other deferred payment plan of either of the parties.

FIGURE 1.3   Continued

Q. **Real Estate Documents:** All documents relating to real estate in which you have an interest currently or had an interest from _____ to the present, whether as sole or joint owner, beneficiary of a trust, holder of an option to purchase of mortgagee. Such documents shall include:

   1. Deeds, policies of title insurance, and closing statements.

   2. Trust agreements and certificates of beneficial interest;

   3. Mortgages and notes and documents relating to payments of the mortgage or note;

   4. The most recent real estate tax bill and receipt for payment of such bill;

   5. Appraisals, market analyses, or written opinions of value;

   6. Leases relating to the use of the real estate and records relating to any rental income received and expenses paid;

   7. Documents indicating the source of all funds used in purchasing the property;

   8. Homeowners and all other insurance covering the real estate and contents of the real estate.

R. **Rented Property:** A copy of your current lease for any premises being rented by you, whether solely or with another or for any premises at which you currently reside.

S. **Debts:** All documents evidencing your current debts including:

   1. All existing notes, installment notes, and contracts to purchase; and

   2. The latest available monthly statements on all outstanding installment credit accounts including, but not limited to, the latest statement of all credit card accounts.

   3. Other Credit Card and Charge Card Documents: All records relating to credit cards and charge accounts to which you have the right to charge, whether held by you or by another, together with all statements received by you in connection with the use of such credit cards and charge accounts, and all credit applications whether or not such credit was approved.

(continued)

FIGURE 1.3 Continued

T. **Personal Property or Assets:** All documents reflecting the acquisition, whether by purchase or otherwise or the disposal, whether by sale or otherwise from _____ to the present of any of the following:

1. Automobiles, boats, airplanes;

2. Stocks, bonds, securities, or stock options;

3. Commodities contracts;

4. Gold, silver, or any other precious metals;

5. Gas, oil, or mineral rights or leases;

6. Artwork worth $500 or more;

7. Jewelry worth $1,000 or more;

8. Antiques, oriental rugs, any item of personal furnishings worth $500 or more;

9. Fur coats;

10. Coins, stamps, and other collections, if the collection is worth more than $500; Foreign currencies;

11. Other items of personal property worth in excess of $500.

U. **Value re Personal Property or Valuation of Other Assets:** All appraisals, opinions of value, and policies of insurance covering all of the items listed in paragraph T, immediately above.

V. **Safety Deposit Boxes or Rental/Storage Space:** All documents relating to the rental and use of a safe deposit box and rental storage space, whether rented by you jointly or solely, by you as trustee, guardian, or custodian for another; or by another who has given you a right of access, from _____ to the present. Documents shall include:

1. Rental agreements;

2. Records relating to changes in names of persons allowed access to the box or storage facility;

3. Records relating to entities in the box or facility; and

4. Inventories of all contents.

FIGURE 1.3   Continued

W. **Intellectual Property Rights:** All documents concerning all intellectual property rights, including but not limited to patents or copyrights in which you have an interest or for which you have filed or plan to file an application, as well as the status of each patent and the registration number(s).

X. **Club Memberships**—All documents concerning any club membership of yours, including but not limited to, membership documents and documents evidencing the value of membership, purchase price, mandatory spending requirements, suggested contribution, and transfer price.

You should also request that your spouse produce an affidavit stating whether or not the production they submit is complete.

Additionally, when issuing subpoenas to either your spouse's accountant or their company's accountant make sure to include a request for their complete correspondence file as they may have been planning the divorce or other transactions with their accountant and this could lead to hidden assets. After obtaining information directly from the spouse through the means previously listed, look to other sources that have information about you, your spouse, and your family's finances. Some of these are:

- *Employers.* Valuable information can be obtained from your spouse's employer, and if your spouse owns the business, the review of corporate documents will be even more important. Additional information to be obtained from the employer beside the Federal Form W-2 include benefits that your spouse receives as an employee: health and medical coverage; life insurance; disability insurance; portable telephone (The detailed monthly billing can provide important information on your spouse's activities and acquaintances.); retirement plan information; company care and/or auto allowance; profit sharing; and liberal expense accounts to name a few. Depending on your state, employment benefits may have value to the marital estate. Obtaining your spouse's personnel file may also provide unknown information about a pending promotion; issuance of stock options; pending ownership; potential bonuses and pending raises, as well as other benefits. You may also discover the amount of control your spouse has over the amount of his/her compensation, the timing of it and how he/she receives it. If your spouse is the owner of a closely held

FIGURE 1.4   Request for Copy or Transcript of Tax Form

Form **4506**

(Rev. May 1997)

Department of the Treasury
Internal Revenue Service

Request for Copy or Transcript of Tax Form

▶ Read instructions before completing this form.

▶ Type or print clearly. Request may be rejected if the form is incomplete or illegible.

OMB No. 1545-0429

Note: *Do not* use this form to get *tax account information. Instead, see instructions below.*

1a Name shown on tax form. If a joint return, enter the name shown first.	1b First social security number on tax form or employer identification number (see instructions)
2a If a joint return, spouse's name shown on tax form	2b Second social security number on tax form

3   Current name, address (including apt., room, or suite no.), city, state, and ZIP code

4   Address, (including apt., room, or suite no.), city, state, and ZIP code shown on the last return filed if different from line 3

5   If copy of form or a tax return transcript is to be mailed to someone else, enter the third party's name and address

6   If we cannot find a record of your tax form and you want the payment refunded to the third party, check here . . . . . . ▶ ☐

7   If name in third party's records differs from line 1a above, enter that name here (see instructions) ▶

8   Check only one box to show what you want. There is **no charge** for items 8a, b, and c:

a ☐ Tax return transcript of Form 1040 series filed during the **current calendar year** and the **3 prior calendar years** (see instructions).

b ☐ Verification of nonfiling.

c ☐ Form(s) W-2 information (see instructions).

d ☐ Copy of tax form and all attachments (including Form(s) W-2, schedules, or other forms). **The charge is $23 for each period requested.**
   Note: *If these copies must be certified for court or administrative proceedings, see instructions and check here* . . . . . ▶ ☐

9   If this request is to meet a requirement of one of the following, check all boxes that apply.
   ☐ Small Business Administration   ☐ Department of Education   ☐ Department of Veterans Affairs   ☐ Financial institutic

10 **Tax form number** (Form 1040, 1040A, 941, etc.)	12 Complete only if **line 8d** is checked. Amount due:
11 **Tax period(s)** (year or period ended date). If more than four, see instructions.	a Cost for each period . . . . $ 23.00
	b Number of tax periods requested on line 11
	c Total cost. Multiply line 12a by line 12b. . $
	Full payment must accompany your request. Make check or money order payable to "Internal Revenue Service."

Caution: *Before signing, make sure all items are complete and the form is dated.*
I declare that I am either the taxpayer whose name is shown on line 1a or 2a, or a person authorized to obtain the tax information requested. I am aware that based upon this form, the IRS will release the tax information requested to any party shown on line 5. The IRS has no control over what that party does with the information.

Please
Sign
Here

▶ Signature. See instructions. If other than taxpayer, attach authorization document.   Date

Title (if line 1a above is a corporation, partnership, estate, or trust)

Spouse's signature   Date

Telephone number of requester
(   )

Best time to call

TRY A TAX RETURN TRANSCRIPT (see line 8a instructions)

Instructions

Section references are to the Internal Revenue Code.

TIP: If you had your tax form filled in by a paid preparer, check first to see if you can get a copy from the preparer. This may save you both time and money.

Purpose of Form.—Use Form 4506 to get a tax return transcript, verification that you did not file a Federal tax return, Form W-2 information, or a copy of a tax form. Allow 6 weeks after you file a tax form before you request a copy of it or a transcript. For W-2

information, wait 13 months after the end of the year in which the wages were earned. For example, wait until Feb. 1999 to request W-2 information for wages earned in 1997.

Do not use this form to request Forms 1099 or tax account information. See this page for details on how to get these items.

Note: *Form 4506 must be received by the IRS within 60 calendar days after the date you signed and dated the request.*

How Long Will It Take?—You can get a tax return transcript or verification of nonfiling within 7 to 10 workdays after the IRS receives your request. It can take up to 60 calendar

days to get a copy of a tax form or W-2 information. To avoid any delay, be sure to furnish all the information asked for on Form 4506.

Forms 1099.—If you need a copy of a Form 1099, contact the payer. If the payer cannot help you, call or visit the IRS to get Form 1099 information.

Tax Account Information.—If you need a statement of your tax account showing any later changes that you or the IRS made to the original return, request tax account information. Tax account information lists

(Continued on back)

For Privacy Act and Paperwork Reduction Act Notice, see back of form.   Cat. No. 41721E   Form **4506** (Rev. 5-97)

company, a whole other issue arises: what is your spouse's true economic income? This issue and the discussion of Recently Acquired Income Deficiency Syndrome (RAIDS) as well as personal assets hidden inside the company are discussed in detail later in this chapter.

■ *Banking institutions and credit reports.* Banking institutions will have all sorts of information on you and your spouse. If there are any loans or credit cards there will be credit applications that can have valuable information. They may also have a credit report which will show you and your spouse's credit history. Many people are surprised to find what is on their credit report. I recommend that you pull your own credit report which can be obtained from any number of credit reporting agencies. They can also be obtained through the Internet. The information such as a list of current credit cards, credit available, and reported income and other financial information can be used in comparing what your spouse has produced in individual disclosures. Typically, a bank that handles the corporation will have the loan or account officer prepare a relationship summary which gives an overview of the entity. If there is bank financing involved, look at their notes for the reason for approving the financing and the support provided for it. You may find out about a direction the company is going that is different from what your spouse is presenting to you, either directly or through an attorney or valuation expert. You will want to look at what security the bank has taken collateral for any financing provided. You may find assets that you were not aware of as well as values that again are quite different than what has been presented to you by your spouse or his experts. Additionally, it is not uncommon that the bank files may have cash flow projections with regard to the business. They may also have other due diligence records about the company or your spouse individually.

■ *Personal and/or corporate accountant.* The accountant's work papers can be a wonderful source of information. The key is to make sure that you get the accountant's notes and correspondence file. Include in your request to obtain anything that they maintain on their computer or on disk to see if there has been any planning and changes in corporate assets or the accounting of things to disguise personal usage. Additionally, obtain any and all of the following documents from the accountant: engagement letters; engagement planning memorandums; tax planning worksheets; in addition to the current workpapers, ask for the permanent file as well; representation letters; management letters; attorney letters; the accountant's billing file which contains all invoices and time records, and any summaries describing the services performed and who performed them. You should also ask for copies of any letters on internal control that the accountant may have issued.

- *Investment broker or advisor.* When opening an account there are numerous forms that need to be completed. Included in these forms are all sorts of information regarding net worth and income. The advisor may also have a file on your spouse containing notes from planning meetings as well as a list of accounts that have been opened by your spouse or on their behalf.

- *Insurance agent.* The insurance agent's file will contain applications for all life insurance and will provide any information on changes to beneficiaries. Also, you may be able to find insurance coverage on hidden assets or assets being used by parties outside of the marriage. For example, I have pulled an auto insurance package that the insurance agent put together only to find that the premiums covered more than just the two cars that were driven by the husband and his wife. Needless to say, the other auto covered was not one driven by any of their children. In other cases, it not uncommon to find an umbrella policy or an extension to the home owners policy which covers jewelry or other valuables. This can provide a good list of assets to look for and a first attempt at their current values.

- *Social Security.* The government provides a summary of an individual's social security benefits. Don't forget a copy of this report. Remember, if you have been married for 10 years, you may be entitled to a piece of your spouse's benefits. This statement also shows a summary of reported earnings.

The Concept of Marital versus Nonmarital (Separate) Property

Become familiar with the law in your state regarding property. You may have heard the terms community property or marital property. What are these terms and how will they affect your divorce? A minority of states are community property states including Arizona, California, Idaho, Louisiana, Nevada, New Mexico, Texas, Washington, and Wisconsin. A community property state assumes that all property acquired during a marriage belongs to both spouses equally. However, only three of the community property states, California, Louisiana, and New Mexico require that community property be divided equally upon divorce. The other states are called marital property states. If you live in such a state, all property acquired during the marriage is presumed to be marital property, subject to several exceptions. The most common exceptions include property acquired by gift or through an inheritance.

In some states, there is a presumption that either marital property or community property will be divided equally. In those states the starting place for the lawyers and the court is an equal property division. The property can be divided unequally but the person seeking an unequal division has to prove that he or she is entitled to more than half the property.

In most states there is no presumption that the marital or community property should be divided equally. Instead, the law provides that this property is to be divided equitably or fairly. Equitable does not necessarily mean 50/50. For example, suppose that a woman has been a homemaker for the entire length of her 25 year marriage and gave up a career to support her husband's career. The husband has climbed the corporate ladder and will have the ability to replace his assets. In order to maintain her lifestyle it maybe necessary for her to obtain a greater share of the assets. The unequal allocation of the assets in this situation would probably be considered equitable. Again, as discussed earlier, to be truly equitable the tax consequences on the ultimate property and support settlement will need to be considered. Though each state will have its own guidelines, there are some common factors that the court uses in dividing such property fairly. These factors include: the length of the marriage; the contribution made to the other spouse's education; the non-economic contribution of the children's custodian to the marriage; the health of the parties, and so on.

Having discussed this distinction in community property states, a more general rule in defining what non-marital property (also called separate property) may be as follows: generally all property acquired during the marriage is marital property, subject to certain exceptions. The common exceptions are:

- In all marital property states, inheritances are considered separate (non-marital) property.

- In most states gifts from third parties are the separate property of the acquiring spouse, even if they were received during the marriage. However, this does not affect gifts made to both parties jointly. Therefore, consider whether any substantial gift was made to one of the parties or jointly to the parties. Often evidence of such gifts may include the submission of gift tax returns, the manner in which the funds were paid, and so on. States are divided in terms of treatment of gifts from one spouse to another made during a marriage. Some states consider gifts such as birthday gifts, to be gifts while other states presume that such gifts are marital in character. Thus estate planning by an individual's parents should be reviewed very carefully, and the consequences of divorce should be considered in their drafting.

■ Property acquired in exchange for separate property remains separate property, even if acquired during the marriage. If the parties going through a divorce do not agree at the time of a divorce on whether the asset was acquired in exchange for separate property, determining its character may require tracing the source of funds used to acquire the property. In most states, when this tracing exercise provides an ambiguous result, the property is presumed to be marital. Again, the use of the financial expert with divorce experience can prove to be invaluable.

■ In some states property acquired during the marriage is defined as meaning after the parties are married but before the service of a petition for divorce (assuming the petition ultimately results in a decree of divorce), unless the court specifically sets forth written findings of fact establishing that the use of other dates (such as the date of the divorce) is necessary to avoid a substantial injustice.

■ Generally, all property acquired before the marriage is considered as separate property. In some states, the courts will occasionally treat property acquired in anticipation of the marriage such as a marital home purchased shortly before the marriage as marital property if certain conditions are met. Other states reject such claims entirely.

One of the jobs that a financial expert with expertise in divorce can assist in is the tracing of marital and non-marital assets. This becomes very complicated when non-marital assets are sold and utilized in the acquisition of another asset. When non-marital assets are sold, the acquired property must retain its separate identity and either you or your financial expert must be able to trace back to the exchanged property. When doing a tracing of marital versus non-marital assets the use of charts and flowcharts is extremely helpful for the courts.

How Does One Handle the Personal Efforts that the Spouse Puts into the Non-marital Business' Appreciation?

Issues of marital and non-marital become more complex when working with closely held businesses. Determining whether the marital estate should be reimbursed because of the efforts expended by an owner spouse during the marriage on a marital or non-marital business can be difficult, especially in complex business valuation contexts where the marital efforts of the owner spouse are used to enhance the value of the non-marital business. States have generally relied upon two traditional approaches: the *Pereira* approach and the *Van Camp* approach. The *Van Camp* approach focuses on the value of a spouse's efforts expended to improve non-marital property. In *Van Camp v. Van Camp,* 199 P. 885, 890-891

(Cal. 1921), the court heard evidence as to the value of services rendered by the spouse to the business and determined whether the value of these services had already been paid to the spouse in the form of salary (or otherwise) or whether such services had been unpaid. The value of the unpaid services would be deemed marital property and subtracted from the earnings and increased value of the business. The remainder would be deemed the owner spouse's separate property. The holding in *Van Camp* emphasized the fact that the husband had been adequately paid by the corporation for his services and that the balance of the profits derived from the business were accredited to the use of the capital previously invested (his premarital property). Thus, under *Van Camp* the focus is on the reasonableness or adequacy of the compensation.

On the other hand, the *Pereira* approach relies upon the assumption that the non-marital property owner is entitled to a reasonable rate of return on his or her separate property. The *Pereira* approach provides:

[W]hen one spouse owns separate property at the time of the marriage and devotes significant time and effort to the care and management of that property over and above the minimum amount needed to preserve the assets, the community will be credited with an increase in value of the separate estate over and above the ordinary return on a long-term secured investment.

The focus under *Pereira* is the reasonable rate of return. Using the *Pereira* approach may result in a more generous award to the non-business owning spouse because the burden is on the owner spouse to prove that an amount less than the reasonable rate of return should be applied. Thus, if the business is not profitable or actual capital return is less than the reasonable rate the difference weighs in favor of the non-owning spouse if the owning spouse cannot carry his burden to show otherwise. (*Pereira v. Pereira*, 103 P. 488 (Cal. 1909)).

Parties will need to review their individual state law, but this issue should be raised with your attorney if a non-marital closely held business is part of the estate and you were involved in creating the increase in value during the marriage. For example, under the Illinois Marriage and Dissolution of Marriage Act (IMDMA) the marital estate may be entitled to reimbursement for marital energies (personal efforts) to a non-marital business if "the effort is significant and results in substantial appreciation of the non-marital property." Illinois has adopted an approach which follows a reasonable compensation inquiry. When the appellate courts in Illinois reviewed the issue of whether the marital estate was entitled to reimbursement from the non-marital business because of the contribution of the personal efforts of the husband, the court has found that the marital estate was not entitled to reimbursement if the salary was found to be reasonable compensation for services rendered. Accordingly, for there to be reimbursement for the marital estate due to the marital energies of a spouse with respect to a non-marital business, it must be shown that: 1) the compensation received during the marriage was not reasonable; 2) the efforts by the business owner spouse are significant; and 3) it is a result of these efforts that the business has substantially increased in value. Thus, in business valuation matters, an expert may be needed to testify as to the elements necessary for a reimbursement claim to succeed, including an analysis of the reasonableness of the compensation. In addition to the issue of personal efforts, another issue is whether the assets of a premarital business acquired after the marriage may be determined to be marital. Understanding how and when the assets were acquired becomes very important. A review of your individual state law will be important, but the facts of your case should be brought to the attention of your attorney. In another Illinois case (*In re Marriage of Kennedy*, 94 Ill.App.3d 537, 418 N.E.2d 947, 49 Ill.Dec. 927 (1st Dist. 1981)), which involved the acquisition of specific assets, during the marriage, from nonmarital property. In *Kennedy*, the husband owned four music stores before marriage. During the marriage more stores were acquired. The trial court awarded the entire music store business to the husband. The appellate court held that the stores acquired before the marriage were clearly nonmarital property. With respect to the stores acquired after the marriage, they were classified as new and distinguishable property and were marital property even though the new stores were bought primarily on the credit of the ongoing nonmarital business of the husband. Each case needs to be looked at on the merits of its own case. So the tracing of the acquisition of assets during the marriage is important and the facts need to be brought to the attention of your attorney. Whenever an asset is purchased during the marriage a closer look needs to be taken to determine its character.

Understanding Your Spouse's True Economic Income

In most divorce cases in which maintenance or child support is involved, the issue of the spouse's true income becomes important. This is usually even more of an issue when the spouse is an owner of his own business in which his salary as reported on his W-2 is not necessarily his true income. It is not uncommon that, when faced with a divorce, one's income and value of the business becomes troubled and reduced. A divorce attorney friend of mine gave me a good term for this phenomenon: RAIDS (Recently Acquired Income Deficiency Syndrome). This is most common for those spouses who are the owners of their own businesses. Businesses that were very profitable suddenly go into the toilet during the divorce. There is often an amazing correlation between the date of divorce and the decline of the business as represented in Figure 1.5. So what can be done?[1]

A business valuator who also has the skills of a forensic accountant can be a valuable member of the divorce team in situations like this. They are used to having to dig into the depths of the corporate books to develop the normalized earnings of the business that they are valuing. In these cases the business valuator serves two purposes: to value the business and to develop the economic benefits that the owner(s) receive from the business. A valuation expert will also need to work closely with the attorney in developing proper discovery requests, assist in depositions, and interpret financial records that are produced. Additionally, the expert should be prepared to assist the attorney in discovering what drives the value of the business and the controls the owner spouse has over the business.

The spouse's annual W-2 is only the beginning. I will attempt to provide you with samples of places to look and items to address in the never-ending saga of the true income of the owner of a privately held business. The following discussion will give you an understanding of the issues and a sample of the things to look for. It is not exhaustive and each case will have its own specific issues to address.

FIGURE 1.5   Graph Representing RAIDS

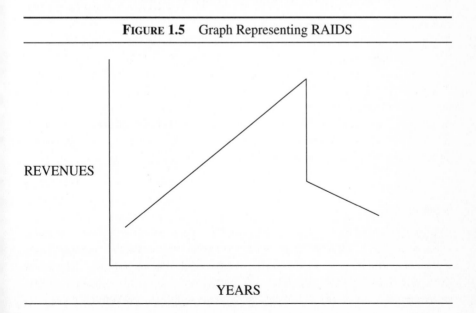

REVENUES

YEARS

Net Worth Analysis

One analysis that can sometimes indicate an individual's missing income is a net worth analysis. This may be a good place to start especially if your available budget for the divorce, as well as needed records are limited. In this analysis, the net worth of the spouse is compared at two specific periods of time. Remember that the assets need to be valued at cost. Basically, compare the change in net worth (determined by looking at the net worth of the estate at cost at the beginning of the selected period and comparing it to the net worth at cost at the current period) and then add living expenses for each year and subtract known income for each of those years. The concept is summarized as follows:

Start with: Change in the spouse's net worth

Plus: Total expenses paid out or incurred

Subtract: Sources of Income

The net amount will indicate the amount of unknown income

If the change in the net worth is greater than the income which is reported on the spouse's affidavit, the difference may represent unreported income. The IRS also uses this net worth method to reconstruct income for tax payers who are suspected of fraud or just underreporting of income. The sources of information can come from the federal income tax returns, loan applications, and the expense affidavit filed in your case. Under this analysis, the expense affidavits play an important part, especially when your spouse has signed under oath that the income and expense disclosure is true and accurate. Lying or misrepresenting facts on your income and expense affidavit can come back to bite you under this analysis. For example, if your spouse is downplaying the lifestyle, it will come to light in an unexplained variance in the use of the family's income or a possible claim of dissipation. Another similar analysis is to compare the expense affidavits to the income being reported. It is amazing how one can have twice as much in expenses as the income they are generating without reducing one's net assets.

Documentation

Information to begin the process will come from your discovery process and the valuator's site visit and interview with management or through deposition. You will want to obtain credit reports on the spouse, bank statements, cancelled checks (front and back), deposit slip details, debited and credit memos, check registers, signature cards, monthly credit card statements, applications for credit cards or checking accounts, loan applications, and so on. Requesting a copy of you and your spouse's credit report can sometimes yield some revealing information. It can provide you with bank accounts, credit cards, and other loans you may not have been aware of.

With respect to the business, you will want to obtain items such as: detailed general ledgers; cash disbursement journals; payroll records; copies of contracts for services; lease agreements; bank statements; deposit slips; credit card statements; loan files; any brokerage statements; and telephone records. This is where the spouse of the company owner can be useful in reviewing and highlighting the personal nature of certain expenditures. Also, obtaining the individual's gift tax returns may be helpful in identifying assets that have been transferred.

Economic Benefits Received from the Company

Some of the more straightforward items that are typical benefits, perks, or additional economic income to the owner are automobile usage and personal use of the credit cards that are paid for by the company. In looking at the automobile, follow up with the related expenses such as gas, insurance, maintenance, and parking expenses. Identifying the true nature of the spouse's job and the perks provided to other non-related employees can downplay the argument of "business need."

In reviewing the cash disbursement journal you should be able to identify which credit cards the company is paying for. It will also be important to identify all people who have credit cards that are paid for by the company and the relationship they have to your spouse. There are situations where the spouse, in an attempt to hide the personal use of the credit cards, would have other company employees charge items on his behalf so they wouldn't show up on his credit card even though the company is still paying for them.

As you go through the cash disbursement journal or cancelled checks, identify those payments directly to the spouse as there may be non-payroll checks that are being cashed for cash. Additionally, look at the back of the checks as they may show the deposit into accounts that you are not aware of. The review of the payroll records may also indicate payments to relatives or girlfriends that do not even work at the company. You may also need to look for fictitious employees by comparing payroll records to health insurance policies (business owners will not usually bother to insure a phantom employee) or other records. You may also notice the loss of key employees who are either aware of the activities of the owner spouse or may have actually been involved in helping the spouse obtain the various perks. These former employees may be great people to talk to, especially if they did not leave on good terms.

In reviewing the detailed expenses of the company for the past few years and common-sizing them, look for unusual increases or trends in a particular expense category that will require further investigation. Common-sizing is taking each expense as a percentage of revenues. For example, if property taxes had been 1.2 percent of revenues for four years straight and then in the last year increased to 2.5 percent it would raise questions as to why. In one instance, after further investigation, including the review of the real estate tax bills and discussions with the controller of the company, it was determined that the owner spouse had acquired a condo for his girlfriend and the expenses were paid for by the company. Increases in the repairs and maintenance account or capitalized leasehold improvements when there have been no changes at the company's facilities can lead to either activities at the spouse's personal residence being paid for by the company or even a condo or house that you were not aware the spouse had.

Another source may also be the company's depreciation lapse schedules. These detailed depreciation schedules are usually maintained by the company or its outside accountants and are usually more detailed than what you may find as part of the corporate income tax return. This may also lead to the discovery of unplanned remodeling, upgrading, and replacement of corporate facilities. This is a subtle way of using profits/funds that may have ordinarily been paid out to the owner spouse, thus in essence a reinvestment by the spouse into the business. This becomes even more important if the business is non-marital, and the spouse has devised a plan to take funds that would be marital if paid out as salary to now reinvest in the non-marital asset. A key is to talk to your financial expert, the company's controller, bookkeeper, or secretary/office manager. They may unknowingly provide information that is needed.

Detailed review of the insurance policies that the company pays for can indicate payments for the spouse's home, car, or life insurance policies that are not business-related. A detailed review of the insurance policies may also indicate assets that you were not aware of as well. For example, the property and casualty policy may show an automobile driven by the owner spouse's significant other or a side condo being maintained by the company. Life insurance policies paid for by the company should be reviewed to see who the beneficiaries are as well as the insured. The company's pension plan(s) should also be reviewed for unusual or extraordinary payments credited to the owner spouse's account.

Another source of a perk is for house accounts or direct pays. The company may have house accounts at a florist, liquor store, or travel agency. The subpoenaing of these records and deposition of the individual may also uncover extensive personal spending by the company on behalf of the owner. For example, the company may have a house account with a local florist. After subpoenaing the florist's records, the routing sheets may show that the flowers were not delivered to the office but rather to the girlfriend of the owner spouse. This same concept can work with the company's travel agent.

The obtaining of shareholder loans can be a disguise of income. This can be a way of providing funds to the spouse without including it on his W-2 as wages. Additionally, the sudden paying off of previous loans made to the company by the spouse may also be a way of changing the characteristic of funds obtained by the spouse. Regardless of what it may be called, this is another source of economic benefit to the spouse. Look for trends. Has the company ever borrowed money from the owners in the past? If there had been loans from shareholders on the books has the company paid down shareholder loans or even interest in the past? Compare these payments with other related items. Have shareholder/ officers' salaries gone down but are shareholder loans now being paid off? Remember that loans to the company may be a marital asset.

We must also not forget to investigate financial arrangements between the business and a party related to the spouse. For example, the building may be leased from a parent of the spouse with the rent above current market rents. Also, look for gifts. After collecting the rent the spouse's parents may be turning over the net profits to the spouse as a gift. Have the real estate appraiser address this issue as part of their work in determining the fair market value of the property by looking at proper rents.

You should also be aware of the concept of parking profits with friends. The business may have a venture relationship where it is not formally written in the agreement but there is an unwritten understanding that a share of the vendor's profits would be given back to the owner spouse. Look out for changes in customers and vendors and be aware of how the company conducts its business. Be aware of sudden shifts in costs of goods sold without increases being passed on to the customer or sudden changes in customers or suppliers. Also look for significant purchases of inventory at year-end when the owner can possibly understate profits until after the divorce. In one case the owner spouse paid significant commissions and bonuses to a member of his management team and after further investigation it was found that the manager had bought a boat which the owner spouse just happens to have the right to use at his leisure.

Most business owners will need assistance with RAIDS, thus a review of invoices from professionals is needed to determine whether services were performed with respect to the business or were personal. Even more important, does the detailed billing indicate any changes in business patterns, transfer of assets, ownership changes, or any other type of planning? It is not uncommon for an owner spouse's salary to decrease but their lifestyle does not seem to change because the company is now paying for the owner spouse's personal expenses.

The detailed review of the entertainment and travel category on the financial statements always needs to be reviewed. Look for trends and the number of meals taken in any one particular day. Compare this pattern prior to the divorce proceedings.

Another item will be the use of cell phones. Determine how many phones the company is actually paying for and to whom the numbers are assigned. Ask for the employee's expense reports. Look at how they are recorded on the books of the company, how they compare to industry standards, how they compare to others in the company, and how they relate to the role that the owner spouse plays in the company.

When the company is in the manufacturing business, a review of the scrap sales can lead to significant unreported cash. Talking with the shop foreman or former employees can help in this area. Discussion with the bookkeeper as to how this is recorded is also helpful. This might also lead to the issue of sales that are not recorded or out the backdoor sales. Compare bank deposit slips to day sheets or other company reports that record company daily sales and collection activity.

Lastly, review the company's assets for significant prepaid assets; prepayment of credit cards; or annuities that are part of insurance policies.

Looking beyond the W-2 is the key. The best cure for the case of RAIDS is the presentation to the court of the true economic income of the spouse. It is amazing how a case of RAIDS usually becomes cured upon the finality of the divorce proceeding or the obligations under it.

Developing Your Lifestyle Analysis

Maintenance (alimony) is court-ordered financial support that one spouse pays to the other in the event of a divorce. Three common types of maintenance are: temporary maintenance; rehabilitative or reviewable maintenance; and permanent maintenance. Temporary maintenance (often called by the Latin term *pendente lite* maintenance) awards are made while the divorce case is still pending. Rehabilitative or reviewable maintenance awards are generally made for the time period necessary for the person to receive maintenance to "rehabilitate" herself or himself by improving her or his earning potential to narrow the income difference between the parties' incomes. Permanent maintenance means there is no set time for the maintenance to end. Unless the parties otherwise agree, the maintenance will end when either spouse dies, the spouse receiving maintenance remarries, or the spouse receiving maintenance co-habitats on a resident, continuing conjugal basis.

A maintenance award is based on the needs/lifestyle of one spouse during the marriage and the ability of the other spouse to pay it. The law in all states that have maintenance is gender neutral. Though in most cases the wife is awarded maintenance, husbands may be awarded maintenance also. Many factors go into determining whether a spouse qualifies for maintenance. Specific factors include the duration of the marriage, the income and property of each party, age, physical and emotional problems and the standard of living established during the marriage. Concerning physical health, the courts are looking at that spouse's ability to work and what their health costs and needs will be. Additionally, many courts will consider, especially with long-term marriages, the ability of the spouse to work and the type of employment he or she can realistically expect to get. In these situations a medical expert or vocational expert may be necessary to prove your case. As discussed in Section II, the tax consequences of maintenance should be reviewed in negotiating an amount.

How Much Maintenance Is to Be Awarded?

There is no set amount. Understanding your state's statutes and case decisions is important. Having said that, many court cases and maintenance laws often speak of the economic lifestyle of the parties as being a very significant factor in determining the amount of maintenance awarded. While the lifestyle factor is important, and maintenance awards all vary, averaging out the maintenance awards tends to show that maintenance increases based upon the length of the marriage. It appears that judges find the income disparity and the length of the marriage are the most significant factors in determining the amount of maintenance awards. Additionally, many judges will have a perceived cap in terms of potential maintenance awards, with this cap increasing based upon the length of the marriage. Another consideration is based on the property settlement regarding what sources of income each party will have. The key is to review what kind of after-tax income your assets will provide to you. This is where a financial expert will come into play in providing the attorney with a detailed analysis and alternative case scenarios. An expert should analyze the parties' marital assets and demonstrate to the court under various allocations of the assets what amount of after-tax cash flow will be generated to the nonworking spouse. The figure arrived at will have a direct impact on the amount of maintenance the court awards her.

Most people cannot live as cheaply in two households as one and thus in many cases the maintenance one spouse receives generally does not allow the less monied spouse to continue to live at the lifestyle established during the marriage. However, this is why it is so important to properly complete and analyze a true standard of living during the marriage by completing an expense affidavit or lifestyle report. The affidavit will list all expenses either on an annual or monthly basis to determine what your needs are. Again, the financial expert or certified divorce planner can assist in developing this information for the attorney. Looking at the check book, cancelled checks, credit cards, and adding in what is paid by the spouse's closely held business are all factors needed to put together a complete affidavit. Figure 1.6 is a sample of how to gather and report this

---

FIGURE 1.6   Financial Disclosure Statement

Mr. NOAH BOATMAN

Case Number: _____

FINANCIAL DISCLOSURE STATEMENT
STATEMENT OF MONTHLY LIVING EXPENSES

2001

1. HOUSEHOLD

Main Residence located at 10 Main Street, Boatville, MA

a.	Mortgage	$ -
b.	Home equity payment	_____
c.	Real estate taxes, assessments	_____
d.	Homeowners insurance	_____
e.	Heat/Fuel	_____
f.	Electricity	_____
g.	Telephone	_____
h.	Water and Sewer	_____
i.	Refuse removal	_____
j.	Laundry/dry cleaning	_____
k.	Maid/cleaning service	_____
l.	Furniture and appliance repair/replacement	_____
m.	Lawn and garden/snow removal	_____
n.	Food (includes Groceries, Restaurants, Supplies)	_____
o.	Liquor, beer, wine, etc.	_____
p.	Other (specify):	
	Electronics	_____
	Maintenance	_____
	Home Improvement	_____
	Flowers	_____
	Other	_____
	China	_____

SUBTOTAL of main residence HOUSEHOLD EXPENSES: $ -

FIGURE 1.6   Continued

1a. Summer House located in Nonboatville, Vermont

    a. Mortgage   _____
    b. Home equity payment   _____
    c. Real estate taxes   _____
    d. Homeowners insurance   _____
    e. Heat/Fuel   _____
    f. Electricity   _____
    g. Telephone   _____
    h. Water and Sewer   _____
    i. Refuse removal   _____
    j. Laundry/dry cleaning   _____
    k. Maid/cleaning service   _____
    l. Furniture and appliance repair/replacement   _____
   m. Lawn and garden/snow removal   _____
    n. Food (groceries, household supplies, etc.)   _____
    o. Liquor, beer, wine, etc.   _____
    p. Other (specify):   _____

SUBTOTAL of Vacation Home HOUSEHOLD EXPENSES: $ -

2. TRANSPORTATION

    a. Gasoline   _____
    b. Repairs   _____
    c. Insurance/license/city stickers
                 Insurance   _____
                 License/city stickers   _____
    d. Payments/replacement   _____
    e. Alternative transportation   _____
    f. Other (specify)   _____

SUBTOTAL of TRANSPORTATION EXPENSES: $ -

(continued)

FIGURE 1.6 Continued	

3. PERSONAL

a.	Clothing	$ -
b.	Grooming	_____
c.	Medical (after insurance reimbursement)	
	(1) Doctor	_____
	(2) Dentist	_____
	(3) Optical	_____
	(4) Medication	_____
d.	Insurance	
	(1) Life (term)	_____
	(2) Life (whole)	_____
	(3) Medical/Hospitalization	_____
	(4) Dental/Optical	_____
e.	Other (specify):	
	Fitness	_____
	Jewelry	_____
	Other	_____

SUBTOTAL OF PERSONAL EXPENSES: $ -

4. MISCELLANEOUS:

a.	Club/social obligations/entertainment	$ -
b.	Newspapers, magazines, books, and CD's	_____
c.	Gifts	_____
d.	Donations, church or religious affiliations	_____
e.	Vacations (includes Airplane Tickets, Baggage, Car Rental, Hotels, Entertainment, Foreign Currency, and Restaurants)	_____
f.	Other (specify):	
	Annual fee—AMEX	_____
	Charity	_____
	Computer Expense	_____
	Dues & Subscription	_____
	Education	_____
	Legal and Consulting fees	_____
	Photography	_____
	Postage	_____

FIGURE 1.6   Continued

Other Expense	_____
Spending Cash/ATM	_____
Sporting Goods	_____
Income Taxes	_____
Video Rental	_____

SUBTOTAL of MISCELLANEOUS EXPENSES: $_____ -

5. DEPENDENT CHILDREN:

a.	Clothing	$ -
b.	Grooming	_____ -
c.	Education	
	(1) Tuition	_____ -
	(2) Books/Fees	_____ -
	(3) Lunches	_____ -
	(4) Transportation	_____ -
	(5) Activities	_____ -
d.	Medical (after insurance proceeds)	
	(1) Doctor	_____ -
	(2) Dentist	_____ -
	(3) Optical	_____ -
	(4) Medication	_____ -
e.	Allowance	_____ -
f.	Child care/after school care	_____ -
g.	Sitters	_____ -
h	Lesson and Supplies	_____ -
i.	Clubs/Summer Camps	_____ -
j.	Vacation	_____ -
k.	Entertainment	_____ -
l.	Other	_____ -

SUBTOTAL of DEPENDENT CHILDREN: $ -

TOTAL EXPENSES $ -

information. An easy way is to use a program such as Quicken to set up the categories in the same format as in Figure 1.6. Then enter all activity from all bank accounts, credit cards, and investment accounts. Quicken will summarize the data and provide a good work paper outlining the detail that makes up each category of expense. Then use your Quicken reports to complete the income and expenses affidavit, which can also be summarized in an Excel spreadsheet.

Another frequently asked question, in addition to the amount of alimony, is how long it will have to be paid. The answer to this varies. Spouses will need to look at their state rulings, however, some general items that are usually considered include: financial ability of the spouse; time until retirement of the spouse; age of the spouse; length of the marriage; and health of the spouse. Sometimes the spouse will receive reviewable maintenance or rehabilitative maintenance. In this situation the period of maintenance is for a set period of time, say 3, 5, or 7 years, and at the end of that time period the burden will be on the spouse to petition the court for additional maintenance. In other cases the non-working spouse may get permanent maintenance. In this case the spouse will usually pay maintenance until he/she retires at which time it will be adjusted. Regarding adjustment, if the economic circumstances significantly change, the spouse paying the maintenance can usually petition the court to reduce the amount of maintenance that he or she is paying. For example, Noah, at the time of the divorce from Dez, was a president of a major company making $2,000,000 a year in salary. The court had determined that he was to pay Dez $35,000 per month in alimony for 5 years reviewable. In the third year Noah lost his job and could only get a job which paid him $250,000 per year. This change is substantial and Noah petitioned the court to reduce his support obligation. Noah could not reduce the amount of his obligation on his own but needed a court order to adjust his obligation. Reduction in the amount of alimony will usually also occur when the spouse retires. To settle a case, the spouse may agree to non-modifiable maintenance which is when the spouse agrees to pay maintenance for a certain period of time with no rights to change the amount due, even if his economic situation changes significantly.

What Is This Thing Called Dissipation?

Another common statutory term for spending marital assets outside of the family unit is often called dissipation or economic misconduct. What is dissipation? The definition varies from state to state. Often dissipation may be defined as expenses by a party which are personal in nature—not expenses for the family [incurred outside of the family unit]—that are made at a time the marriage has undergone an irretrievable breakdown, or at least is on the rocks (perhaps due to one party's affair). For example, in Illinois it is held that dissipation refers only to a spouse's improper use of marital property during a time in which the marriage is undergoing irreconcilable breakdown. In states that follow dissipation at the time after the breakdown of the marriage the big litigated point is the date on which the marriage broke down. The financial expert can assist in this area by investigating the financial records to find signs of this breakdown such as expenditures on marriage counselors or temporary housing. In some states there is no requirement to prove that the marriage was broken down at the time of the expenditure. In other states there is a requirement to prove this. The thinking in those states is that if dissipation was not limited to the time period when the marriage was on the rocks it would open the floodgates to allow the parties to litigate over a laundry list of expenses throughout their marriage.

What types of expenses might be considered dissipation? This varies from state to state. Generally, expenses paid to or on behalf of a boyfriend or girlfriend are considered dissipation. Thus, expenses for such items as jewelry, flowers, and so on, are often considered as dissipation. Gambling expenses might also be considered a dissipation of marital assets. In some states if one party moves out of the marital residence without good cause and incurs a substantial rental expense, this might be considered a dissipation. For this reason, consult with a lawyer before moving out of the marital residence and incurring separate living expenses.

The issue of dissipation should be addressed early on in the divorce case. Depending on your state, jurisdiction will dictate when the claim must be raised. On the other hand, the attorney should be consulted in order to understand what constitutes dissipation so that not only can the potential exposure be quantified but also the dissipation acts by the spouse can be limited. As mentioned above, each state will control what is considered to be dissipation. For example, courts have found dissipation to include, but not limited to, the following: significant gifts to children during the divorce; excessive drinking and gambling (a case held that a husband's expenditure of most of his salary on alcohol was dissipation of marital assets), and loans or gifts to relatives. In a 1982 Illinois case, where the husband already owned a yacht and went out and bought a very expensive racing boat, this was considered dissipation. If a spouse has sufficient funds but still lets a marital property go into foreclosure, this may be considered dissipation. Other situations found to be dissipation include: money spent on a companion while still married; the failure to file a joint return resulting in additional income taxes to be paid may be considered dissipation in the amount of the additional taxes incurred; marital funds spent on drugs; and the spouse's intentionally mismanagement of the marital assets such that the value of such assets are significantly reduced. Again, guidelines for your specific states should be addressed with the attorney and/or certified divorce planner. Your certified divorce planner/financial expert can play a big role in putting together the dissipation claim by searching out unexplained uses of marital funds or actual misuses such as purchases for hotel rooms, dinners, trips, jewelry, and gifts as discussed above.

Once the issue of dissipation is raised by one spouse, the spouse that is charged with dissipation usually must prove by clear and convincing evidence how the marital funds were spent. Just providing general and vague statements regarding unaccounted-for expenditures will probably still be claimed to be dissipation.

Because of the potential dissipation issue, it is not a good idea to have an affair while going through a divorce even if no money is spent on this person. Also consider the potential additional cost of litigation if your spouse takes an unreasonable position if he or she finds out about your affair. It is for this reason that family lawyers will often give advice to try to avoid your spouse learning about an affair (or your having an affair) during the course of your divorce.

Note

[1]Excerpts taken from an article written by Bruce L. Richman for the Family Advocate entitled "Determining the true income of an entrepreneur" published by the ABA Family Law Section.

Mediation in Settling Cases and Collaborative Divorce

Mediation

Mediation in the framework of family law cases is an attempt by a disinterested third party, a mediator, to bring about an agreement on contested issues in a family law case, such as divorce or custody cases. A mediator makes no decisions, but can provide information or have a financial expert come in and provide information to you and your spouse. The mediator simply facilitates the negotiations and settlement of a dispute between the parties. The mediator cannot and should not force any decisions on you or your spouse. In mediation, the control of the divorce process is in the hands of the divorcing parties rather than in the hands of the courts. Mediation is successful if, with the aid of the mediator, the parties reach an agreement. If there is no agreement, the parties must continue in the litigation.

In most states mediation is not mandatory, though the courts often require divorcing parents to attempt to mediate their differences in regard to custody and visitation before the issue can be litigated. Some states such as Texas and Florida require mediation before trial. Before entering mediation, check to see if under your state law mediation will be confidential. If this is the case, the mediator would not be called into court to testify as to what was said during your mediation process. The key to settling the couple's issues is to be able to talk about the issues freely, and if the mediation is not confidential, this might hinder the process.

Mediation is not for everyone. Knowledge is power, and if you have one strong partner with all the knowledge and one weak partner, then mediation usually does not work well. Settlements are made when both parties have equal negotiating and financial power and equal access to financial information, but that doesn't happen often. A good lawyer and financial advisor can sometimes balance the scale. A mediator should attempt to make up the imbalance between the parties, but the danger is that the mediator may go too far and step out of his or her role as a mediator. In situations where there is no communication or there is clear mental or physical abuse by one spouse or the other, mediation will probably not be recommended.

Mediators are usually mental health professionals or lawyers who have completed a minimum level of mediation training, though a good financial advisor with extensive divorce experience and mediation training could work well in select situations. A source for mediators is The Academy of Family Mediators (AFM). The Academy of Family Mediators is a nonprofit educational organization founded in 1981 to support professional and public education regarding mediation. They have a referral service to find a family mediator in your area. The American Academy of Matrimonial Lawyers can also assist you in finding a qualified family mediator. Being licensed as a lawyer, or being licensed or registered as a mental health professional, and taking a course in mediation does not necessarily equip the mediator to sort out the complexities and advise as to the consequences in the highly complicated field of family law. The issues of divorce-property division and maintenance (alimony) are complex and in my view should be mediated only by those who have a thorough understanding of matrimonial law. A good mediator will seek out a neutral financial advisor who is well-versed in the issues of divorce to present the various financial issues in assisting in the mediation. When deciding on a mediator, always review their credentials, their technical training in the area of mediation, and their practical experience in family mediation.

The advantage of mediation is that the process is less adversarial and therefore less stressful, and the resultant agreement may be a better product because it had the open input of both parties, and therefore each party may be more satisfied with the agreement. You and your spouse will make the decisions, not the mediator. A good mediator will be able to assist in identifying what decisions need to be made and what documents and information are needed. The good mediator will have control of the session so that you will be able to speak freely without your spouse interrupting you or putting you down and belittling you. Most mediators mandate that you and your spouse show respect to each other during the process. It is not uncommon for the mediator to meet not only with both of you together, but to meet with each of you individually to understand how you are feeling and whether your issues are being addressed. The mediator will keep track of the issues and decisions that you and your spouse agree to and will put together a mediation memorandum, which each party can provide to their attorneys as the basis for writing up a settlement agreement.

People tend to believe that mediation is less expensive than litigation. If you compare a successful mediation to a contested trial, the mediation is much cheaper. If you compare mediation to negotiations between lawyers, the mediation may or may not be cheaper. If, as is usually the case, the mediated issues are complex, the parties will still need lawyers to advise them while they are going through mediation and to finalize the agreement. If the mediation is unsuccessful, the mediator will still have to be paid and the parties will start over with attorneys. Thus, as you can see, it is difficult to say whether mediation will be less expensive, but usually, in the smaller cases this works best.

Collaborative Divorce

There is a growing trend in many states where the lawyers use a process called "collaborative divorce" to encourage the parties to come to a fair agreement. Collaborative law is a process whereby both you and your spouse and your attorneys commit yourselves to resolving your differences justly and equitably without resorting to or threatening to go to court to litigate your divorce. The key to this type of dispute resolution is based on honesty, cooperation, integrity, and respect. The goal in this dispute resolution method is to work together with the parties and the lawyers to find a win-win solution to the divorce. There is a distinct difference between mediation and collaborative law. In mediation there is a neutral party that gets you and your spouse to talk. Unlike the collaborative process, the mediator cannot step over to assist in the decision process or be an advocate to a position they think is right for the parties. Collaborative law allows the attorneys to get involved with both sides in an open discussion of the issues and the positions of the parties. In mediation if either spouse is not happy with the process or a position the other spouse is taking, they can always put a halt to the process and decide to just go to court and litigate; however, in a collaborative divorce both spouses and the attorneys that are involved are committed to continuing the process until a satisfactory solution is reached since litigation is not an option.

Under a collaborative divorce, you, your spouse, and each lawyer would all sign an agreement providing that if either lawyer files a contested motion, then both lawyers must withdraw and other lawyers will take over your and your spouse's representation. The advantage is that this system provides a financial incentive for everyone involved to come to an agreement without the aid of the court. Additionally, the agreement that is signed should include that the parties will agree to provide a proper disclosure of all documents and information. Even if one spouse's attorney has made a mistake, and the other attorney is aware of it, he/she should bring this up without taking any advantage of the mistake. Instead, the attorney should correct the mistake. This applies to the theory of working together with respect. As the team approach is also a key in a collaborative divorce, the agreement will also indicate that you and your spouse will share experts where needed, such as a child counselor, a financial expert, or a business valuator. Because of this team approach it is not uncommon for creative solutions to be devised. The strangest thing about a collaborative divorce is watching two lawyers work together in an open and honest setting, treating each other with respect, and showing the highest level of integrity.

Glossary of Common Legal/Divorce Terminology

As you go through the divorce process you will be blitzed with words you have never heard of before. I call this the legal jargon of divorce. Be familiar with these terms so that you can follow what your attorney is talking about. The following is a list of the common divorce terms you are likely to encounter:

A.D.R. (Alternative Dispute Resolution): There are various forms of A.D.R. One form is arbitration, which may be a hearing before an impartial arbitrator or panel of arbitrators. Another form of A.D.R. is mediation. Mediation is not a formal hearing but involves a series of meetings between you and your spouse (possibly including your lawyers), which is used in an attempt to help negotiate a fair settlement.

Affidavit: Written statement made under oath and signed before a notary public.

Alimony: Spousal support. (In many states alimony is now known as maintenance).

Allegation: Statement made in a pleading or affidavit.

Annulment: A legal action that makes the marriage null and void, as if it did not occur.

Answer: Pleading filed by defendant in response to complaint for divorce.

Appeal: The process of appellate court review of a trial court decision.

Appearance: Document filed by defendant informing the court and the plaintiff's counsel where papers may be served on the defendant.

Arrearages: The amount of past due alimony or child support that is required to be paid.

Attorney of Record: This is the attorney recognized by the court as officially representing you in the divorce proceeding.

Cause of Action: The basis upon which the litigation is premised.

Change of Venue: Transfer of the case from one county to another.

Child Support: Financial support paid to the custodian of a child. All states have child support guidelines, but the amount of child support that is paid under the guidelines varies significantly from state to state.

Cohabitation: Living with someone on a consistent basis. Each state may have its own more refined definition, so look to your local laws.

Collaborative Divorce: A process used to encourage the parties to come to a fair agreement. Under a collaborative divorce, you, your spouse, and both lawyers all sign an agreement providing that if either lawyer files a contested motion, then both lawyers must withdraw and other lawyers will take over your and your spouse's representation.

Community Property: Property acquired during marriage. (Only applicable in community property states.)

Contempt of Court: Intentional failure to abide by a court order without legal justification.

Contested Case: Any case in which a court must decide one or more issues.

Cross-examination: Questioning of a witness by the opposing party at a hearing.

Custodial Parent: The parent who has physical custody of the child or children.

Custody: The parent who has the legal right and responsibilities for the care of the child or children. This can be shared with a former spouse and then is called joint custody. Look at your specific state laws for further rights and explanation.

Default Judgment: A judgment granted when the defendant has failed to appear to plead.

Defendant: The respondent to the complaint for divorce.

Defined Benefit Plan: A type of retirement benefit which is often called a pension plan. A pension plan of this type is payable as an annuity; that is, it is generally payable over the course of the life of the pension-holding spouse (called the plan participant).

Defined Contribution Plan: A type of retirement benefit. Think of a defined contribution plan as a "what you see is what you get" type of plan; that is, generally there is an account statement showing the current balance.

Deposition: Oral examination of a party or other person to obtain evidence about the case.

Direct Examination: Testimony of a party when questioned by that party's attorney.

Discovery: Process of gathering data to present evidence to the court.

Dissolution of Marriage: Divorce. The termination of marriage.

Divorce Decree: The court order that grants your divorce. The decree will either spell out the terms of the divorce or make reference to a marital settlement agreement and parenting agreement which details your rights and obligations.

Emancipation: The point when a child is treated as an adult and when support for that child terminates.

Equitable Distribution: A system of distributing property in connection with a divorce that is based on fairness and not based on who holds title to property.

Evidence: Documents, testimony, or other material submitted to the court to prove or disprove allegations.

Ex Parte: Literally means one-sided. The process by which a party seeks relief from the court without the other party being present.

Grounds for Divorce: Legally accepted reasons for the granting of a divorce.

Guardian ad Litem: A lawyer who is assigned to represent and protect the rights of the children.

Hearing: Any proceeding before a court for the purpose of resolving contested issues.

Hold Harmless: Situation in which one spouse assumes responsibility for a debt.

Indemnification: Situation in which one spouse agrees to reimburse the other spouse in the event the creditor collects money from the other spouse despite the other spouse's hold harmless agreement.

Injunction: A court order prohibiting acts by a party.

Interrogatories: Written questions answered under oath by a party to a case.

Joint Custody: Both parents have equal rights and responsibilities for making the major decisions in raising their child or children with respect to such items as education, medical care, and religion. This is different from physical custody, which deals with where the child or children spend their time living.

Judgment: An official court ruling.

Jurisdiction: The authority of a court to rule on issues relating to the parties.

Legal Separation: A judgment authorizing spouses to live separate and apart which may make support provisions but does not divide property of the marriage.

Maintenance: Spousal support. (Formerly known as alimony.)

Marital Property: All property acquired during the marriage, unless the property was acquired by inheritance or gift.

Marital Settlement Agreement: Agreement of the parties resolving all issues incident to their divorce (child custody, child support, division of property, etc.).

Mediation: A process by which a neutral third party facilitates negotiations between the parties.

Motion: A pleading filed with the court seeking relief such as temporary custody, child support, etc.

Neutral Valuator: A neutral valuator is an agreed-upon expert who is mutually chosen by the parties. In the traditional situation, if there is a disagreement as to the valuation of a significant asset such as a business interest, each spouse will hire his or her own expert, thereby increasing the cost of litigation. In many cases the use of a neutral valuator may be a cost-effective means of reducing the overall cost of litigation.

No-Fault Divorce: Granting of a divorce without the need for proof that a party was the cause of the divorce.

Non-Marital Property: Term used in many states to define an individual's separate property not subject to allocation, such as property from gifts and inheritance.

Offsetting Property: Trading an item of value for an item of similar value. For example, the value of the house may be offset to compensate for the present value of a pension plan.

Order of Protection: An order entered against the one spouse to refrain from having any contact with the other spouse.

Party: A person involved in a divorce.

Pension Plan: A form of deferred compensation.

Perjury: Lying under oath.

Petition (complaint): The pleading filed with the court seeking a divorce.

Plaintiff (petitioner): The person filing for divorce.

Pleading: A written document which is filed with the court to request an action by the court on a particular matter.

Prenuptial Agreement: Prior to getting married, the parties enter into an agreement outlining their rights with respect to property allocation and spousal support in the event of divorce.

Pre-Trial Conference: This is a meeting of the attorneys with the judge, (sometimes with the experts and sometimes with the parties), for the purpose of trying to settle the case. The judge is usually in charge of the meeting.

Pro Se: Representation of one's own self in a divorce.

QDRO (Qualified Domestic Relations Order): This is an order which will provide for an allocation of a pension plan. The domestic relations order portion of the title is merely a way of saying that the order is from the divorce court. The qualified portion of the title means that a person called the plan administrator will have to approve of the QDRO. The negotiation and the entry of a QDRO in your case should be done before you are divorced. Especially if you are the person receiving benefits under a QDRO, you should not agree that the QDRO will be drafted at some time following the entry of your divorce decree.

Relief: What the court is asked to grant by a pleading or motion.

Request for Production of Documents: Form of discovery in which a party asks another party to provide documents.

Respondent (see defendant): The person sued for divorce.

Retainer and Retainer Agreement: The contract that you sign with your attorney and experts outlining their scope of services and fees that they will be charging you. The retainer is the initial amount of money that you must pay upon engaging them.

Rule (order) to Show Cause: Order requiring a party to explain why his actions were not a contemptuous violation of the court's order.

Rules of Evidence: Rules that govern the admissibility of all evidence, documents, oral testimony, etc.

Settlement: The agreed resolution of disputed issues.

Sole Custody: One parent has the sole responsibility for making the primary decisions and authority over the raising of the children.

Stipulation: An agreement between the parties.

Subpoena: A document served on a party or a witness to require appearance in court and/or the production of documents.

Summons: A written notification that a complaint has been filed.

Temporary Motions: Application to the court for relief while the divorce is pending.

Temporary Restraining Order: An order for a short duration prohibiting a party from certain acts. Similar to injunction.

Testimony: Statements made by a witness under oath.

Transcript: A typewritten record of testimony.

Trial: A formal court hearing to decide disputed issues.

Uncontested Divorce: The rare situation where the parties are immediately in full agreement on all issues and present this agreement to the attorneys for drafting and to the court for approval and entry of judgment.

Visitation: The time and right of the nonresidential parent to spend time with one's children.

SECTION

II

THE TAX SIDE
OF DIVORCE

CHAPTER

4

Taxation of Financial Support

Introduction

One of the more complex issues in divorce is understanding the tax side of divorce. There are many accountants who are good accountants, and there are many doctors who are good doctors, but would you want your general doctor or internist to be performing brain surgery for an aneurism or would you prefer a brain surgeon or some other type of specialist? The same is true with your divorce. The divorce forensic accountant is a good place to start, but the accountant should be a specialist in the area of divorce taxation. This issue becomes very important in a divorce case in that judges in many states may consider the tax consequences of their decision, but it is still the responsibility of the individuals through their attorney to present the facts and demonstrate the tax consequences. These consequences must be presented by your attorney or through the use of an expert who can present a report or an exhibit of the impact of taxes on either the property settlement or maintenance or any other issues of the case.

Your goal is to make sure that the tax consequences are made part of your record. It is also important to be aware that your marital settlement agreement in itself does not dictate the tax consequences to the IRS. This is another reason to make sure that your agreements are reviewed by a professional in divorce taxation so that the tax results you have negotiated and structured are the ultimate result you can expect. The tax laws as contained in the U.S. Internal Revenue Code ultimately set the standard, not what you necessarily say or intended to say in your agreement. This section of the book will provide you with details, but in a straightforward and understandable format, the basics to divorce taxation.

Alimony and Child Support

In many states, financial payments from one spouse to the other is called "maintenance." The term used by the Internal Revenue Code (IRC) is alimony. Thus, alimony is actually a tax term and is covered under Section 71 of the IRC. Whatever term you use, it generally represents an amount paid by one former spouse to the other former spouse as specified in a divorce or separation agreement. The important distinction here is that just because you may have maintenance payment requirements in the divorce agreement, these payments, if not structured properly, may not be considered alimony for tax purposes. This will become more important as we discuss the tax consequences of alimony and you will see why proper drafting of your divorce agreement becomes so important. If you intend payments to be treated as alimony, the intention of the parties should be clearly spelled out in specific detail. Ambiguity regarding the parties' intentions or poor drafting of the divorce agreement creates additional litigation down the road. Your divorce agreement should contain very precise language when relying on specific sections of the IRC and the intentions of the parties should also be explicit.

If the payments received by the former spouse qualify as alimony, then under IRC Section 71, the payee must include the payments received as part of their taxable income. The payments would be taxed in the year they are received. On the other side of the transaction, under IRC Section 215(a) the Code states that the general rule in the case of an individual is that there shall be allowed as a deduction an amount equal to the alimony or separate maintenance payments paid during such individual's taxable year. Further, IRC 215(b) goes on to define "alimony or separate maintenance payment" to mean any alimony or separate maintenance payment as defined in IRC Section 71(b), which is includible in the gross income of the recipient under IRC Section 71. To ensure that both sides of the transaction take place in the same year, IRC Section 215(c) requires:

- Any individual receiving alimony or separate maintenance payments is required to furnish such individual's taxpayer identification number to the individual making such payments, and

- The individual making such payments is required to include such taxpayer identification number on such individual's income tax return for the tax year in which such payments are made.

Section 71(b) provides for the qualifications of payments to be treated as alimony. The Code under Section 71(b)(1) states that the term "alimony or maintenance payment" means any payment in cash if:

- Such payment is received by (or on behalf of) a spouse under a divorce or separation agreement.

- The divorce or separation agreement does not designate such payment as a payment which is not includible in gross income under this section and not allowable as a deduction under Section 215.

- In the case of an individual legally separated from his spouse under a decree of divorce or of separate maintenance, the payee spouse and the payor spouse are not members of the same household at the time such payment is made; and

- There is no liability to make such payment for any period after the death of the payee spouse and there is no liability to make any payment (in cash or property) as a substitute for such payments after the death of the payee spouse.

Under IRC Section 71(b)(1), the Code defines the term "divorce or separation agreement" to mean:

- a decree of divorce of separate maintenance or a written instrument incident to such a decree,

- a written separation agreement, or

- a decree requiring a spouse to make payments for the support or maintenance of the other spouse.

Based on the IRS Regulations under Section 71 and various other authorities such as court cases, the requirements have payments properly qualify as alimony and can be summarized in the checklist shown in Figure 4.1. (I recommend the use of this checklist when reviewing a marital settlement agreement to make sure that the intentions of the parties to have the payments treated as alimony are met.) A more detailed discussion on each item in the checklist is provided following the checklist.

If any of the items on this checklist are marked "NO," the payments probably do not qualify as alimony, or at the very least, any issue(s) checked "NO" should be reviewed.

FIGURE 4.1 Qualification as Alimony Checklist		
	YES	NO
(1) Are the payments to the former spouse in cash?		
(2) Are the payments made pursuant to a divorce or written separation instrument?		
(3) Do the divorced or legally separated spouses reside in separate households when payment is made?		
(4) Are payments made to a third party on behalf of the payee spouse evidenced by a writing?		
(5) Does the liability for the payments to the former spouse cease at the death of the payee spouse?		
(6) The payor and payee do not file a joint return?		
(7) The divorce instrument does not designate nonalimony treatment of the payments (the designation rule)?		
(8) Have the payments, in whole or in part, not been designated as support for children of the payor spouse?		
(9) Have the rules relating to excess frontloading (alimony recapture rules) not been violated?		

Payments to Be Made in Cash

Cash means cash! According to the IRS regulations under Section 71 (Q&A-S) a debt instrument issued by the payor is not within the definition of cash. The regulations further indicate that cash includes checks and money orders payable on demand or any other legal tender or order to pay money to the payee. In order to meet this test, the medium used must be convertible immediately into cash. I like to quote the saying "In God we trust, but all alimony is in cash." If the payments by the payor are given to the former spouse in cash, it is recommended that the payor spouse request and receive a written receipt. The transfer of services or other property will not meet this requirement.

Payments Made Pursuant to a Divorce or Written Separation Agreement

In order for the cash payment to qualify as alimony it must be made pursuant to a divorce or a separation agreement. The following would fall under this definition:

- A decree of divorce or a written instrument incident to such decree

- A decree of separate maintenance or a written instrument incident to such decree, sometimes referred to as a legal separation

- A written separation agreement

- An order for support

Included in the above would be any court orders or agreed orders for temporary support pending the outcome of the divorce or separation. Any voluntary payments made by one spouse or former spouse to the former spouse, even if agreed to orally, will not qualify as alimony. Along those same lines, any payments made in excess of the required payments under the divorce or a separation agreement would not be considered alimony. At the same time if any of the above agreements are modified the payments must follow the modification.

There are several tax cases where the former spouse either decided to voluntarily increase the maintenance or to continue the payments after his obligation was over and in these cases the judge thought it was honorable of the former spouse to do this but unfortunately the payments did qualify as alimony under IRC Section 71. Additionally, payments made prior to the time an agreement or divorce is executed is considered a voluntary payment, even if the divorce agreement made the obligation retroactive to an earlier date.

For example, Josh and Talia get divorced, and Josh is obligated to pay Talia $1000 per month as alimony. A year after the divorce, Talia loses her job and Josh, feeling bad for her, decides to increase the payments to $2500 per month. The additional $1500 per month will not qualify as alimony under IRC Section 71.

The courts, however, have determined that written letters between the former spouses would qualify as a written separation agreement because the letters were in writing and constituted a meeting of the minds. This was also similar to the case where the court felt that a letter from the one spouse's lawyers to his spouse's wife constituted a written separation agreement and thus the payments would qualify as alimony under IRC Section 71. A document calling something alimony does not qualify because the parties to the divorce cannot have documents that change the tax laws.

If payments relate to the payment of arrearages, those amounts that were due under a previous divorce instrument qualify as alimony during the year it is paid. For example, if your spouse was required to pay $10,000 per month for five years and after the fourth year he stopped making payments and after three years of battling he decided to give you the balance that was due under the original agreement, the amount paid would be treated as alimony in the year paid.

Separate Households

The regulations under IRC Section 71 are very specific in that a payment made at the time when the payor and payee spouses are members of the same household cannot qualify as an alimony or separate maintenance payment if the spouses are legally separated under a decree of divorce or of separate maintenance.

Physical separation via separate residences is required. The regulations are quite clear that for purposes of this test, a dwelling unit formerly shared by both spouses shall not be considered two separate households even if the spouses physically separate themselves within the dwelling unit. However, the IRS does give the parties a break in that once one of the parties is preparing to leave the marital residence the payments will qualify as long as the one spouse leaves within 30 days.

The separate household rule does not apply if there is no legal separation or divorce. Thus, payments made under a written separation agreement or a temporary support order would still qualify as alimony even if the parties cohabitate within the same residence.

Payments Made to a Third Party

A payment to a third party by one spouse for the benefit of the other spouse can qualify as alimony under IRC Section 71 provided all of the other provisions are met. The key is that the payee spouse must have received an economic benefit from the payment as if the payee had paid the amount directly. This falls under a tax theory known as the "step transaction" doctrine because it omits the intermediate step of deposit and remittance by the payor spouse (see Figure 4.2).

To have this qualify, an economic benefit must be received by the recipient spouse (former spouse) and must not be for the benefit of the payor. For example, a payment relating to a property that the payor owns in which he lets the payee live would not qualify as alimony as the economic benefit was not received by the payee spouse. However, payments could be for the former spouse's rent, tuition, and direct liabilities. In fact the regulations (1.71-1T(b), Q&A-6,7) provide that term or whole life insurance premiums paid on a policy owned by the payee, insuring the payor's life, qualify if all other conditions are met. There does not appear to be any restriction concerning the nature of the payee's obligations to be paid directly by the payor former spouse as long as they are for any legal obligation of the payee spouse.

The following checklist can be used to determine if the third-party payments qualify as alimony:

- Do the payments meet all of the other requirements for alimony treatment under IRC Section 71?

FIGURE 4.2   Step Transaction Graph

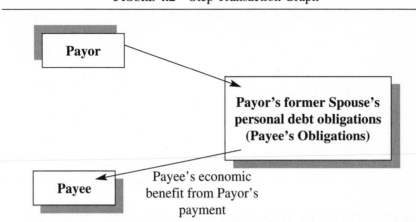

- Were the payments by the payor for obligations and/or economic benefit of the payee spouse?
- Do the parties intend to have the payments treated as alimony?
- Is there a signed written agreement classifying the payments as alimony, either as part of the divorce agreement or in a separate written instrument signed by both parties?

The IRS regulations indicate that the consent or agreement between the two parties be received by the payor prior to the due date of the payor's first tax return for the tax year in which the payment is made. The consent must explicitly express the parties' intention to have the transaction governed by IRC Section 71. The following sample language in Figure 4.3 can by used as a paragraph to be included in the divorce agreement or as a separate statement to be signed by both parties and attached to the payor's tax return.

Having said this, one needs to be careful how to structure payments relating to housing costs when one spouse is given the legal right of possession while the other, who may own it solely or jointly with the former spouse, is the one paying the expenses. Mortgage payments on property owned by the payor and used by the payee are not alimony within the context of IRC Section 71. The interest paid would be governed by other sections of the IRC dealing with the deductibility of interest expense. So when real estate is involved, a thorough review of how ownership is maintained is critical in determining the deductibility of the payments.

FIGURE 4.3   Third-Party Sample Language

Josh Do and Talia Do expressly consent to have the payments by Josh Do directly for the tuition obligations of Talia Do (describe the transaction of the payments) to be subject to the alimony provisions of IRC Section 71 and IRC Section 215 and therefore includable in the taxable income of Talia Do and deductible for federal income tax purposes by Josh Do.

_____   _____

Josh Do   Talia Do

Payments to End at Death of Payee

The IRC under Section 71(b)(1)(D) requires that the obligation for the payment of alimony terminates at the death of the payee spouse. Additionally, as discussed later, the regulations require that such transfers that occur after date of death be reviewed for "substance over form." Under the current rules, a marital settlement agreement does not have to state in writing that the alimony obligation will cease at the death of the payee spouse. When it is not stated in the agreement, the IRS will probably challenge the qualification of the payments as alimony and will shift the burden of proof back to the payor spouse to prove that the state alimony statutes provide for termination. Thus, regardless of the state statutes, payments to the payee spouse must terminate upon the payee's death. To avoid any conflicts and misinterpretations of the state statute, it is always best to include the following language in your marital settlement agreement to be safe:

". . . . all maintenance paid to payee from payor shall cease / terminate upon the death of the payee unless designated to end sooner"

Any payments to the estate for arrearages after the death of the payee would not be considered .

The other problem in this area is when one has arrangements to provide for a post-death substitute for continuation of payments to a decedent or his or her estate. When this takes place, all previous payments will be disqualified as alimony. The concept of substitute payments comes into play when you have a maintenance arrangement calling for a number of payments and upon death of the payee spouse, the payments are accelerated in time. This goes to the concept of substance over form, as indicated earlier. The IRS regulations under Section 71 provide a good example of this issue:

.... under the terms of a divorce decree, A is obligated to make annual alimony payments to B of $30,000, terminating on the earlier of the expiration of 6 years or the death of B. B maintains custody of the minor children of A and B. The decree provides that at the death of B, if there are minor children of A and B remaining, A will be obligated to make annual payments of $10,000 to a trust, for the benefit of the children until the youngest child attains the age of majority. These facts indicate that A's liability to make annual $10,000 payments in trust for the benefit of his minor children upon the death of B is a substitute for $10,000 of the $30,000 annual payments to B. Accordingly, $10,000 of each of the $30,000 annual payments to B will not qualify as alimony or separate maintenance payments.

One of the important things to observe from this example is if the payments are deemed not to terminate at death, then none of the payments made before the date of death, as well as those after the date of death, would qualify as alimony. The IRS regulations also provided another example where any unpaid maintenance at the date of death of the payee would be due in a lump sum to the estate. They determined that such a lump sum payment would be treated as a substitute for the full amount of each of the annual maintenance payments due to the payee spouse and accordingly, none of the maintenance payments would qualify as alimony.

When we deal with structuring marital settlement agreements and the settlements are based on assumed tax positions to be taken by the parties or how something will be treated by the IRS, I would recommend including a tax indemnification agreement as part of the final settlement agreement. Basically, the agreement should indicate what tax positions the parties are assuming and if either side would take a different position than originally agreed to, they would be responsible for the tax consequences, including any penalties, interest, and professional fees incurred. If the parties are intending the maintenance payments to be treated as alimony for tax purposes and they end up not qualifying, the payments would be adjusted downward such that the payor would be out of pocket the same amount after considering his tax deduction. Tax indemnifications are a good tool in making sure that everyone does what they agree to. If one party balks at such an agreement it is usually a good indication that they may have other motives after the divorce agreement becomes final.

The Designation Rule

The IRC Section 71(b)(1)(B) provides us with some latitude in planning when it comes to the tax treatment of alimony. The IRC allows the payor and payee, or a court may direct, to elect not to have the maintenance payments treated as alimony, thus the payments would not be taxable to the payee spouse and not deductible to the payor spouse. The non-alimony designation establishes what the tax treatment will be on a going forward basis. An example of what the language in the divorce agreement or in a separate statement should be is:

> As set forth in IRC Section 71(b)(1)(B), the parties hereby expressly agree to designate, and do designate, all payments required and referenced at [*identify the relevant paragraphs or sections in the agreement that discuss the maintenance payments*] as excludable/nondeductible payments for purposes of IRC Section 71 and IRC Section 215 respectively.

The IRS regulations under this section seem to indicate that one can make this election in any year, providing that the payee spouse gets an agreement signed by the payor spouse and attaches a copy of the agreement containing the election with the first income tax return for that year, including extensions. Based on this requirement, one can assume that this election cannot be made with an amended return. However, it does appear that taxpayers can control and plan tax consequences of maintenance payments on a year-to-year basis. Though an election is needed, an omission of one is important only if the payor and payee take inconsistent positions with respect to the treatment of the payment.

Payments Designated as Child Support

If the payment made by the payor spouse is treated as child support then it will not qualify as alimony. IRC Section 71(c) and the related regulations thereunder make it clear that the general provisions of IRC Section 71 (payments treated as alimony) will not apply to any part of any payment which the terms of the divorce or separation instrument fix the sum which is payable for the support of a child or children of the payor spouse. Payments classified as child support are not taxable to the payee spouse and not deductible to the payor spouse. If the divorce or separation instrument has both taxable/deductible alimony and child support, the child support amount must be completely paid before any amount is treated as alimony (IRC Section 71(c)(3)). Thus, if an agreement requires the payment of both alimony and child support and in any particular year you pay less than the total required amount due under the agreement, the amount paid would be credited toward the child support amount first and then to the alimony portion. For example, Josh is required to pay Talia $1000 per month as alimony and $1000 per month as child support. Josh is short on cash and only pays Talia $1500 per month. Only $500 of the $1500 would be considered as alimony.

In order for payments to be treated as child support, the payments structured in the divorce or separation agreement must be fixed or treated as fixed for support of payor's children. Payments by the payor for the benefit of children other than the payor's children are not child support. For example, if the payor spouse makes payments to the payee spouse on behalf of step-children, these payments are not qualified as child support. The IRC does not require the funds to actually be spent on the children, just that the payments are made to the payee spouse. Even if the obligation is beyond the parents' obligation to support, the payments will be treated as child support.

The payments treated as child support will qualify if a payment(s) is (are) fixed in amount and identified specifically as child support or a payment(s) is (are) DEEMED to be child support.

Deemed child support payments are those that are:

- Payments made by the payor spouse to the payee spouse which will be reduced on the happening of a contingency event that relates to a child; or

- Payments made by the payor spouse to the payee spouse which will be reduced at a time which can clearly be associated with a contingency relating to a child.

Under the first scenario, the Temporary IRS Regulations Section 1.71, Q&A – 17, provides that a contingency relates to a child if it is dependent on an event relating to the child, regardless of whether the event is certain to or likely to occur. The regulations as well as the IRC under Section 71(c) identify several events that are examples of an event relating to a child, though the following list of examples is clearly not exhaustive:

- Reaches a specified age
- Reaches a predetermined level of income
- At the time the child dies
- At the time the child marries
- When the child graduates or leaves school
- The child leaves the parents' residence
- The child accepts full-time employment

Section 71 of the IRC does not define what is meant by "clearly associated" with the contingency. However, the regulations provide two situations in which otherwise qualifying alimony payments are presumed to be reduced at a time "clearly associated" with the happening of a contingency relating to a child of the payer and payee spouses. There is a rebuttable presumption that the payments are for child support if:

- The payments are to be reduced not more than six months before or after the date the child is to attain the age of 18, 21, or local age of majority (the "six-month" rule); or

- The payments are to be reduced on two or more occasions that occur not more than one year before or after a different child of that payer spouse attains a certain age between the ages of 18 and 24, inclusive (the multiple reduction rule).

Either one of the above situations can be rebutted by an evidentiary showing that the time of reduction was an independent event having nothing to do with the child or children or if the reduction is a total cessation of alimony at the time of the first payment reduction.

Examples of both of these safe harbors are worth demonstrating.

Example 1

Assume that there is a divorce agreement and that Josh is required to pay Talia $5,000 per month, where all of the payment is designated as alimony. The parties have one child named Noah who was born January 1, 1990. The divorce agreement states that Josh's payments to Talia will be reduced to $2,500 starting on January 1, 2008. Because Noah will turn 18 within six months of the date on which Josh's payments are to be reduced, the payment reduction is assumed to be clearly associated with a contingency relating to a child. Thus, the $2,500 reduction will be treated as child support regardless of the intention of the parties, unless it can be rebuffed. This is an example of the six-month rule.

Example 2

This example will demonstrate the analysis needed if there are multiple reductions in the payment of support. Notice how complicated it is, thus the use of flow charts is the best way to analyze these sets of facts. Assume the following example, which was similarly presented the temporary regulations under Section 71, Joshua and Talia are divorced on July 1, 1985, when their children, Noah (born July 15, 1970) and Dez (born September 23, 1972), are 14 and 12, respectively. Under the divorce decree, Joshua is to make alimony payments to Talia of $2,000 per month. Such payments are to be reduced to $1,500 per month on January 1, 1991 and to $1,000 per month on January 1, 1995. On January 1, 1991, the date of the first reduction in payments, Noah will be 20 years, 5 months, and 17 days old. On January 1, 1995, the date of the second reduction in payments, Dez will be 22 years, 3 months, and 9 days old. Each of the reductions in payments is to occur not more than one year before or after a different child of Joshua attains the age of 21 years and 4 months. Accordingly, the reductions will be presumed to be clearly associated with the happening of a contingency relating to Noah and Dez. Unless the presumption is rebutted, payments under the divorce decree equal to the sum of the reduction ($1,000 per month) will be treated as fixed for the support of the children of Joshua and therefore will not qualify as alimony or separate maintenance payments.

Obviously, to avoid the above applications one can do some thoughtful planning by planning the dates for the reduction of payments to be on specific dates that are not involving a contingency relating to a child or one that is "clearly associated" with the occurrence of a contingency relating to a child of the payor. For example: if you have one child, you can structure the maintenance payments such that they will be reduced on a specific date that just so happens to be seven months before the child becomes 18. Just do not mention that fact. Drafting will be important as the language in your divorce agreement may very well control the ultimate tax consequences.

Joshua and Talia have one child named Noah. Noah was born January 1, 1980. The divorce agreement is written as follows: Joshua is to pay Talia in the form of maintenance the amount of $1,500 per month until June 1, 1997 and at that time it will be reduced to $1,000. This language is not presumed to be clearly associated with a contingency related to a child. However, if the language read that Joshua is to pay Talia in the form of maintenance the amount of $1,500 per month until Noah becomes 17 years and 6 months old, this language would be presumed to be a contingency relating to the child.

In a 1994 tax case, it was determined that a divorce agreement that provided that any future court-ordered increase in child support will correspondingly decrease spousal support was not deemed a contingency under the previously mentioned IRS regulations. The legal right to petition for an increase in child support under local statutes is not a contingency.

Another approach that some suggest is to set the dates of the reductions but not indicate the exact amount of any reductions. The reductions can be determined at a later date or some criteria can even be set up to determine the amount at the time of the reduction. For example, Joshua is to pay Talia $5,000 per month as maintenance and this will be reduced at the time Noah, their son, graduates from high school or becomes 18. When this occurs, Joshua's payment of maintenance to Talia will be reduced by 20% of Joshua's net income (this section should be a reduction to be determined at a later date which is determined by a method that is agreed to by both sides). Under this scenario the argument will be that the reduction is not associated with a contingency relating to a child and thus the payments should qualify as alimony.

In many instances, what we are trying to do is classify what normally would be child support and have it treated as alimony. In this case we call it unallocated support. Because alimony is deductible and child support is not, there can be significant tax reasons to want to do this. The larger the spread in taxable income levels between the parties and ultimate spread in tax rates they fall in can provide for a larger benefit in planning the structure of the payments. Take the following examples:

Assume the following facts: If Joshua makes $100,000 per year and his tax rate is 36%, he is required to pay $20,000 a year in support. Joshua's ex-wife Talia makes $30,000 per year and has a tax rate of 20%.

Assume all is treated as child support:

	JOSHUA	TALIA
Taxable income before payment of child support	$100,000	$ 30,000
Income Tax	(36,000)	(6,000)
Child Support Payment	(20,000)	20,000
Net Cash Available	$ 44,000	$ 44,000

Now assume that the payments are all treated as alimony:

	JOSHUA	TALIA
Taxable income before payment of child support	$100,000	$ 30,000
Alimony	(20,000)	20,000
Income Taxes	(28,800)	(10,000)
Net Cash Available	$ 51,200	$ 40,000

Note that if the payments are all treated as child support the net cash flow to the total family unit is $88,000. If the payments are treated as alimony, the net cash flow to the total family unit increases to $91,200. Thus you could structure the payments such that the excess to Joshua is shared with Talia by increasing the payments to Talia from Joshua as follows:

	JOSHUA	TALIA
Taxable income before payment of child support	$100,000	$ 30,000
Alimony	(25,000)	25,000
Income Taxes	(27,000)	(11,000)
Net Cash Available	$ 48,000	$ 44,000

Notice that Talia is in the same position after tax on whether the payments are treated as child support or alimony by increasing her payments by $5,000; however, Joshua's net cash available to him has increased by $4,000 even after increasing the payments to Talia by $5,000.

Recapture Rules Relating to Alimony Payments

Given the deductibility of alimony, many creative people have tried to convert what would have been a property transfer (non-deductible) into tax-deductible alimony. To prevent this practice, the IRS provides that any payments that are excessive in the early years will be recharacterized as non-deductible property settlement as outlined in IRC Section 71(f) and thus not qualified as alimony. A spouse whose alimony payments decrease or terminate during the first three calendar years may be subject to the alimony recapture rules. The impact of the alimony recapture recharacterization occurs by requiring the payor spouse to pick up income in later years and allow the payee spouse a deduction in later years for the amount of the determined excess (as discussed below, this is determined in the third year of payment.) The tax treatment of payments made in the early years is not disturbed.

Calculation of the Alimony Recapture

As mentioned above, we are dealing with looking at a three-year period to determine recapture. The three-year period starts with the first calendar year when a payment is made that qualifies as alimony under a decree of divorce or separate maintenance. Thus, it does not include any time in which payments may have been made under a temporary support order. As long as there is no decrease in alimony payments in excess of $15,000 in year two or year three the alimony recapture rules won't come into play. The impact of any recapture does not occur until the third year. If there is recapture, in the third year the payor spouse will include the amount of the recapture into income and the payee spouse will get a deduction from gross income equal to the amount of the recapture.

Application of the Rules

IRC Section 71(f) provides that the Excess Alimony Payments, which is the recapture, is equal to the excess payments for the first post-separation year and the excess payments for the second post-separation year. The amount of the excess payments for the first post-separation year is the excess (if any) of:

1. The total amount of alimony or separate maintenance payments paid by the payor spouse during the first post-separation year

OVER

2. The average of:
   - The alimony paid by the payor spouse during the second year, reduced by the excess payments for the second year, and
   - The alimony payments paid by the payor spouse during the third year, plus
   - $15,000

The excess payments for the second year is the excess of (if any):

1. The alimony paid by the payor spouse during the second year;

OVER

2. The sum of:
   - The amount of alimony payments paid by the payor spouse during the third year, plus
   - $15,000

Typically, the way to calculate the amount of recapture is to first calculate the excess second-year payments and then calculate the excess first-year payments. The next scenario is an example of how the calculation of alimony recapture works.

Talia and Joshua are divorced and enter into a marital settlement agreement whereby Joshua will pay Talia alimony in the following amounts:

Year 1: $100,000
Year 2: $ 60,000
Year 3: $ 30,000

Joshua had agreed to this arrangement because he had agreed to pay for Talia's college tuition for the next two years as well as buy her a new car and wanted to make these payments tax deductible to him to minimize his cash outflow. Joshua figured that Talia would get a job in the third year and thus ended alimony at the end of that year.

Unfortunately, his planning did not work out as planned, as in the third year Joshua would have to recapture $72,500 into income and Talia would receive a deduction from her gross income in the same amount (see Figure 4.4).

By adding the excess second-year payments and the excess first-year payments together Joshua will have a total alimony recapture in year three in the amount of $72,500. Figure 4.5 is a worksheet that can be used for calculation of alimony recapture.

FIGURE 4.4 Excess Payments

Excess Second—Year Payments

Total second-year payments:		$60,000
Total third-year payments:	$30,000	
Statutory Floor	15,000	
Less: Sum of third-year payments		45,000
Excess second-year payments		$15,000

Excess First—Year Payments

First-year payments:		$100,000
Second-year payments:	$60,000	
Less: excess second-year amount	(15,000)	
Net second-year payment	$45,000	
Plus third-year payments	30,000	
Sub-total	$75,000	
Sub-Total divided by 2		$37,500
Statutory Floor		15,000
Total subtraction from first-year payments		$42,500
Excess first-year payments		$57,500

FIGURE 4.5   Alimony Recapture Worksheet

Excess Second-Year Payments

1. Alimony paid in the second year $ _____
2. Alimony paid in the third year   _____
3. Statutory Floor $15,000
4. Sum of lines 2 and 3 $ _____
5. Excess second-year payments [line 1 less line 4] $ _____

Excess First-Year Payments

6. Alimony paid in the first year $ _____
7. Adjusted Second-Year Payments
   [Line 1 less Line 5]   _____
8. Third-year alimony payments   _____
9.   Subtotal [add line 7 and line 8]   _____
10. Divide the Subtotal [line 9] by two   _____
11. Statutory Floor $15,000
12. Subtraction from First-Year Payments [Line 10 plus Line 11]   <_____>
13. Excess First-Year Payments [Line 6 less Line 12] $ _____
14. ALIMONY RECAPTURE [Line 5 plus Line 13] $ _____

The Internal Revenue Code under Section 71(f) (5) provides exceptions where the alimony recapture rules do not apply:

- If either spouse dies before the close of the third year and the alimony payments cease because of such death

- If the payee spouse [the spouse receiving the alimony] remarries before the end of the third year and the alimony payments cease by reason of such remarriage

- Payments of alimony made under a court decree or order that qualifies as temporary support do not apply in the calculation of alimony recapture

- Payments will not be considered in the alimony recapture calculation to the extent that they are made pursuant to a continuing liability over a period of not less than three years to pay a fixed portion or portions of the income from a business or property or from compensation for employment or self-employment. An example of this exemption would be where Joshua would pay Talia as maintenance, qualifying as alimony, 20% of his annual net profits from his law practice for a period of five years. Under this scenario even if in year-one Joshua's practice produces $1,000,000 in net profits (thus Talia's alimony payments would be $200,000) and in the second year his practice produces net profits of only $200,000 (thus Talia's alimony payments would be only $40,000) this reduction will not produce alimony recapture.

Since these are the only exceptions that are available, any other reductions to alimony payments may create alimony recapture. The IRS regulations are clear that a decline in payments during the first three years due to a failure by the payor to make timely payments; a modification of the divorce; a reduction in the support needs of the payee; or a reduction in the ability of the payor to provide support will not be a reason to avoid recapture.

It is important to note that when we talk about years, we are talking about calendar years. Thus if the parties are divorced in November and the first alimony payment is made in December, this would be considered the First Year.

Alimony Trusts

Many times it is not unusual to feel uncomfortable with prospects of hope that the payor spouse will continue to make his/her payments as required or possibly the payor is in a risky business and the payee does not want to worry about the risk of losing his/her payments. This may also be very important if the payee is relying on the maintenance payments to live on. One way to handle this situation is to set up an alimony trust under IRC Section 682. Under this section, the payor spouse can transfer money or other property into a trust for the benefit of the payee spouse. Under this structure, the trust would then make the distributions to the beneficiary (the payee spouse).

By using the trust vehicle the payee spouse will have some security that future alimony payments will be made. The payor spouse may be the trustee and has investment discretion pursuant to his fiduciary capacity under state law and other standards set forth in the trust document.

The key of using this vehicle is that there is no tax to the trustee or the payor spouse upon the creation of the trust unless there are liabilities in excess of the basis of the assets contributed. As the trust earns income on the corpus, it pays tax on the income net of any distributions of income to the payee spouse. The deduction to the trust and the income to the payee spouse is calculated based on the income of the trust. Thus, it is possible that the actual distributions received by the beneficiary are in excess of trust income and thus the trust would be distributing corpus. Income-producing property, such as bonds, or possibly a rental property, would be good assets with which to fund an alimony trust.

CHAPTER

5

Transfers of Property in Connection with a Divorce— IRC Section 1041

General Rules

In general, IRC Section 1041 provides for the nonrecognition of gain or loss on transfers of marital property between spouses pursuant to the divorce. The terms gain or loss are important as this section does not provide for the shifting of ordinary income from one taxpayer to another. This distinction is based on the long-standing principles contained in the "Assignment of Income" doctrine. Basically, if the property being transferred has any deferred income attached to it, the accrued income must be recognized by the transferring spouse. Thus, IRC 1041 does not shield the transferring spouse from recognizing ordinary income associated with the property transferred. An example of this is the transfer of Series EE Bonds. In this situation the transferring spouse has accrued interest income on the bonds but has not recognized the income yet, thus, the transferring spouse must recognize the accrued interest up to the date of transfer.

In order to transfer current income that is generated from property, it is necessary to transfer the underlying property. The transfer must be total and complete in fact and appearance. Thus, the transferring spouse must divest all ownership and control. If the transferring spouse retains an influence over the management of the property, this could result in a challenge to the validity of the entire transfer. For example, Josh and Talia get divorced and Josh transfers a rental property to Talia. Talia takes complete title to the property and takes over the management of it. No gain or loss will be recognized on the transfer and all future rental income generated from the property (ordinary income) will be taxable to Talia.

Beware! The transfer of a nonqualified stock option incident to a divorce may be taxable under these same principles of the Assignment of Income Doctrine.

Though not to be cited as precedent, in a recent ruling by the IRS, [IRS FSA 200005006 – February 4, 2000], they have indicated that a transfer of a nonqualified stock option, which is transferred to a spouse as part of a property settlement in connection with a divorce, would be taxable to the transferring spouse. Additionally, the spouse receiving the options would receive a carryover basis in the options.

The basis of the IRS ruling is their interpretation of IRS Code Section 83 and the assignment of income doctrine.

Facts
As part of a divorce settlement, the Wife was awarded one half of the Husband's incentive stock options and nonqualified stock options which the husband received from the company where he was employed. It is important to note, that because of rules prohibiting the transfer of qualified incentive stock options, upon the transfer of these options, these became nonqualified stock options and thus would now be taxable under IRC Section 83.

Subsequent to the transfer, the Wife exercised these options and then sold the stock. The company issued the Ex-husband a Form 1099 for the difference between the fair market value of the stock and the exercise price paid by the Wife. The Ex-husband reported this gain on his tax return and subsequently filed an amended return claiming a refund for the taxes paid.

The Issues at Hand and the Related Law
We have two issues at hand: (a) When is income relating to the nonqualified stock options recognized under IRC Section 83; and (b) What applies— IRC Section 1041 or the assignment of income doctrine.

Looking at the first issue, in general, if property is transferred to an individual in connection with the performance of services, the excess fair market value of the property, on the first day that the rights to the property are either transferable or not subject to a substantial risk of forfeiture over the amount paid for the property is included in the individual's gross income. This does not apply if we are dealing with a qualified stock option or the transfer of an option without a readily ascertainable fair market value. Under this situation, the taxability of this transaction would apply at the time the option is exercised or otherwise disposed of.

In this situation, the Husband transferred one-half of his stock options to his Ex-wife as part of the property settlement as required by the divorce decree. Though normally no income is recognized in a transfer under IRC Section 1041 in connection with a divorce, in the case of United States v. Davis, 370 U.S. at 71 (62-2 USTC 9509) it was recognized that the parties to a divorce that exchanged stock did so for the release of other marital rights or property in an arm's length transaction and that the properties exchanged were of equal value. In applying this theory, the IRS believes that the transfer of the options to the Ex-wife was an arm's length transaction. In continuing with the same line of thinking, the property that the Husband received as part of the property settlement in the divorce is presumed to equal the value of the options at the time they were transferred to his Ex-wife. Thus, the Husband would receive compensation income equal to the fair market value of the options over his basis in the stock options when they were transferred to his Ex-wife. Additionally, since the Husband has recognized compensation due to the arm's length transaction, there would be no taxable event to the Husband upon the time when the Ex-wife exercises the options. The Ex-wife would recognize any gain on the subsequent sale of the underlying stock and her basis for determining her gain would be equal to the amount includable in her Ex-husband's gross income.

The other argument that the Husband might make is that he should not have to recognize any income because the transfer of the options was made pursuant to a divorce and should be covered under IRC Section 1041. IRC Section 1041 is very clear in providing that no gain or loss shall be recognized on a transfer of property between spouses and former spouses if the transfer is incident to divorce. However, the subtle difference here is that the compensation that the Ex-husband is recognizing is ordinary income, not gain, and thus Section 1041 should not apply. The IRS looked to the tax case [Gibb v. Commissioner, T.C. Memo, 1997-196] in which it was stated that IRC Section 1041 does not provide for the exclusion of income, just the nonrecognition of gain or loss.

The other argument that can be made to support the fact that the Ex-husband should be taxed on the transfer is the application of the assignment of income doctrine, which requires the transferor, rather than the spouse receiving the property, to recognize the assigned income. We have seen this before in dealing with the issue of transferring Series E government bonds to a former spouse. In this case, the taxpayer must include in their gross income the amount of interest that has accrued but not recognized at the time of transfer. The IRS in Revenue Ruling 87-112 states that although IRC Section 1041 shields the taxpayer from recognition of gain that would ordinarily be recognized on a sale or exchange of property, it does not shield the taxpayer from recognition of income that is ordinarily recognized upon the assignment of that income to another taxpayer. The ruling makes it clear that because the income at issue was accrued but unrecognized interest income, rather than gain, IRC Section 1041 did not shield the income from recognition. One can easily see how the IRS would take a similar position in dealing with nonqualified stock options/deferred compensation and that Section 1041 would not shield the recognition of the Husband's compensation income on the transfer of the stock options to the Ex-wife.

These potential problems can and should be addressed when developing the value of the marital estate and considering the tax implications of such transfers and the value to the marital estate.

Though the provisions of Section 1041 tend to be rather broad, there are certain restrictions to be aware of as follows:

- Nonresident aliens are excluded from the nonrecognition provision. Alien status is determined as of the time the property transfer is made. It does not matter whether or not the alien is subject to federal income taxes in the year of transfer.

- This section does not apply to the transfer of services.

- The nonrecognition provisions of this section overrides any other non-recognition provisions of the tax code. For example, suppose that Joshua has a piece of land titled in his name, which was inherited from his father. The land has a basis of $20,000 and a fair market value of $100,000. Joshua decides to sell this land to his wife, Talia, for its current value. No gain would be recognized by Joshua. This sale is automatically considered a Section 1041 transfer of property between spouses.

In addition to transfers between spouses, Section 1041 clearly applies to those transfers that are incident to the divorce. The IRC states that for the transfer to be incident to the divorce, the transfer must have occurred within one year of the divorce, or must be related to the cessation of the marriage.

Given the way the language of Section 1041 is written, transfers within one year of divorce need not be related to the cessation of marriage and the term cessation of the marriage must be for those transfers that did not take place within one year of the divorce. So, for the definition of what is meant by the "cessation of the marriage," the temporary regulations under Section 1041 state that a transfer of property is treated as related to the cessation of the marriage if the transfer is:

1. Pursuant to a divorce or separation instrument (note that this includes a modification or amendment of such decree or instrument), and
2. The transfer occurs not more than six years after the date on which the marriage ceases.

Although the presumption is that if you do not meet these tests, the transfer would be presumed to be not related to the cessation of the marriage, this presumption can be rebuffed only by showing that the transfer was made to effect the division of property owned by the former spouses at the time of the cessation of the marriage. An example of rebuffing the presumption is as follows:

Noah and Dez have been divorced for eight years, at which time Noah transfers to Dez the rental property that they had held during their marriage. Though Noah was to transfer the property per their settlement agreement, legal and business impediments hampered an earlier transfer of the property. The property was transferred immediately upon the conclusion of the business dispute and settlement of all legal matters. Under this situation, the transfer would probably be treated as falling under Section 1041.

The regulations under Section 1041 make it clear that to rebuff the previous rules, the transfer must have not met the safe harbor test because of factors which hampered an earlier transfer of the property such as:

- Legal or business impediments to transfer of the property
- Disputes concerning the value of the property owned at the time of the cessation of the marriage

The transfer is effected promptly after the impediment to transfer is removed.

Basis in the Property Received

When one spouse receives property pursuant to the divorce, they also receive the same attributes that the property carried with it in the hands of the transferor. These attributes would include items such as its basis, holding period, and all potential recapture relating to the property.

The code and the regulations under 1041 are clear that the basis of the transferred property in the hands of the transferee is the adjusted basis of such property in the hands of the transferor immediately before the transfer. It is also important to note that the carryover basis rule applies whether the adjusted basis of the transferred property is less than, equal to, or greater than its fair market value at the time of transfer. The basis in the transferred property is used for purposes of determining loss as well as gain upon the subsequent disposition of the property by the transferee.

The issue of liabilities associated with the property being transferred is important, as no gain is recognized even if the liabilities transferred exceed the adjusted basis of the property. For example, assume that Talia receives a building as part of the property settlement for which she has a tax basis of $5,000 and a current fair market value of $100,000 and related debt which encumbers the property of $30,000. No gain would be recognized on the transfer. However, if the property was transferred into a trust for the benefit of the spouse, the nonrecognition provisions would not apply to the extent that the sum of the liabilities assumed, plus the amount of the liabilities to which the property is subject, exceeds the total adjusted basis of the property transferred.

In computing the gain on the subsequent sale of the property by the acquiring spouse, the basis of the transferring spouse is used. Additionally, the holding period of the transferring spouse is also used. For example:

> Assume the same real estate that Talia received from her former husband was held by him for 10 years. After receiving the property, Talia turns right around and sells the property for its current FMV of $100,000. The gain on the sale would be $95,000 and would be a long-term gain.

If the property being transferred is a partnership interest or property that has passive loss carryovers, the basis of the interest in the passive activity is increased by the unused carryover losses allocated to the interest transferred. Thus, the losses are not allowable as a deduction. For example, if property with unused passive losses is transferred to the former spouse in the divorce settlement and later has some passive income, the unused passive losses from the property transferred in the divorce would not be used to offset the current passive income.

With respect to any passive loss carryforwards, the losses will continue to be available only to the party which owned the activity. Thus, the most beneficial division of the passive loss property is a matter of careful consideration in which one needs to consider the nature of the assets owned by each party.

The regulations under Section 1041 mandate that a transferor spouse of property must provide their transferee spouse sufficient records to determine the adjusted basis and holding period of the property transferred as of the date of the transfer. This information is to be provided at the time of the transfer. As this type of information should be reviewed in connection with reviewing any proposed settlement, this requirement should be written into the marital settlement agreement so there are no arguments later. In addition, this information should be made as an attachment to the marital settlement agreement.

Recapture

Since transfers under Section 1041 are treated as acquired by gift, the depreciation recapture provisions of IRC Sections 1245 and 1250 do not apply to the transfer of property to a spouse as part of a divorce settlement. However, other recapture provisions do apply. For received property that was used in business and an IRC Section 179 deduction taken, the receiving spouse may encounter a potential problem if the usage of the property changes. IRC Section 179 provides for recapture any time property ceases to be used predominantly in a trade or business. Additionally, IRC 280F(b)(3) requires recapture of excess depreciation on any listed property if the qualified business use percentage falls to 50 percent or less. Listed property includes luxury automobiles and personal home computers. This may be easy for the transferee spouse to meet but still can raise unexpected problems to the receiving spouse. The lesson here is to carefully review what the usage of the property was in the hands of the transferor spouse and what prior tax positions were taken. Though the recapture provisions under IRC Section 1245 and 1250 may not apply on the transfer of property under Section 1041, this recapture potential still remains with the transferee spouse and may be triggered by the subsequent disposition of the property by the receiving spouse.

Transfers to Third Parties

Though the application of Section 1041 applies to transfers from one spouse to another, transfers may still qualify if they are made to a third party on behalf of the spouse (former spouse). In order to have a transfer to a third party qualify, the transfer must fall under one of the following three situations:

1. The transfer to the third party is required by a divorce or separation agreement.
2. The transfer to the third party is pursuant to the written request of the other spouse (former spouse).
3. The transferor receives from the other spouse (or former spouse) a written consent or ratification of the transfer to the third party.

Under this third situation, the written consent or ratification must:

- State that the parties intend the transfer to be treated as a transfer to the nontransferring spouse (or former spouse) subject to the rules of Section 1041, AND
- Must be received by the transferor prior to the date of filing of the transferor's first return of tax for the taxable year in which the transfer was made.

If done properly, under each of the above situations the transfer of property to the third party will be treated as if the property was made directly to the nontransferring spouse and the nontransferring spouse will be treated as immediately transferring the property to the third party. It is also important to note that the deemed transfer from the nontransferring spouse to the third party does not qualify for any nonrecognition rules of Section 1041.

Special Issues in Property Transfers

Transferees of Closely Held Businesses and the Issue of Stock Redemptions

It may be possible to structure a stock redemption agreement as a nontaxable transfer of assets between spouses. Such stock redemptions may occur where both spouses have an ownership interest in a marital corporation. The big question that arises is whether the transaction will be treated as a redemption or a transaction under IRC Section 1041 and thus a constructive dividend to the remaining spouse. In essence the questions to be answered are:

■ Was the redemption part of a step transaction to relieve the transferor spouse of his/her obligation under the marital settlement agreement, or

■ Was the redemption an independent and separate transaction?

This issue of stock redemptions and divorce was addressed in the famous case of *Arnes v. U.S.*, (*Arnes I*), 981 F.2d 456 (9th Cir. 1992); and *John A. Arnes v. Commissioner*, 102 T.C. 522 (1994), *Arnes II*. The husband and wife in the *Arnes* cases owned a McDonald's franchise. The parties' California divorce decree (California being a community property state) provided that the corporation would redeem the wife's 50% stock interest. The ex-wife first reported a gain on the sale and paid the tax but later filed a suit for refund in the district court claiming the nonrecognition rules of IRC §1041 applied to the transfer because it was made between former spouses incident to a divorce. The Ninth Circuit Court of Appeals held that the transfer qualified for nonrecognition treatment. However, the Ninth Circuit did not address the tax ramifications to the former husband because he was not a party to the lawsuit. *Arnes II* involved a case before the Tax Court to determine the former husband's tax liability. The IRS argued that the former husband was personally liable for the purchase of his ex-wife's stock as part of the corporate division. Because of the stock redemption, the IRS urged that the corporation relieved the ex-husband of a legal operation, which constituted a constructive dividend. The tax court rejected the argument that a constructive dividend should be imposed because of the ex-husband's obligation. The interesting aspect of the Arnes decisions is that both spouses eluded responsibility for payment of tax. The same issue was addressed in *Blatt v. Commissioner*, 102 T.C. 77 (1994) , where the Tax Court ruled that when the divorce decree requires the corporation to redeem all of the wife's stock, the wife may be subject to tax on her realized gain. The key under these cases was whether or not the husband had a primary and unconditional obligation on the payment from the company to the wife for the redemption of her stock.

In a recent case the Eleventh Circuit court of appeals rebuffed the position of the Internal Revenue Service that a woman must pay tax on payment to her under the stock redemption provisions of the divorce agreement. In *Craven v. United States*, 11th Circ. No. 99-12803, 6/19/00), the former husband and wife had owned a 51% and 49% interest, respectively, in a pottery business. The husband and wife entered into a settlement agreement in which the wife agreed to sell and the corporation agreed to redeem her stock for $48 million through the issuance of a promissory note. The payment was to occur in monthly payments of $15,000 for ten years (beginning in June 2000), and then lump sum payments of $1 million occurring in five-year increments (beginning July 2000). The husband guaranteed the note, acknowledging that the terms of the note were of direct interest, benefit, and advantage to him as the sole remaining shareholder of the company. Any payment not made by the company by the tenth of each month was to be made by him. Furthermore, either he or the corporation could make discounted prepayments, which occurred four times. The wife did not report any capital gain on the redemption from the prepayments on the note.

The 11th Circuit opinion found that the redemption proceeds received by the ex-wife qualified for nonrecognition treatment pursuant to Section 1041 of the Internal Revenue Code (IRC) because it "facilitates the division of a marital estate incident to divorce without taxation to the spouse who is withdrawing assets from the marital estate." Thus the Eleventh Circuit agreed that the redemption was tax-free to the wife because: (1) she was redeeming her stock pursuant to the divorce settlement, (2) the husband guaranteed the note, and (3) the husband acknowledged in the note that its terms were of direct interest, benefit, and advantage to him. What is key in this ruling is that the Court stated that the first item alone was enough to qualify the wife's transfer to the corporation for non-recognition under Section 1041 and that the other two fact simply reinforced that conclusion. In redeeming her stock, the wife was acting "on behalf" of the husband since the divorce settlement reflected his wishes on the matter. Therefore the transfer qualified under Section 1041 and Reg. Section 1.1041-1T (c), Q&A9.

The *Craven* court also noted that Section 1274 of the IRC does not operate to tax the imputed interest on the corporation's note in connection with the transfer of stock because the transfer fell within the nonrecognition provision of Section 1041.

The key is to properly structure the settlement so that its possible tax consequences in the event of a corporate redemption of stock to buy out a spouse's interest in a closely held corporation is upheld. Make sure that there is a concurrence and understanding among all parties as to the substance of the transaction and than a concise and unambiguous drafting of the required documents. In the marital settlement agreement there should be specific reference to the intentions of the parties with regard to the tax consequences. Be sure to include in the tax indemnification section that holds the transferee spouse liable for any tax assessed against the transferor spouse if either the transferee spouse takes a different position on their tax return than agreed to in the settlement agreement or simply if the transaction is audited by the IRS and it is challenged.

Some professionals may suggest that if you are doing a transaction you want to qualify as a redemption, request a revenue ruling from the IRS in advance. The problem here is that it is usually expensive and time-consuming and will vary based on the facts of the case. Thus even if you get a positive ruling, if your facts in the actual transaction change from those that were submitted for the ruling, the IRS would not be bound by the ruling.

If you want the redemption to be respected, you can also try to structure the redemption separate from the divorce settlement agreement to try to fall outside of IRC Section 1041. No mention of the redemption should be made in the divorce settlement agreement. The key in this situation is to structure the transaction such that the nonredeeming shareholder spouse should avoid any personal obligation to redeem the stock.

Overview of Retirement Plans and the Tax Impact on Transfers During Divorce

A major asset in many marital estates is retirement benefits. There are many types of retirement arrangements, and the workings of these plans can be quite confusing. There are qualified and nonqualified plans. In general, two common types of qualified plans are defined contribution and defined benefit plans. Defined contribution plans have a percentage of income contributed to the plan each year by the individual employees or by the employer on behalf of the employee. Each employee has his or her own individual account which the plan administrator maintains and manages. Valuing an individual's interest in a defined contribution plan can be done easily by looking at a current statement to determine its current value based on the market value of the investments that it holds. A common type of defined contribution plan is a 401(k) plan; a profit sharing plan; or a money purchase plan. Determining the portion that is marital or non-marital is also straightforward, though time consuming, because one can look to the balance at the date of marriage and allocate the growth on a specific basis or make some allocation based on invested dollars.

Defined benefit plans are those where the end benefit at retirement is determined and then an actuary determines what amount will be needed annually to fund such benefits. Determining the value of such benefits is more complicated as one needs to make assumptions, such as when the payout will begin, the life expectancy of the individual receiving the benefit, and how long they expect to work, just to name a few. Based on the various assumptions, a present-value calculation of the expected benefits are then calculated. Other factors that may come into play in determining the benefits to be received may be the spouse's final salary or an integration with Social Security benefits. In determining marital and non-marital allocations an analysis of years employed during the marriage and number of years after the marriage until benefits are to be received needs to be analyzed and ratios calculated. This is more complicated than for defined contribution plans. Additionally, it is important to review the choices as to how the benefits will be paid out: over one's life, over the joint lives of you and your former spouse (rights of survivorship), or possibly in certain years.

A nonqualified plan would be an individual retirement account (IRA) or possibly a nonqualified deferred compensation plan.

In dividing retirement plans there are three common approaches: the immediate offset approach, immediate allocation of benefits, and the reserved jurisdiction approach. The immediate offset approach will only work if the marital estate has significant assets beyond the retirement benefits. Under this approach, the present value of the retirement benefits that the employee spouse may have or might be given are determined and credited with this asset. The nonemployee spouse is then given other marital property to offset the value of the retirement benefits that are being kept by the employee spouse.

In some instances it may make sense to provide the nonemployee spouse with some amount of retirement benefits or the marital estate may simply lack other marital property or liquidity sufficient to offset the working spouse's interest in the retirement benefits. In this case, the benefits or interest in the retirement plans can be allocated between the two spouses. In a defined contribution plan it is simply a determination of the account balance to be allocated. In the defined contribution plan, which promises to pay the employee spouse a certain amount per month or annually at retirement, the expected benefit is allocated based on a percentage when it eventually pays out.

When the value cannot be determined or ultimate benefits are contingent on certain events, the reserved jurisdiction approach is used. Under this approach the court will retain the authority to divide and distribute the benefits from the retirement plan at the time it pays or some other predetermined time. This is difficult because it keeps the parties from having their litigation be truly final until sometime in the future, leaving the ultimate resolution of one's economic situation unknown. This is not only seen in division of certain retirement benefits but is common in the area of stock options, especially when the employee spouse is not totally vested in the options at the time of the divorce.

Understanding the concept of vesting is an important item. In many defined contribution plans, the employer will contribute to the employee's retirement account. This is common with 401(k) plans with employer-matching programs, in which an employer will match an employee's contribution up to a certain percentage. However, if the employee is to leave the company, some plans are designed such that unless you have been with the company for a specified number of years, you forfeit a portion of those contributions made by the employer. For example, the plan may call for only 40% vesting after two years, 50% vesting after three years, and so forth. So, in looking at the value of your spouse's retirement plan you will need to consider the impact of the vesting provisions. Naturally, all dollars invested by the employee spouse are automatically 100% vested. Consider the following example: Joshua has been employed by the Noah Boat Company for two years and has contribution to the company's 401(k) plan plus the growth attributed to the portion he has contributed to be $15,000 over this time. Also assume the company has matched Joshua's contributions into his account, and this amount plus accrued earnings is $5,000. Assuming that Joshua is only 40% vested in the plan, the value of his retirement plan at the time of the divorce is only $17,000, not the $20,000 currently showing in his account statement.

Use of a QDRO

The problem in dividing qualified plans is that any early distribution (prior to the age of 59½) from a qualified plan will be subject to a 10% penalty by the IRS in addition to the amount withdrawn by the participant spouse, which will be taxed as an early distribution. To avoid this problem in divorce situations, there is IRC Section 401(a)(13)(B), which provides that the creation, assignment, or recognition of a right to any benefit will be permissible if it is done in conjunction with a qualified domestic relations order, normally referred to as a QDRO. IRC Section 72, which provides for a 10% penalty on early distributions, also provides an exception for payments to an alternate payee pursuant to a QDRO. Thus, even if the alternate payee does not roll over his or her share of the retirement account, he or she will not be subject to the 10% penalty; however, the amount not rolled over would be included in the alternate payee's income if a QDRO is used.

The Code defines a QDRO as a domestic relations order that creates or recognizes the existence of an alternate payee's right to receive all or a portion of the benefits payable with respect to a participant under a plan or assigns that right to an alternate payee. Within this definition, additional terms need to be defined.

In order to have a qualified domestic relations order you first must have a domestic relations order. In addition, you will hear the term "alternate payee" in connection with the concept of a QDRO. The individual who will be getting paid or receiving the benefits from the qualified plan is referred to as the alternate payee. The alternate payee is defined as any spouse, former spouse, child, or other dependent of a participant child, or other dependent of a participant who is recognized by a domestic relations order as having a right to receive all or a portion of the benefits payable under a plan with respect to such participant.

The Basic Items Every QDRO Must Have

The form of the QDRO is critical. If you do not have a proper QDRO, the distribution from the qualified plan could end up being taxed to the paying spouse in addition to a 10% penalty. In order for a QDRO to qualify, the following basic items must be clearly stated:

- The name and the last known mailing address of the participant (It will not fail to be a QDRO if the current mailing address is missing if the plan administrator has reason to know the address independently of the order.)

- The name and mailing address of each alternate payee covered by the QDRO (It will not fail to be a QDRO if the current mailing address is missing if the plan administrator has reason to know the address independently of the order.)

- The amount or percentage of the participants' benefits to be paid by the plan to each such alternate payee, or the manner in which such amount or percentage is to be determined

- The number of payments or period to which such order applies
- Each plan to which such order applies

The real key here is that the alternate payee steps into the shoes of the participant. Thus, the alternate payee receives no greater rights or benefits than the participant had under the plan. IRC Section 414(p)(3) is clear that the order should not require a plan to provide any type or form of benefit or any option not otherwise provided under the plan, nor should it require the plan to provide increased benefits or require the payment to an alternate payee of benefits that are required to be paid to another alternate payee under another order previously determined to be a QDRO. Having said this, there is some leeway in that the QDRO can be structured such that the alternate payee can begin to receive payments of benefits after the participant's earliest retirement age, even though the participant has not yet retired. The Code defines the term "earliest retirement age" as the earlier of:

- Date on which the participant is entitled to a distribution from the plan, or
- The later of: (1) the date the participant attains age 50, or (2) the earliest date in which the participant could begin receiving benefits under the plan if the participant separated from service.

One of the key people involved in a QDRO is the plan administrator, who is:

- In charge of fulfilling the requirements of any QDRO
- In charge of determining the qualified status of the domestic relations order
- Responsible for notifying the participants and each alternate payee of the receipt of such order and the plan's procedures for determining the qualified status of the QDRO

It is wise to have the QDRO in place at the time the divorce is being proved and before it is final. Many a mishap has occurred because the QDRO was not in place and the divorce had already been finalized. For example, if the employee spouse dies before a QDRO is drafted, the nonemployee spouse may be frozen out of any benefits. As another example, if the employee-participant retires without a QDRO and elects a single-life annuity, the ex-spouse's right to a survivor annuity may be lost. Even worse, if the participant remarries prior to the QDRO's entry and then retires, the surviving spouse's pension benefit will probably vest in the new spouse, thereby forever depriving the prior spouse of this benefit. The right to survivor benefits is very important and you need to make sure that you are covered so that such coverage cannot be waived without your written consent. If done correctly, your rights as the former spouse should override the rights of the new spouse of your former spouse.

Planning with QDROs

There are many creative planning opportunities in using QDROs. Two of the opportunities to be considered are security interest and payment of professional fees during divorce.

Security Interest

Normally the creation of a security interest in a qualified plan would cause a constructive distribution of the portion pledged or even possible disqualification of the plan. The IRC is very clear that a trust (retirement plan) shall not constitute a qualified trust unless the plan provides that the benefits provided under the plan are not assigned or alienated [IRC Section 401(a)(13)(A)]. The planning opportunity comes into play with the very next section of the Code [IRC Section 401(a)(13)(B)], which provides that the creation of a security interest or a right to any benefit payable with respect to a domestic order that would normally be disallowed under IRC Section 401(a)(13)(A) will not apply if the security interest is pursuant to a QDRO. This was also supported by an IRS letter Ruling 9234014 which indicated that a creation of a security interest in a husband's qualified retirement plan as part of a judgement of divorce to cover potential income taxes and indemnify his former wife for certain contingent tax obligations which was covered by a QDRO was a permitted assignment.

The use of the QDRO in making the qualified retirement plan a piece of collateral for divorce obligations can be a great tool to use. In general, in addition to life insurance to cover divorce obligation upon death of the payor spouse for payments due over time, if the spouse has a significant retirement plan, placing the spouse's retirement account into a QDRO and tying it to a collateralized agreement might add additional security. This might also give the payee a sense of comfort knowing that there are real funds available to cover the payor's divorce obligations. It might also be an incentive for the payor spouse to follow through with his/her obligations.

I have not seen any cases or rulings directly on this point but based on the actual reading of the law, it would appear that you could set up a security interest in the retirement plan with a QDRO that upon default on his/her obligations a specified amount and the specific timing of the payments would be made from the plan to the alternate payee. Two good scenarios that would be perfect for this type of security interest would be the payment of alimony and child support obligations.

Alimony Payments Collateralized with the Qualified Retirement Plan

Assume that Joshua, as part of the divorce agreement with Talia, is obligated to pay Talia $5,000 per month in qualifying alimony. Joshua, who is an executive, has a qualified profit sharing plan which is currently worth $2,000,000, and he is fully vested. He is also a high roller and a gambler. Talia is very nervous that he will spend his money elsewhere and does not want to constantly chase him for her monthly payment. To alleviate this problem, or at least give Talia some comfort, a QDRO was set up covering Joshua's qualified retirement plan, naming Talia, the former spouse, as the alternate payee and specifying the amount of the payment ($5,000) and the period it will cover (the same period of the maintenance obligation) indicating that payment would be made if Joshua does not make his monthly obligation. This plan will also leave each of them in the same tax position as if he was paying the alimony out of his current earnings and taking an alimony deduction from his adjusted gross income. Demonstrating this, assuming Joshua does not pay his obligation and Talia has the administrator of the plan then make a payment directly to her as the alternate payee, she would receive a taxable distribution from the qualified plan (assuming she didn't roll it over) and Joshua picks up no income and receives no tax deduction. If Joshua had paid the alimony directly, Talia would still have picked it up as income. Joshua's cash flow is improved because he was able to remove funds from his qualified retirement plan without incurring any tax consequences.

Child Support Payments Collateralized with the Qualified Retirement Plan

Assume the same facts as above except that the payments by Joshua are for child support of their son, Noah. Based on Joshua's history, Talia obtains from the court a QDRO that provides for child support, payable to a child in the custody of his mother, Talia. The QDRO could be written one of two ways:

1. It could direct the plan administrator to make the support payments directly from the participant's (Joshua) account until the child (Noah) reaches a certain age, at which time the payments stop, or
2. It could set up the QDRO as a collateral arrangement in which payments are made to the alternate payee if the participant defaults on his obligation of child support.

When we looked at the QDRO in connection with alimony, the IRC provided that the distributions to the spouse or former spouse who is an alternate payee are generally includable in their income of that spouse or former spouse. However, there is no similar provision for distributions to nonspouse alternate payees, such as a child. Because of this one would assume that the distribution to an alternate payee who is a child of the participant, or on behalf of the child, would not be includable in the income of the child but rather would be includable in the gross income of the plan participant for whom the QDRO was set up.

As in the alimony situation, the plan participant, Joshua, would be in no worse tax position than if he had paid the child support out of his earned income. Since the child support from Joshua's earned income is nondeductible, in essence he is paying the child support with after-tax dollars. The payments from the QDRO to Noah or to his mother, Talia, on behalf of Noah, as an alternate payee would be tax-free and the tax burden would still remain with Joshua, the participant. Thus, Joshua, Noah, and Talia are in the same tax situation as if the payments were made directly from Joshua. Again, the only difference to Joshua is that his cash flow was helped by being able to dip into his qualified retirement plan without any penalties.

Payment of Professional Fees During Divorce

Through the use of a QDRO funds can be obtained to pay for legal and other professional fees during the divorce without incurring an early withdrawal penalty. You have now just found another source of funds.

When dealing with distributions from retirement plans please keep in mind the mandatory 20% withholding tax that applies to any eligible rollover not deposited directly into another plan. In these cases it may be important to gross up the amount that is truly needed.

Individual Retirement Accounts

We have all heard about "substance over form," but when it comes to transferring IRAs, it is form over substance. The IRS is very clear that an early distribution from an IRA is subject to a 10% penalty as provided in Section 72(t) of the Internal Revenue Code (IRC). The IRC also provides that any amount distributed from an IRA ". . . shall be included in gross income by the payee or distributee, as the case may be, in the manner provided under IRC Section 72." Because an IRA is not a qualified plan, a QDRO cannot be used to avoid the penalties associated with an early withdrawal. However, the IRC does provide for an exception, which is contained in IRC Section 408(d)(6), whereby a transfer of an individual's interest in an IRA to his or her spouse or former spouse under a divorce or separation instrument is not considered a taxable transfer. This exception applies only if the following two requirements are met:

1. There must be a transfer of the IRA participant's interest in the IRA to his or her spouse or former spouse, and
2. Such transfer must have been made under a divorce or separation instrument.

It is important to note that IRC Section 408(d)(6) deals with the "transfer" of an individual's *interest* in an IRA and does not deal with "distributions" from an IRA.

If, as part of the divorce or legal separation, you are required to transfer some or all of the assets in a traditional IRA to your spouse or former spouse, there are two commonly used methods to effect this transfer. IRS Publication 590 describes the two methods for transferring an interest in an IRA tax-free as follows:

1. If you are transferring all of the assets of the IRA, you can simply make the transfer by changing the name on the IRA from your name to the name of your spouse or former spouse.
2. For a direct transfer, simply direct the trustee of your traditional IRA to transfer specific assets to the trustee of a new or existing IRA set up in the name of your spouse or former spouse.

This appears to be rather straightforward. However, so often these simple rules are not followed and problems arise. This is illustrated in two recent tax cases, which demonstrate the importance of form over substance. In *Jones v. Commissioner* TC Memo 2000-219, the taxpayer had an IRA. In 1992 the taxpayer and his wife filed for divorce. In April 1994, the husband and wife drafted a marital settlement agreement requiring the husband to transfer his IRA to his wife as part of the property settlement. In May 1994, the husband cashed out his IRA (he received a check for $68,000) and endorsed the check he received to his wife. The IRS sought to have the $68,000 included in the taxpayer's income for 1994. It was the court's opinion that the endorsement of the check to the wife was not a "transfer" of the husband's interest in the IRA because his interest in the IRA was depleted at the time he withdrew the funds. The check for the IRA balance was endorsed rather than deposited into the husband's account and did not affect the outcome of the case. The Court stated that the transfer of IRA assets by a distributee to a nonparticipant spouse does not constitute the transfer of an interest in the IRA under IRC Section 408(d)(6). The purpose of IRC Section 408(d)(6) was to offer a means to avoid having the interest transferred treated as a distribution. It does not permit the IRA participant to allocate to a nonparticipant spouse the tax burden of an actual distribution.

Following the same logic was the case of *Bunney v. Commissioner* 114 TC No. 17 (April 2000). The husband and wife, both residents of California, a community property state, were divorced in 1992. Per their divorce settlement, the husband's IRA, which was funded with contributions that were community property, was to be divided equally between the husband and wife. The husband withdrew the $125,000 balance of his IRA and deposited the proceeds into his money market savings account. During the same year, he transferred $111,600 to his former spouse as part of the divorce settlement. Mr. Bunney reported only $13,400 of the IRA distribution on his 1993 federal income tax return.

Just as in the *Jones* case, the main issue revolved around the question of whether the husband's gross income should include the distributions he received from his IRA. Again, the court turned to the two requirements that must be fulfilled in order for the exception of IRC Section 408 (d) (6) to apply, and again the husband did not satisfy the first requirement calling for a "transfer" of the IRA interest to the spouse. Mr. Bunney cashed out his IRA, deposited the funds into his money market savings account, and followed this by paying his former spouse some of the proceeds.

As demonstrated by these two cases, the simple "form over substance" is important in transferring an IRA tax-free pursuant to a divorce or separation agreement. An easy way to avoid any potential problems is to have the actual transfer papers made available and incorporated into the divorce settlement. The timing and nature of the transaction are critical in the transfer. If the transfer of an IRA from one spouse to another is made prior to a divorce settlement or sometime after and not part of the divorce settlement, in all likelihood it would be deemed to be taxable to the participant as an early distribution. So be careful! A mishap with the form of the transaction can have significant tax consequences.

Social Security Benefits

This item is so often forgotten about that it is worth making a clear point here. An ex-spouse may be entitled to half of a former spouse's Social Security benefits under the following four conditions:

1. The couple were married for ten (10) years before they were divorced.
2. The ex-spouse is not married at the time she or he is looking to collect on the former spouse's Social Security.

3. The ex-spouse is age 62 or older.

4. The ex-spouse is not entitled to Social Security benefits that equal or exceed half of the former spouse's benefits.

If you have worked in the past, currently work, or plan on working, you will need to get a schedule of what your current or expected Social Security benefits are to determine if your benefits would be greater than one-half of your former spouse's. Another thing not to worry about is that the former working spouse's benefits normally will not be reduced upon retirement, due to such a claim by your former spouse.

Other Types of Retirement Benefits

Qualified plans for certain government and public employees (police, school-teachers, firefighters, etc.) do not fall under the QDRO rules. In fact, many of these plans may not allow for a division of these benefits and thus are not assignable. However, under the recent tax bill passed in the summer of 2001, the availability of QDRO usage was extended to IRC Section 457 plans. IRC Section 457 sets forth the types of eligible plans that can be established for a state or local government or tax-exempt organizations. A thorough review of all deferred compensation plans for state and local government and tax-exempt organizations should be reviewed very carefully if you or your spouse is employed by such an organization. In addition to the QDRO issue, many government employee plans are set up such that the employer's contribution doesn't kick in until the employee retires. The amount of the employer's contribution is determined based on the timing of the employee's retirement and his or her current compensation. In these cases looking at a statement showing what you or your spouse contributed into the plan may not show the whole picture and may underestimate the value of the plan. For example, because some plans have you contribute based on the age you retire and the number of years of service, your monthly retirement benefits will be based on a percentage of your compensation; thus your amount contributed to the plan does not show the true picture.

The Sale of the Personal Residence— When, How, or Does One of the Spouses Get It?

It may be desirable for the custodian of the children to remain in the marital residence for a time after the divorce. This decision has both psychological and financial considerations. For example, it may be psychologically desirable for the children of a divorcing couple to remain in the same marital home and same school system to ease their adjustment to the divorce. It may also be practical if the payments on the marital residence are lower than rental or mortgage payments on another residence.

In negotiations the custodial parent often urges that he or she should be awarded the marital residence "for the sake of the children." If the custodial parent's interest actually is only to live in the residence for some period of time with the children, it is not necessary to make a present disposition of the ownership of the residence. This goal can be accomplished by merely giving the custodian possession of the residence for a period of time.

In negotiating over the time period the custodian is to stay in the marital residence, the time frame should be a logical one. The justification of the custodian to remain in the residence is that the divorce itself is a formidable adjustment for the children to make, and they should not also be required to adjust to a new residence, new friends, and new schools. The length of time, therefore, should be related to the adjustment factor and other transitions that a child will go through. For example, if a child is two or three years old, a transitional time might be when the child enters school. Other transitional events might be a child entering, or finishing, high school.

The situation in which the custodian is granted possession of the residence for a period of time presents many of the same problems as when the parties agree that the real estate is to be sold shortly and the sale proceeds to be divided. Who makes mortgage, tax, insurance, repair, and maintenance payments until the residence is sold?

One solution is that both spouses continue living in the residence until it is sold and share the expenses of the residence and other living expenses in accordance with an agreement. This, however, only works in a friendly divorce.

If the former wife stays in the residence until it is sold and pays the mortgage, she will raise the issue of why the husband should take advantage of the principal mortgage reduction without having contributed to it. The wife also takes a position that her plans were to rent a residence and the rental would be lower than the mortgage payments. The husband on the other hand contends that the wife would have to pay rent wherever she goes and therefore she would pay the mortgage. In most cases the result is that the former wife should be credited out of the sale proceeds for the reduction in the principal balance of the mortgage during the time she had possession of the house and paid the mortgage.

This type of arrangement allows for the nonpossessory party's investment to grow or diminish in accordance with the market. It also allows the possessory party to recover some of the sums spent on the residence through reimbursment for the amounts by which the principal balance of the mortgage was reduced. If the parties will divide the proceeds equally upon the sale, then, in effect, by reimbursing the possessory party off the top, she is only reimbursed by the amount by which the mortgage has been reduced. The balance that the possessor of the real estate has spent on the residence, by way of interest payments, real estate taxes, etc., may be viewed as an expense he or she would have incurred under any circumstances for living quarters.

Another resolution to the problem is to have the real estate appraised at the time of the divorce, or agree to its value, and agree as to what the parties' present interest in the real estate is (e.g., 50/50). Thus if, for example, the appraised value is $150,000 and the mortgage balance is $50,000, the parties would have a $100,000 equity interest. If there is to be an equal division the nonpossessory party would have an equity interest of $50,000. The agreement would further provide that the equity interest of the nonpossessory party will be adjusted in a ratio to the eventual sale price.

For example, if the residence eventually sells for $225,000, the value would increase by one-third. The nonpossessory party's equity interest of $50,000, would therefore be increased by one-third, or $16,500. Under this formula the party in possession obtains full benefit of the amounts she invested in the property by way of mortgage payments, and other payments and the nonpossessory spouse will have the benefit of the increase in the value of his or her interest in the residence.

There is a caveat to the above arrangement if the possessory spouse substantially improves the real estate and the increase in value, in part, is on account of the improvement to the real estate. To cover this possibility the agreement should provide that the spouses either pay for the improvement in proportion to their ownership interest, or that there will be an appraisal of the property to determine what its value would have been without the improvement. The equity value to be divided will then exclude the value of the improvement. While the agreement could merely provide for deducting the cost of the improvement, improvements to residential property seldom bring a 100% return.

Attention must also be given to the cost of necessary repairs and maintenance of the family residence until it is sold. If each of the parties will be sharing equally in the proceeds of the sale, such expenses should be shared equally. If the proceeds are not shared equally, such expenses should be paid in proportion to the division of the proceeds of the sale.

Tax Deductions

An often overlooked item in negotiations where one spouse pays some or all the housing costs for a home occupied by the other spouse is the tax consequences. This is important because the characterization of the payment of those costs depends upon various factors including how the title is held to the property and whether a spouse is primarily liable on the mortgage note.

Knowledge and use of the tax laws in the deductibility of interest payments and tax payments may help minimize the resulting tax consequences for the parties. In negotiations on behalf of the husband in instances where he shall pay the housing costs for the wife, the husband's attorney should recommend that the form of ownership not be as tenants in common, but in a form of joint ownership.

Where the husband is the only party liable on the mortgage, he may deduct both interest and tax payments, while if the parties are co-obligors on the mortgage, the husband may deduct one-half of the interest paid and all the tax payment made. However, where the form of ownership is as tenants in common, the husband could deduct only one-half the interest and tax paid, while if the wife is the sole owner, the husband may deduct neither taxes nor interest paid. Therefore, knowledge of the tax laws in negotiations as to the disposition of the marital residence may help parties implement their intentions and minimize the tax consequences.

The Ultimate Sale of the Personal Residence

Even if the real estate is to be sold immediately, it is most likely that the sale will not actually be immediate, and even in a good market it will usually take several months to sell the residence. This delay raises the following questions which will have to be resolved in the negotiating process.

- At what price shall the residence be listed?
- What happens if the residence is not sold at the listed price within a reasonable time?
- Who will occupy the residence until sale?
- What if the party in occupancy is not motivated to sell?
- What if the residence is sold before the entry of the judgment of a dissolution of marriage?

The negotiating solutions to the problems are:

- If the parties cannot agree to a listing price, an appraiser selected either by the parties or their lawyers determines the listing price.
- Inflate the listing price, for example, 10%, over the appraised fair market value to leave room for negotiations. Anticipate that the property may

not sell within a certain amount of time. A well-negotiated and drafted settlement provides for the price to be lowered by a certain amount or percentage periodically at the insistence of either party. Below a certain point both parties must agree to a reduction of the sale price, and that any offer which meets or is greater than the agreed-upon sale price (as adjusted from time to time) will be accepted at the insistence of either party.

- Under some marital settlement formulas it may be financially advantageous to the spouse who remains in the marital residence to continue residing there. Anticipate that the remaining spouse may not fully cooperate in selling the house. A well-drafted agreement, therefore, will provide that the remaining spouse shall cooperate with brokers in the sale of the residence and keep the residence repaired and attractive.

- If under the settlement formula the spouse who is not occupying the residence is contributing to, or paying all of, the mortgage, the formula may provide for an incentive for the occupant to sell the residence. The formula could provide for reductions in that spouse's contribution toward the mortgage if the real estate agent does not sell in a certain amount of time, thus giving the remaining spouse an incentive to cooperate in the sale of the residence.

- If the residence is sold before the judgment of a dissolution of marriage, a fair method to resolve the issue of what to do with the proceeds is to place the money into a joint account subject to withdrawal by both the parties. Such a provision provides the parties with a no-cost solution to the problem and facilitates settlement where certain debts are to be paid from the proceeds of the sale of the marital residence.

New Rules Under IRC Section 121

The sale of a personal residence is such that if there is a gain, the IRS will recognize it. However, since it is considered personal in nature, if there is a loss, it is not recognized.

After the Taxpayer Relief Act of 1997, the old rules on the replacement of a personal residence to avoid tax on any gain has been replaced with IRC Section 121 as amended. Under this amended section, $250,000 of gain per taxpayer is excluded if the property is *owned* and *used* as your principal residence for at least two of the last five years preceding the date of sale. For purposes of this exclusion, it is only permitted to be used once every two years. In other words, more than two years will have to have elapsed since the date of a previous sale of a house where the exclusion was taken. If this time period is not met, the gain excluded would be limited to the shorter of the following ratios:

- The total periods during the five-year period ending on the date of such sale of the residence which has been owned and used by the taxpayer as his or her principal residence over two years, or

- The period after the date of the most recent prior sale or exchange by the taxpayer which qualified for an exclusion and before the date of the current sale over two years.

$$\frac{\text{Days owned and used}}{2 \text{ years}} \times \text{Full Exclusion} = \text{Exclusion Allowed}$$

The exception to this rule is if you had to sell your house within this two-year period because of a change in place of employment, health problems, or for some unforeseen circumstances. Further analysis needs to be made if both parties had owned their own houses prior to marriage and sell both houses during the time they are married or if one party had sold a house within two years and now they file a joint return during the time they sell another house within the two-year period. Under this situation, the rules will not prevent a couple filing a joint return from excluding up to $250,000 of gain from the sale or exchange of either spouse's residence provided that either one would have been permitted to exclude up to $250,000 of gain if they had filed separate returns. For example:

Assume that Noah and Dez are married and file a joint return. Noah has owned a house for five years which he has lived in as his principal residence for at least two years. Dez has owned a house for 10 years which she has always lived in. Now that they are married they decided to sell both houses to buy a new one together. Noah and Dez may each exclude up to $250,000 assuming that they would have qualified to have excluded up to $250,000 of gain if they had filed separate returns. If the facts were that Noah had within the past two years sold and bought a new house, Dez would still be entitled to a $250,000 exclusion.

Joint Returns

If you and your spouse file a joint return, the amount of the exclusion is increased to $500,000 provided that:

- Either spouse meets the ownership requirements, and
- Both spouses meet the use requirements, and
- Neither spouse used the exclusion on a sale within the past two years.

For example, Noah and Dez are married and file a joint return. They have lived in the same residence since they were married two years ago. Noah has owned and lived in this house for 10 years. They both have decided to sell the house today for $500,000. Noah had purchased the house for $100,000. On their joint return, they will be able to exclude the entire $400,000 of gain.

Assume the same facts as above, but assume that Dez has lived with Noah since they were married only one year ago. Under this situation, only $250,000 would be excluded on their joint tax return.

For Those Involved in a Divorce

Congress, realizing the problem in meeting the various requirements for those who move out of their principal residence due to a divorce, made certain exceptions to assist in these situations. This section of the code addresses the ownership and use period for those involved in a divorce:

- If property is transferred to you from your spouse in a transaction qualifying under Section 1041, the period of time such spouse owns the property shall include the period the transferor spouse owned the property.

- You will be treated as using the property as your principal residence during any period of ownership while your spouse or former spouse is granted use of the property under a divorce or separation instrument. (Divorce or separation instrument means a decree of divorce or separate maintenance, written separation agreements, and support orders.)

This is an important change, since under the old rules when in a divorce situation where one spouse leaves the residence and the other spouse remains in the marital home for some time, even if the parties ultimately agree to sell the house later as part of the divorce settlement, the IRS was usually successful in making the argument that the spouse who moved out had abandoned the marital home as his or her principal residence. Thus, they would not qualify in rolling over the gain under the old IRC 1034 rules.

For example, assume that Josh and Talia had owned a residence together for 10 years prior to getting a divorce. As part of the divorce settlement, Talia was allowed sole possession of the house until their last child graduated from high school, which was in five years. At that time the house was to be sold and the proceeds to be split equally based on their joint ownership. Even though Josh is not living in the house during this five-year period, he will be deemed or treated as using the property as his principal residence during this period of time and thus qualify for the exclusion of his share of the gain up to $250,000.

Business Use of Portion of Personal Residence

In allocating assets in a divorce settlement, the future potential tax consequences should not be overlooked. This holds true with respect to the personal residence. In addition to the potential gain on the sale previously discussed, which is subject to an exclusion, the owner of the personal residence must recognize gain on the sale to the extent of any depreciation allowable with respect to the rental or business use of the personal residence. If not planned for in advance, it can be a big surprise for the unprepared spouse who takes the house as part of the property settlement. Look at the big surprise in the following example:

Noah and Talia were married for a long time. As a consultant, Noah worked out of a home office. They filed a joint return each year of their marriage in which they depreciated a portion of the house and took an expense deduction each year in connection with Noah's home office. The total depreciation taken over the period of the marriage was $100,000. As part of the property settlement in connection with Noah and Talia's divorce, Talia received sole possession and ownership of the house. Five years later after her last child graduated from high school, Talia decided to sell the house. The house had appreciated in value such that the total gain was $250,000. Talia did not concern herself about this because she had always anticipated that this gain would be excluded under the current tax rules. Now the surprise: Because of the depreciation recapture of the previous $100,000 of depreciation expense deductions taken while she was married, Talia may only be able to exclude $150,000 of her gain and must take the remaining $100,000 into her taxable income.

Filing Status

One question that is always asked is, "What status do I use to file my federal and state income taxes?" The next question is "Should I have 'our' accountant do mine or should I get a new accountant?" The first question you have to ask is whose camp the accountant is in. If your spouse has a company in which the accounting firm does accounting and tax work, the answer will be quite clear. Other times when there is only a once-a-year 1040, the choice may not be as clear. In those situations, and where you have enjoyed working with the accountant in the past, let the accountant know that you are uncomfortable with him/her handling both you and your soon-to-be former spouse's work. If you end up filing a joint return with your spouse, arrange to have a draft of the return for you and your tax accountant to review it before you sign it. Additionally, if you do file a joint return with your soon-to-be former spouse, make sure that he/she signs a tax indemnification agreement. Figure 7.1 is a sample of a tax indemnification agreement.

There will be four basic filing categories from which you can choose to file: (1) married filing jointly, (2) head of household, (3) single, and (4) married filing separately. Your filing status for the entire year is determined based on your status as of the last day of the taxable year.

In order to file a joint return, you must be married on the last day of the taxable year. When couples are in the process of getting a divorce they may still be married for tax purposes at the end of a particular tax year. Thus, the question always comes up as to whether or not to file a joint return. One issue to consider

---

FIGURE 7.1   Tax Indemnification Agreement

JOSHUA DOE ("JOSH") will cause to be prepared joint federal and state income tax returns for the year 2000. JOSH acknowledges that TALIA DOE ("TALIA") will not participate in the preparation of such returns except to supply information with respect to her income and deductions within her sole control.

TALIA agrees to execute said returns upon JOSH's representations and warranties that the information on the returns is true and correct. Further, that JOSH warrants and acknowledges that all relevant information as to his income from all sources and as to the deductible expenses has been provided to the preparer of the joint income tax return. Except as provided for herein, JOSH shall assume any and all liability with respect to such returns, including, but not limited to, taxes, penalties, interest, and attorneys' fees or accountants' fees with regard to filing such returns, amendments to such returns, or relating to the audit of such returns, and he shall indemnify and hold TALIA harmless with respect to such liability.

TALIA shall assume all liability relating to errors in reporting her income and deductions relating exclusively to her, and she shall indemnify and hold JOSH harmless with respect to such liability.

Any taxes due and owing relating to the 2000 federal and state tax returns shall be paid by JOSH at the time of the filing of such returns. If there is a deficiency assessment in connection with the 2000 returns, JOSH shall notify TALIA immediately in writing. Any amount ultimately determined to be due on such deficiency, together with interest and penalties, and any and all expenses that may be incurred in contesting the assessment, including without limiting, accountants' fees and attorneys' fees, shall be paid by JOSH, who shall indemnify and hold TALIA harmless thereon.

Any refunds or overpayment relating to the 2000 returns shall be deposited into a joint interest-bearing account requiring the signature of both JOSH and TALIA and shall be allocated by written agreement of the parties.

JOSH DOE	TALIA DOE
Dated: _____	Dated: _____

---

is the tax savings. This can be determined rather simply by having your accountant compute the taxes under both married filing jointly and married filing separately and compare the tax liabilities. The filing of separate returns by married individuals usually increases the aggregate tax liability. Another issue is the actual tax liability. When a couple files a joint return, they are jointly and severally liable for any tax, penalty, and interest due to the IRS. Even though you may sign a tax indemnification agreement, this will not have any bearing with the IRS. The IRS could still go after you for the taxes and then you would have to go after your former spouse in a separate action. Another issue to consider is that once a joint return has been filed, an amended return cannot be filed to elect a change in filing status. However, if you file separate returns, they can be amended within the statutory three years, and the filing status of married filing jointly can be elected.

For determining when you are no longer married for tax purposes, you (1) must obtain a final decree of divorce, (2) must obtain a court decree of separate maintenance, or (3) will possibly fall under the abandoned spouse rules or obtain a decree of annulment. The final decree of divorce is rather clear; however, the other situations may not be so clear. A court decree of separate maintenance is a court decree (which can be different from a court order) that orders the parties to live apart and alters the matrimonial bond and is required for unmarried filing status. This court decree has nothing to do with the payment of support. A court decree that merely provides for the payment of support is not a decree of separate maintenance, nor is a court order for temporary alimony, alimony *pendente lite*, or an interlocutory decree (under any of these situations the couple will remain married for tax filing purposes). So even if you are living apart, you may find that for tax purposes you are still married. Thus, if you want unmarried filing status before the final divorce decree, you will need a formal decree that legally separates the parties, ordering or authorizing them to live apart.

A decree of annulment holds that no marriage ever existed. Additionally, in this situation, you will need to file an amended return for any year still opened by statute for which you claimed a married status.

Head of Household

First to qualify as head of household for filing status, you, as a parent, must satisfy the following requirements as of the end of the tax year:

- As a parent you must be divorced or legally separated, or
- Qualified as married and living separate and apart pursuant to a qualified decree of separate maintenance.

Again, understanding the issues facing those going through divorce, the Code provided for head of household status if you meet the following four requirements:

1. You must file a separate return.
2. You must have paid for more than half of the cost of keeping up the home for the tax year for yourself and a qualified dependent.
3. Your spouse did not live in your home for the last six months of the tax year.
4. For over half the year, your home was the principal residence of a child whom you can claim as a dependent or could claim except that you released the exemption by written declaration to allow the noncustodial parent to take the exemption.

The benefits of being able to file as head of household are numerous. An example of some of these advantages are:

- The standard deduction for head of household is larger than what is available for one who files as single or married filing separately.
- Under married filing separately if one spouse itemizes, the other spouse must itemize; however, if you file as head of household, you can use your standard deduction regardless of what your spouse does.
- Save taxes as the lower incremental tax rate schedule is lower than married filing separately.
- There are certain credits that are available only when electing head of household status as opposed to married filing separately.

Allocation of Income

When one is married and filing a separate return, the allocation of income and deductions is important. Generally, for noncommunity property states, you will need to look at whose name the asset is held in. You should also be aware of state property law. For example, Talia and Joshua are in the middle of a divorce and decide to file as married filing separately. In deciding who will pick up the interest income earned on various investment accounts—those in Talia's sole name will be picked up by her and those in joint name will be split equally. If the house is sold, the person who has the title will be responsible for recognizing the gain as opposed to who received the sale proceeds.

For community property states, I would recommend that you refer to IRS Publication 555, Community Property and the Federal Income Tax. This publication provides a straightforward guide for filing separate tax returns in community property states. In general, if you are filing in a community property state, you will need to include 50% of those items attributable to the period of time that the community existed. The presumption is that each spouse owns an undivided half interest in all items of the community. When we use the word community, this is in many respects the same as marital property. Note that an allocation schedule of community income and deductions must be attached to each spouse's income tax return. If not, the statute of limitations may be extended beyond the normal statutory three years.

Under the following situations, community income would be allocated to a specific spouse as follows:

- Earned income is taxable to the spouse rendering the service.

- Trade or business income is allocated to the spouse exercising substantially all of the managerial control.

- Partner's distributive share of partnership income is allocated to the spouse who is the actual partner.

- Community income derived from separate property and not covered under items 1 through 3 is taxable to the owner of the specific property.

Having indicated that in community property states income shall be shared for tax purposes, if a spouse is abandoned, as defined by the IRC, then the abandoned spouse would not be liable for federal income tax on community income earned by the other spouse and not received, either directly or indirectly. In other words, the community property laws would not be followed in these cases. To be considered an abandoned spouse you will need to establish the following:

- Individual was married for some part of the year.
- Both spouses have lived separate and apart the entire year.
- Did not file a joint return.
- One or both spouses had earned income.
- No portion of the community income was transferred between spouses during the year.

Additionally, if you can establish a lack of knowledge concerning certain items of income that you would have no reason to know of, this too would fall under this relief. In addition to the conditions listed above, for additional relief you would have to show that:

- The income omitted would be treated as income of the other spouse.
- The nonrecipient spouse had no knowledge or reason to know the income existed.
- Based on the facts and circumstances, it would be inequitable to include the income in the nonrecipient spouse's income.

Assignment of Income Doctrine

As discussed earlier, when one spouse has property that has income deferral attached which is transferred, the accrued income must be recognized by the transferor. Remember that IRC Section 1041 deals with the nonrecognization of gain on the transfer to a spouse in connection with a divorce. It does not provide for the non-recognition of ordinary income which would normally be recognized upon transfer. This follows the assignment of income doctrine which basically says that the one who earns the income should be taxed on that income. When one spouse transfers property which produces ordinary income, the issue that is usually challenged is who must report the income. An example of a transfer that would not fall under IRC Section 1041 and should be taxed to the transfers is *EE U.S. Savings Bonds* where the accrued interest is recognized upon transfer. The IRS takes the position that since the interest is accrued but unrecognized income rather than gain, IRC Section 1041 does not shield that income from recognition. Transfer of only the income and not the asset will cause the transferor spouse to pick up income. For example, in a ruling from the IRS, regarding a baseball player who was required to pay 50% of the benefits from his non-qualified deferred compensation plan to his wife, the IRS ruled that the husband should be taxed on the benefits paid to his wife because they were attributable to the husband's personal services. Thus, earnings from personal services are taxed to the spouse who earned it.

In another ruling, the husband, who was an inventor and had patents on various inventions, received some damage payments due to infringement issues. The court ordered 50% of the damages to be paid to the wife. The IRS ruled that the husband was responsible for taxes on the full amount, as the wife was not the owner of an interest in the patent or lawsuit, but merely entitled to payments from her husband's.

In a 1994 Tax Court Case [Kochansky v. Commissioner, 67 T.C.M. (1994)] where an attorney assigned one half of his rights to a contingent fee case to his wife, the court ruled that he was taxable on the entire contingent fee because he earned the income. This supports the argument that you cannot assign income from personal services and that it should be taxed to the person who performed the services.

In summary, be careful and do some proper planning with regard to transfers of property that have

- Accumulated but unreceived income
- Assignment of income from settlement situations
- Assignment of income relating to personal services or earned by one spouse
- Deferred income (avoid)

If you are transferring property that has these types of issues attached to them, consider structuring the settlement that divides the assets on an after-tax basis or structure it such that the payout of the income will be treated as alimony. Again, as previously mentioned in this book, have a tax indemnification clause in your settlement agreement that will keep the parties in the same economic situation if the IRS takes a position that is contrary to what you have agreed to in your settlement.

Deduction for IRA Contribution

In determining a spouse's income for the purposes of determining the amount of an IRA deduction, alimony payments are treated as compensation. Normally, if one spouse participates in a qualified plan, the other spouse's contribution to an IRA is reduced or eliminated. However, if you are still married but file a tax return as married filing separately and you have not lived together during the tax year, your contribution to an IRA will not be limited by the fact that your spouse is covered by a qualified plan.

Dependency Exemptions

Under the general rules, the parent who has custody of a child may claim the dependency deduction, unless otherwise released to the noncustodial parent. Custody is determined by the divorce decree or separate maintenance agreement.

If the agreement is silent, custody is determined by which parent has physical custody during the greater portion of the calendar year.

For the child to qualify as a dependent for the dependency deduction, both parents together must provide more than one-half of the child's support during the year and that the child is either:

- Less than 19 years old
- Less than 24 years old and a full-time student
- 19 years or older and not a student but has income during the year of less than the exemption amount

There are certain situations in which a noncustodial parent may claim the dependency exemption:

- A multiple support agreement is in effect that designates the noncustodial parent as the person entitled to claim the exemption.
- The custodial parent relinquishes his right to claim the exemption to the noncustodial parent. This is done by completing IRS Form 8332.

Notice that the custodial parent has the control over the assignment of this exemption.

Pursuant to the authority accorded by IRC Section 152(e)(2), successful completion and attachment of IRS Form 8332 enables the noncustodial parent to claim the dependency exemption. Satisfying the signature requirement is critical for this to occur.

Along with the signature of the custodial parent confirming his or her consent, Form 8332 requires the taxpayer to furnish:

- The names of the children for which exemption claims were released
- The years for which the claims were released
- The Social Security number of the custodial parent
- The date of the custodial parent's signature
- The name and the Social Security number of the parent claiming the exemption

Under Form 8332 (see Figure 7.2), the assignment of the dependency exemption can be released for the current tax year or you can release the claim to the dependency exemption for all future years or for a specified number of years.

FIGURE 7.2 Release of Claim to Exemption for Child of Divorced or Separated Parents

Form **8332**
(Rev. December 2000)

Department of the Treasury
Internal Revenue Service

Release of Claim to Exemption
for Child of Divorced or Separated Parents
▶ **Attach** to noncustodial parent's return **each year** exemption is claimed.
Caution: Do not use this form if you were never married.

OMB No. 1545-0915

Attachment
Sequence No. **115**

Name of noncustodial parent claiming exemption

Noncustodial parent's
social security number (SSN) ▶

Part I   **Release of Claim to Exemption for Current Year**

I agree not to claim an exemption for_____
Name(s) of child (or children)

for the tax year 20_____ .

_____
Signature of custodial parent releasing claim to exemption

Custodial parent's SSN

Date

Note: If you choose not to claim an exemption for this child (or children) for future tax years, also complete Part II.

Part II   **Release of Claim to Exemption for Future Years** (If completed, see **Noncustodial parent** below.)

I agree not to claim an exemption for_____
Name(s) of child (or children)

for the tax year(s)_____ .
(Specify. See instructions.)

_____
Signature of custodial parent releasing claim to exemption

Custodial parent's SSN

Date

General Instructions

Purpose of form. If you are a **custodial parent** and you were ever married to the child's **noncustodial parent**, you may use this form to release your claim to your child's exemption. To do so, complete this form (or a similar statement containing the same information required by this form) and give it to the noncustodial parent who will claim the child's exemption. The noncustodial parent must attach this form or similar statement to his or her tax return **each year** the exemption is claimed.

You are the **custodial parent** if you had custody of the child for most of the year. You are the **noncustodial parent** if you had custody for a shorter period of time or did not have custody at all. For the definition of custody, see **Pub. 501,** Exemptions, Standard Deduction, and Filing Information.

Support test for children of divorced or separated parents. Generally, the custodial parent is treated as having provided over half of the child's support if:

• The child received over half of his or her total support for the year from one or both of the parents **and**

• The child was in the custody of one or both of the parents for more than half of the year.

Note: Public assistance payments, such as Temporary Assistance for Needy Families (TANF), are not support provided by the parents.

For this support test to apply, the parents must be one of the following:

• Divorced or legally separated under a decree of divorce or separate maintenance, **or**

• Separated under a written separation agreement, **or**

• Living apart at all times during the last 6 months of the year.

Caution: This support test does not apply to parents who never married each other.

If the support test applies, and the other four dependency tests in your tax return

instruction booklet are also met, the custodial parent can claim the child's exemption.

Exception. The custodial parent will not be treated as having provided over half of the child's support if **any** of the following apply.

• The custodial parent agrees not to claim the child's exemption by signing this form or similar statement.

• The child is treated as having received over half of his or her total support from a person under a multiple support agreement (**Form 2120,** Multiple Support Declaration).

• A pre-1985 divorce decree or written separation agreement states that the noncustodial parent can claim the child as a dependent. But the noncustodial parent must provide at least $600 for the child's support during the year. This rule does not apply if the decree or agreement was changed after 1984 to say that the noncustodial parent cannot claim the child as a dependent.

Additional information. For more details, see **Pub. 504,** Divorced or Separated Individuals.

Specific Instructions

Custodial parent. You may use this form to release your claim to the child's exemption for the current tax year or for future years, or both.

• Complete **Part I** if you agree to release your claim to the child's exemption for the current tax year.

• Complete **Part II** if you agree to release your claim to the child's exemption for any or all future years. If you do, write the specific future year(s) or "all future years" in the space provided in Part II.

 To help ensure future support, you may not want to release your claim to the child's exemption for future years.

Noncustodial parent. Attach this form or similar statement to your tax return for **each year** you claim the child's exemption. You may claim the exemption **only** if the other four dependency tests in your tax return instruction booklet are met.

Note: If the custodial parent released his or her claim to the child's exemption for any future year, you **must** attach a copy of this form or similar statement to your tax return for each future year that you claim the exemption. Keep a copy for your records.

Paperwork Reduction Act Notice. We ask for the information on this form to carry out the Internal Revenue laws of the United States. You are required to give us the information. We need it to ensure that you are complying with these laws and to allow us to figure and collect the right amount of tax.

You are not required to provide the information requested on a form that is subject to the Paperwork Reduction Act unless the form displays a valid OMB control number. Books or records relating to a form or its instructions must be retained as long as their contents may become material in the administration of any Internal Revenue law. Generally, tax returns and return information are confidential, as required by Internal Revenue Code section 6103.

The time needed to complete and file this form will vary depending on individual circumstances. The estimated average time is:

Recordkeeping . . . . 7 min.
Learning about the law or the form . . . . 5 min.
Preparing the form . . . . 7 min.
Copying, assembling, and sending the form to the IRS . . . 14 min.

If you have comments concerning the accuracy of these time estimates or suggestions for making this form simpler, we would be happy to hear from you. You can write to the Tax Forms Committee, Western Area Distribution Center, Rancho Cordova, CA 95743-0001. **Do not** send the form to this address. Instead, see the Instructions for Form 1040 or Form 1040A.

Cat. No. 13910F

Form **8332** (Rev. 12-2000)

A signed Form 8332 or its equivalent must be attached for each year the non-custodial parent is taking the exemption.

In order to be in a position to assign the dependency exemption and meet the requirement discussed above, you and your spouse or former spouse (assuming you both are the parents of the child) must (a) be divorced or legally separated, (b) have lived separate and apart at all times during the last six months of the calendar year, and (c) have a child that is in the custody of one or both of you (as parents) for more than half of the calendar year.

For those who have been divorced under an agreement executed prior to 1985 which provides that the noncustodial parent is entitled to the dependency exemption, the noncustodial parent must provide at least $600 of child support to the child. In looking at whether or not you meet this test, if you owed child support for an earlier year, your payments are considered support for the year paid, up to the amount of your required child support for that year.

Phaseout Limitation

Like many other benefits provided by the code, these benefits are taken away or reduced as one earns more money. This is the issue with personal exemptions. The deduction for personal exemptions is phased out ratably for taxpayers once their income gets to a certain level. For the year 2001, these thresholds are as follows: adjusted gross income of $132,950 for single individuals; $199,450 for married individuals filing a joint return; $166,200 for heads of households; and only $99,725 for those that are married filing separately. These thresholds are to be adjusted annually for inflation. Under the tax bill enacted in 2001, the phaseout of the personal exemptions are repealed. The repeal of this phaseout is planned to be over a five-year period. The phaseout is reduced by one-third in taxable years 2006 and 2007, reduced by two-thirds in taxable years 2008 and 2009, and will be fully effective for tax years after 2009.

Because the phaseout is tied to levels of income, in negotiating who will get the exemption(s), keep in mind the levels of the individual incomes. This approach should maximize the tax benefit of the dependency exemptions If the parties can agree and you settle on allocating exemptions back and forth every other year. Why not expand the language in the agreement to include the following:

If it is determined that the spouse who is allocated the dependency exemptions and for that year he/she cannot obtain any tax benefit from them due to their his/her of income or any other reason, the spouse will agree to sign Federal Form 8332 allowing the other spouse to take the various dependency exemptions. Any tax savings generated to the spouse who has now taken the dependency exemptions will be shared equally with the other spouse.

Allocation of Itemized Deductions

Divorce situations have an impact on the itemized deductions that may be taken. An especially important divorce planning item to remember is that if married individuals file separate returns and one spouse uses the itemized deductions, the other spouse does not qualify for the standard deduction and must also itemize his or her deductions. The following is a summary of some of these items.

Medical Expenses

A child of divorced or separated parents whose support test is met is treated as a dependent of both parents for the medical expense deduction. Thus, a parent can deduct medical expenses he or she pays for relating to their child, regardless of which parent is entitled to the dependency exemption. For example, Noah is the child of Josh and Talia, who are currently divorced. Though both contribute to the cost of raising Noah, Talia is allowed the dependency exemption. For the current year, Josh paid $4,000 in various medical costs relating to Noah, directly to various doctors. For the current year Josh will be allowed to include the $4,000 as part of his itemized deductions.

As part of some divorce tax planning, since medical expense deductibility is subject to a floor of 7.5% of adjusted gross income, if one spouse's gross income is expected to be so significant that any medical expenses paid by that spouse will not produce any tax benefit, it may make sense to increase the amount of alimony one spouse pays and have the other spouse pay the medical expenses directly. This would work well for insurance premiums paid. Working together with a former spouse can create many tax savings opportunities for the family unit.

All other rules relating to medical expenses to be treated as an itemized deduction also apply to those for one's dependent child.

Qualified Mortgage Interest

Interest is deductible if there is a mortgage on a qualified residence. A qualified residence includes the principal residence of the taxpayer and one other residence that is used by the taxpayer (if the second unit is rented out, it must be used by you for a number of days exceeding the greater of 14 days or 10% of the number of days during the tax year that it is rented out at a fair rented value). The limitation is for a mortgage in the amount of $1,000,000 for the acquisition or construction of your primary residence and $100,000 for a home equity loan. If, while you are still married and you file married filing separately, the limitations are reduced by half to $500,000 and $50,000. Also, the code provides that married taxpayers who file separate returns are treated as one taxpayer, with each entitled to take into account one residence unless both consent in writing to having only one taxpayer take into account both residences.

The problem is if you move out of the marital house and thus it ceases to be your qualified residence and you do not move into your second residence, the mortgage payments you make on the principal residence would not qualify as deductible mortgage interest.

As an example of this problem, Talia and Joshua are in the process of obtaining a divorce. During the divorce process, the court orders the removal of Joshua from the residence and there are no children living in the residence. Joshua still has a joint interest in the property and is still liable for the mortgage. In fact, the court forces Joshua to continue to pay the mortgage. Under this situation the mortgage interest would be personal interest to Joshua and probably not deductible. In these situations it would be better to have the payments structured as alimony to Talia and let Talia pay the mortgage directly and take the interest deduction.

Dealing with large estates where the house may have significantly increased in value, there may be situations where the house will need to be financed to take out the other spouse. The problem is that the acquisition indebtedness as discussed above cannot exceed the cost of the residence, including improvements.

The IRS has indicated in IRS Notice 88-74 that they expect that regulations will provide that, in general, debt incurred to acquire an interest of a spouse or former spouse in a residence, incident to divorce or legal separation, will be eligible to be treated as debt incurred in acquiring a residence, thus allowing one to finance an amount greater than the original cost and still qualify for interest that is deductible.

Deductibility of Divorce-Related Attorney and Accounting Fees

Generally, expenses paid relating to legal, accounting, and appraisal services incurred relative to proceedings for separation, divorce, and the divisions of marital property are not deductible. The determination of the tax treatment of attorney's fees, litigation expenses, and settlements rests with the classification of such payments, as related to a trade or business (IRC Section 162), for the production or preservation of income (IRC Section 212), or personal (IRC Section 262). IRC Section 162 and Treasury Regulation Section 1.162 provide the statutory framework for the definition of ordinary and necessary business expenses.

There have been Supreme Court cases involving legal expenses incurred by the taxpayer-husband to retain control of income-producing property, a controlling corporate interest, in a marital property partition. It was contended that such a judicial division would cause a financial detriment to the corporation and its stockholders. The taxpayers, similarly, asserted that a portion of the fees were deductible under IRC Section 212(2), as expenses for the conservation of property held for the production of income.

In one of these cases, the taxpayer acknowledged the wife's claim and offered an equalizing payment in satisfaction of the same. The Court's opinion was that "[T]he origin and character of the claim with respect to which an expense was incurred, rather than its potential consequences upon the fortunes of the taxpayer, is the controlling basic test of whether the expense was 'business' and hence whether it is deductible or not. . . ." In applying this test, the intent of the taxpayer in filing the suit is irrelevant.

Divorce is personal and as such, the associated costs of litigation are not deductible. There is strict statutory construction in these instances and the case law specifically reference marital property.

Generally, attorney fees in a divorce or separation are nondeductible since they are personal in nature. On the other hand, counsel fees for tax advice are deductible if the taxpayer itemizes deductions. Also, if the fees are incurred in defending income-producing property from another spouse's claims, such fees may be added to the basis of the property defended. In the case where one party agrees or is ordered to pay the other's legal fees, the deduction may be lost to both. IRC Regulation 1.262-1(c)(7) indicates that legal fees attributable to the production or collection of alimony are deductible. However, a deduction is not allowed for fees attributed to the collection of child support. See the Summary of Deductibility of Divorce Costs in Figure 8.1.

The planning opportunity is to have the professional provide the parties with an itemized bill for the services rendered. The professional should do the allocation, which may be based on time, customary charges for similar services for the locality, or results obtained.

Care should be taken in constructing questionable payments from a corporation or other business entity for these expenses. The courts have denied deduction status to legal and accounting fees paid by a business because the origin was the marital relationship. Further, the professional fees may be treated as a constructive dividend to the shareholder. Even where the company is named defendant in a domestic-related action, the origin of claim test may cause such deductions to be disallowed.

Treasury Regulation Section 1.212-1(I) provides that "Expenses paid or incurred by an individual in connection with the determination, collection, or refund of any tax, whether the taxing authority be federal, state, or municipal, and whether the tax be income, estate, gift, property, or any other tax, are deductible." Rev. Rul. 72-545, 1972-2 C.B. 179 illustrates three hypothetical situations in which a reasonable basis exists for establishing a deduction for divorce-related professional fees. The following is a summary of these situations:

1. A law firm, which limited its practice to issues of federal and state taxation, was engaged solely to provide advice relative to income tax consequences of proposed marital property transfers in release of marital rights.

2. The tax division, a separate department of the law firm which was providing nondeductible divorce-related services, provided advice as to the tax treatment of establishing a trust as a conduit for alimony or child support payments. The professional fees were allocated based on time expended and complexity of the tax issues.

3. For an agreed-upon fee, a law firm was engaged to provide both divorce and income tax consulting services. The mixed services were allocated between tax matters and nontax matters based on the time expended for each, the customary local fees charged for such services, and the results of the divorce negotiations.

FIGURE 8.1   Summary of Deductibility of Divorce Costs

The following summarizes the tax rules related to the costs of getting a divorce:

Type of cost	Tax treatment
Court costs	Not deductible
Legal fees for divorce	Not deductible
Legal fees for tax advice related to divorce	Deductible as misc. itemized deduction subject to 2% limitation
Appraisal fees, actuarial fees, and accountant's fees to determine correct tax or to help collect alimony	Deductible as misc. itemized deduction subject to 2% limitation
Personal advice or counseling	Not deductible
Legal fees for property settlement	Addition to basis of property received
Legal fees paid to spouse's attorney	May be subject to gift tax where no legal obligation to pay exists

Accurate and contemporaneously prepared time and billing records should be maintained from which a reasonable allocation of services can be provided to the client at the conclusion of the engagement. (See Figures 8.2 and 8.3.)

In a Californian appellate decision, a client sued her divorce attorney asserting that he failed to advise her as to the adverse tax consequences arising from the settlement of the marital estate. Although dismissed in appeal for failure of damage proof, this should provide incentive for the professional to maintain accurate time and charges records and refer the client to competent tax professionals. It is not what you know that is dangerous, but what you don't know. It is also important that you inquire about your attorney and financial advisor as to their tax expertise and whether the tax issues have been revised.

FIGURE 8.2   WORKSHEET: Tax Deductible Attorney's Fees

Client Name: _____   Date: _____

Total fees paid in _____
                                (year)

Allocation Summary

1. Nondeductible fees
   (IRC §162; trade legal service for family court)   _____

2. Deductible fees (line 7)   + _____

3. Nondeductible fees; additions to basis (line 8)   + _____

                    Total fees paid in _____   = _____

Deductible Fees

4. Tax deductible fees (IRC §162; trade or business expenses)

   Explanation: _____

   _____   _____

5. Tax deductible fees (IRC §212(1); production or
   collection of income)

   Explanation: _____

   _____   + _____

6. Tax deductible fees (IRC §212(2); management,
   conservation, or maintenance of income-producing
   property)

   Explanation: _____

   _____   + _____

7. Tax deductible fees (IRC §212(3); determination, collection,
   or refund of any tax)

   Explanation: _____

   _____   + _____

                    Total Deductible Fees   = _____

FIGURE 8.3   WORKSHEET: Tax Deductible Attorney's Fees

Fees Increasing Basis of Marital Property Received

8. Nondeductible fees: (IRC §1016 & Treas. Reg. §1.212-1)
   Specify with explanation

   (a) Real Estate: _____

   _____   _____

   (b) Household items & personal effects: _____

   _____

   _____   + _____

   (c) Retirement benefits: _____

   _____

   _____   + _____

   (d) Stocks/bonds/securities: _____

   _____

   _____   + _____

   (e) Commercial and professional business interests: ____

   _____

   _____   + _____

   (f) Miscellaneous property: _____

   _____

   _____   + _____

   (g) Retirement benefits: _____

   _____

   _____   + _____

   (h) Stocks/bonds/securities: _____

   _____

   _____   + _____

                Total Additions to Basis   = _____

Allocation of
Tax-Related Carryovers

Changing from filing a joint return in prior years to filing a separate return will have certain tax benefits that normally would have been carried over to future joint returns that now need to be allocated to each spouse. Some of these have been addressed by the IRC and the related regulations, while others are not addressed and need to be determined by the two spouses or former spouses. It is important to address the handling of carryovers in the marital settlement agreement so that there are no misunderstandings later on. A discussion of some of these tax-related carryovers follows:

Charitable Contribution Carryovers

Normally, a charitable contribution deduction for an individual is limited to 50% of the contribution base. (The contribution base equals the adjusted gross income before deductions for any net operating losses). If you incur excess charitable contributions, this excess is carried forward for five years. After the five-year period, any remaining excess is lost.

The IRS regulations are clear when the carryover of the charitable contributions is from a period when the spouses or former spouses had filed joint returns. In this situation, the charitable contribution carryforwards are to be apportioned between the spouses in the same ratio as separate carryforwards would have been had the spouses filed separate returns for the year in which the excess contributions arose. The regulations provide the following formula (these rules may not be modified in a marital settlement agreement):

1. Divide the amount of contribution computed as if the spouses had filed separate returns in the year the contribution was made by the total carryover available in the contribution year based on the separate contributions.
2. Multiply the ratio in Step 1 by the total amount of the carryover available in the carryover year in which the spouses first file separate returns.

Due to the phaseout rules, it is possible to have no contribution carryforwards in a hypothetical separate return scenario even though the joint return produced a contribution carryforward.

Net Operating Losses

Net operating losses are carried back three years or forward 15 years. The NOL is first carried back until fully absorbed and then forward. However, the taxpayer can elect to forgo the carryback period and carry the NOL forward instead. Just like the carryover of charitable contributions, the regulations under Section 172 of the code provide a mechanism to allocate the NOL carryover to the individual spouses when they arise in a year when they filed jointly and now file separately. The amount of each spouse's separate net operating loss carryover or carryback to the taxable year is apportioned between the spouses in the same ratio as separate NOL carryforwards and carrybacks would have been had each spouse computed income and deductions separately. It is possible that the amount of the NOL will not be used.

Capital Loss Carryforwards

The regulations are very clear on the allocation of capital loss carryforwards when going from the filing of a joint return to a separate return. Capital loss carryforwards must be allocated based upon the separate capital gains and losses of the spouses. Gains or losses on jointly owned or community property are generally divided equally between the spouses. This is very important to consider when allocating marital assets. For example, Talia and Josh have filed joint returns in prior years when Talia had sold her stock portfolio, which was in her name, for a loss of $50,000. Of this loss, only $10,000 of it had been used and

$40,000 was available for future use. The marital estate has, among other things, a stock portfolio with $40,000 in gain. The portfolio was split equally between Talia and Josh as part of the property settlement. After the divorce, when each of them filed a separate return, they each sold their stock portfolio for a profit of $20,000 each. Talia was able to offset her gain with her prior capital loss while Josh would have to pay tax on the full $20,000 gain as none of the capital loss carryforward would be allocated to him as it was created from the sale of Talia's assets. In this scenario, it would have been wiser to have given Talia the entire stock portfolio and given Josh other assets.

Investment Interest Expense

There has been no published guidance on the division of investment interest carryovers. One would presume that the carryover should follow the debt and the debt should follow the individual obligation to repay the loan which created the interest expense. Again, this should be addressed in the marital settlement agreement and the divorcing couple should decide how they will agree to allocate the investment interest expense.

Passive Loss Carryforwards

This issue was discussed earlier in our discussion of allocating various types of property. In summary, if the passive activity which created the passive loss carryover stays with the spouse who owned it, the losses will continue to be available to that spouse. However, if the property that created the passive loss carryover is given to the spouse who did not have the title to it in the marital estate, then the passive loss carryover is added to the basis of the property and any such losses shall not be allowable as a deduction for any year by either party.

Therefore, careful consideration should be given in determining the most beneficial division of the passive loss property and the nature of the assets owned by each party. For example, if the passive loss property was transferred to the spouse who has no other passive activity property and sells the property for a gain that does not exceed the suspended losses, the losses would be wasted.

Other Credit Carryforwards

There are many other tax credits to consider in allocating property or doing tax planning. Some tax credit carryforwards that need to be reviewed in the order that they are used are: rehabilitation tax credit, energy credits, jobs credit, research tax credits, and low income housing credits. Since not all of the credits may have been used on the final joint return that you and your spouse filed, there may be unused suspended credits and credit carryforwards that will need to be allocated to each spouse. Suspended credits or credit carryforwards usually follow the property or business that gave rise to the credit. Because of this, consider this impact when allocating marital property to maximize all tax benefits. In a private letter ruling from the IRS dealing with an investment credit carryforward and the recapture potential, one spouse on a joint return had a rehabilitation tax credit, which, after carrybacks were exhausted, was a carryforward. That spouse transferred the building to the other spouse. The transfer was governed by IRC Section 1041, and thus no gain or loss was recognized. However, the IRS ruled that the credit carryforward and the recapture potential followed the property to the receiving spouse. Based on this logic, other similar types of credits would also be treated in the same manner.

Allocation of Estimated Tax Payments and Tax Refunds

Estimated Tax Payments

The IRS regulations have made it clear that if you and your spouse file a joint declaration of estimated taxes this does not preclude you from filing a married filing separate income tax return. In deciding how to allocate the estimated tax payments between you and your spouse, the IRS allows the estimated tax payments to be treated as if they were paid on behalf of either you or your spouse for the related tax year. The determination as to how or how much of the estimated tax payments are allocated between spouses may be decided on by the two spouses. For example, Noah and Dez have paid $100,000 in estimated taxes for the current year. Having decided to file for divorce at the end of the year, they both have decided to file as married filing separately for the year just ended. Even though their income is such that Noah had earned 75% of the total family taxable income, both Noah and Dez had agreed to split the estimated tax payments equally so that they would each get credited with $50,000 in estimated tax payments. Under this situation the IRS will respect their agreed-to allocation.

If you have a situation where you and your spouse cannot come to an agreement on how to allocate the estimated tax payments made during the year, the IRS will allocate the estimated tax payments between you and your spouse based upon your separate tax liabilities as if they had filed separate returns. I would recommend that this is determined in preparing for a negotiation on the allocation of the estimated tax payments so that you will know what your worst case scenario would be.

Federal Income Tax Refunds

Two questions with respect to tax refunds always arise. First, if during the divorce process you and your spouse decide to file a joint return and there is a tax refund for the current period, how will the tax refund be allocated? Second, if a refund is created from a prior tax year where you and your spouse had filed a joint return, how will the refund be allocated? The tax refund from prior years can be generated from an IRS audit, NOL carryback, or other prior overpayments of tax.

Tax refunds are generally allocated proportionally to the amount of overpayment each spouse actually generated, since merely filing a joint return does not create an interest in the other spouse's income tax overpayment. In a 1974 IRS Revenue Ruling the IRS indicated that the overpayment is the property of the spouse whose income and tax prepayments created the overpayment. The IRS went further in a 1980 ruling that the portion of the tax attributable to each spouse is calculated by means of a separate tax formula. Thus, for purposes of the tax refund allocation the following steps are taken:

1. Calculate each spouse's tax as though you each file a separate return.
2. Determine an allocation percentage by taking the tax calculated in Step 1 and dividing it by the total of the separate taxes computed for each spouse.
3. Each spouse's allocation percentage is then multiplied by the actual joint tax liability incurred on your and your spouse's joint tax return (this determines how much of the joint tax each spouse is deemed to have incurred).
4. Your share of the joint tax refund is now computed by taking your share of the tax liability calculated in Step 3 and subtracting your actual withholding and the actual or allocated tax payments made by you.

In summary, the division of a shared tax refund is based on an allocation of the actual tax created and your share of the payments toward the tax liability.

Having gone through this calculation, if both you and your spouse can agree on an allocation of the tax refund the IRS will respect such allocation. To assure that the allocation will be as you expect, have this issue addressed in your marital settlement agreement. In drafting this provision, be specific in how you are planning to allocate the current year's tax refund if you filed jointly with your spouse and how prior years' tax refunds will be allocated if they are audited or if carrybacks credit a refund of income taxes from a prior year. How the audit of prior years' joint income tax returns will be handled should also be tied into this provision. This should include not only how the refund will be allocated but also who will be responsible for the payment of any additional tax, interest, and penalties and should indicate which spouse will be responsible for dealing with the IRS.

Innocent Spouse Rules, Child Care Credits, and Adoption Credits

Innocent Spouse Rule

When a joint income tax return is filed, both you and your spouse are jointly and individually liable for the entire tax. However, if one spouse qualifies as an innocent spouse, he or she will be relieved of the tax, penalty, and interest. A spouse can get innocent spouse relief through the following means:

- *Qualification as an innocent spouse.* To meet this test, one will need to meet the following requirements:
  - A joint return has been filed for the taxable year.
  - The joint return contains understatement of tax attributable to grossly erroneous items of the other spouse.
  - The other spouse did not know and had no reason to know there was such an understatement of tax at the time the return was signed.
  - It would be inequitable to hold the innocent spouse liable for the deficiency attributable to the understatement, taking into account all facts and circumstances. (In this situation the IRS will consider whether the spouse requesting innocent spouse relief received any substantial benefits from the other spouse's tax deficiency.)

- *Separation of Liabilities.* The spouse, who had previously filed a joint return, may elect to have the deficiency limited to the portion of the deficiency that is attributable to him or her. The burden is on the taxpayer electing the relief to prove that the allocation is proper. One way is to look at what would have been allocated to the individual if the spouse had filed a separate return for the year in question. To qualify for this exception, the spouse electing the relief must be either:

  - No longer married to the other spouse,

  - Legally separated from the other spouse, or

  - Living apart for at least 12 months from the other spouse with whom he or she originally filed a joint tax return.

  This exception is not available to the spouse if the IRS can show that assets were transferred between the joint filers as part of a fraudulent scheme, or that the electing spouse had actual knowledge of the understatement.

- *Equitable Relief.* Taking into account all the facts and circumstances, it is inequitable to hold the individual liable for any unpaid tax or deficiency and relief is not available to the spouse under any of the two exceptions mentioned above.

The spouse may elect separate liability up to two years after the date the IRS begins collection activities. The spouse may also petition the Tax Court within 90 days after the IRS mails a notice denying innocent spouse relief.

The IRS will not automatically grant relief to the spouse even if all conditions are clearly met. The spouse requesting the relief must elect this treatment by filing IRS Form 8857 (see Figure 11.1), Request for Innocent Spouse Relief. If the spouse qualifies for relief under the innocent spouse rule, he or she are relieved of liability of tax, interest, and penalties.

If there is one spouse who handles all of the finances and the other one has no knowledge of any tax issues or business activities within the family, the following statement should be included in the marital settlement agreement to assist in arguing your case for innocent spouse status.

Innocent Spouse Statement:

Wife has no knowledge as to the contents of any of the parties' federal and state income tax returns prepared by Husband or on his behalf, except as to any income that Wife has received. Wife has not been involved in Husband's business and is not aware of the information provided by Husband to his accountant in connection with income and expenses or other

FIGURE 11.1   Request for Innocent Spouse Relief

Form **8857** (Rev. October 1999) Department of the Treasury Internal Revenue Service	**Request for Innocent Spouse Relief** (And Separation of Liability and Equitable Relief) ▶ Do not file with your tax return. ▶ See instructions.	OMB No. 1545-1596

Your name		Your social security number
Your current address		Apt. no.
City, town or post office, state, and ZIP code. If a foreign address, see instructions.		Daytime phone no. ( )

Do not file this form if all or part of your overpayment was (or is expected to be) applied against your spouse's past-due debt (such as child support). Instead, file **Form 8379**, Injured Spouse Claim and Allocation, to have your share of the overpayment refunded to you.

> **TIP** *The IRS can help you with your request. If you are working with an IRS employee, you can ask that employee, or you can call 1-800-829-1040.*

Part I	**1** Enter the year(s) for which you are requesting relief from liability of tax . . . . . . ▶	
	2 Information about the person to whom you were married as of the end of the year(s) on line 1.	
See **Spousal Notification** on page 3.	Name	Social security number
	Current home address (number and street). If a P.O. box, see instructions.	Apt. no.
	City, town or post office, state, and ZIP code. If a foreign address, see instructions.	Daytime phone no. (if known) ( )

3 Do you have an **Understatement of Tax** (that is, the IRS has determined there is a difference between the tax shown on your return and the tax that should have been shown)?

☐ **Yes.** Go to Part II.   ☐ **No.** Go to Part IV.

Part II

4 Are you divorced from the person listed on line 2 (or has that person died)?
☐ **Yes.** Go to line 7.   ☐ **No.** Go to line 5.

5 Are you legally separated from the person listed on line 2?
☐ **Yes.** Go to line 7.   ☐ **No.** Go to line 6.

6 Have you lived apart from the person listed on line 2 at all times during the 12-month period prior to filing this form?
☐ **Yes.** Go to line 7.   ☐ **No.** Go to Part III.

7 If line **4, 5,** or **6** is **Yes,** you may request **Separation of Liability** by **attaching a statement** (see page 3). Check here ▶ ☐ and go to Part III below.

Part III

8 Is the understatement of tax due to the **Erroneous Items** of your spouse (see page 4)?

☐ **Yes.** You may request **Innocent Spouse Relief** by **attaching a statement** (see page 4). Go to Part IV below.

☐ **No.** You may request **Equitable Relief** for the understatement of tax. Check **Yes** in Part IV below.

Part IV

9 Do you have an **Underpayment of Tax** (that is, tax that is properly shown on your return but not paid) or another tax liability that qualifies for **Equitable Relief** (see page 4)?

☐ **Yes.** You may request **Equitable Relief** by **attaching a statement** (see page 4).

☐ **No.** You cannot file this form unless line 3 is **Yes.**

Under penalties of perjury, I declare that I have examined this form and any accompanying schedules and statements, and to the best of my knowledge and belief, they are true, correct, and complete. Declaration of preparer (other than taxpayer) is based on all information of which preparer has any knowledge.

Sign Here Keep a copy of this form for your records.	Your signature ▶		Date

Paid Preparer's Use Only	Preparer's signature ▶	Date	Check if self-employed ☐	Preparer's SSN or PTIN
	Firm's name (or yours if self-employed) and address ▶			EIN
				ZIP code

For Privacy Act and Paperwork Reduction Act Notice, see page 4.   Cat. No. 24647V   Form **8857** (Rev. 10-99) deductions related to his business(es) or amounts included in their joint federal and state income tax returns. Husband has read it and it has been explained to him by his attorney and accountant the definition of an innocent spouse and related rules as provided by IRC Section 6015 and other related sections of the Internal Revenue Code. Husband hereby acknowledges that Wife is an innocent spouse, as defined by the Internal Revenue Code, with respect to the joint federal and state income tax returns filed or to be filed.

Child Care Credits

If you work and incur expenses to care for your children, it is possible that you will be eligible for a credit against your taxes. Form 2441, the Child and Dependent Care Expenses form, is shown in Figure 11.2. The amount of the credit available is computed as the lesser of:

- Qualified dependent child care expenses times 30%; however, the 30% is reduced by 1% for every $2,000 of income over $10,000 of one's adjusted gross income. The maximum reduction in the credit percentage will not go below 20%.

  Or

- $2,400 times the percentage calculated above for one qualifying individual and $4,800 times the percentage calculated above for two qualifying individuals.

Qualified dependent and child care expenses are those paid for household services and care of a qualifying person while you work, such as day care expenses. However, child support payments do not qualify as a qualified dependent child care expense.

A qualified person is defined as:

- Any child under age 13 whom you can claim as a dependent.
- Your disabled spouse.
- Any disabled person who is not able to care for him- or herself whom you can claim as a dependent.

There are several problems in divorce situations that can affect the taking of the credit.

FIGURE 11.2 Child and Dependent Care Expenses

Form **2441**	**Child and Dependent Care Expenses**	OMB No. 1545-0068
	▶ Attach to Form 1040.	**2001**
Department of the Treasury Internal Revenue Service (99)	▶ See separate instructions.	Attachment Sequence No. **21**

Name(s) shown on Form 1040 — Your social security number

Before you begin: You need to understand the following terms. See **Definitions** on page 1 of the instructions.

● **Dependent Care Benefits**   ● **Qualifying Person(s)**   ● **Qualified Expenses**   ● **Earned Income**

Part I **Persons or Organizations Who Provided the Care**—You **must** complete this part.
(If you need more space, use the bottom of page 2.)

1	(a) Care provider's name	(b) Address (number, street, apt. no., city, state, and ZIP code)	(c) Identifying number (SSN or EIN)	(d) Amount paid (see instructions)

Did you receive **dependent care benefits?**
- No ⟶ Complete only Part II below.
- Yes ⟶ Complete Part III on the back next.

Caution. If the care was provided in your home, you may owe employment taxes. See the instructions for Form 1040, line 57.

Part II **Credit for Child and Dependent Care Expenses**

2 Information about your **qualifying person(s).** If you have more than two qualifying persons, see the instructions.

(a) Qualifying person's name — First	Last	(b) Qualifying person's social security number	(c) Qualified expenses you incurred and paid in 2001 for the person listed in column (a)

3 Add the amounts in column (c) of line 2. **Do not** enter more than $2,400 for one qualifying person or $4,800 for two or more persons. If you completed Part III, enter the amount from line 24 . . . .   **3**

4 Enter your **earned income** **4**

5 If married filing a joint return, enter your spouse's earned income (if your spouse was a student or was disabled, see the instructions); **all others,** enter the amount from line 4 . . . .   **5**

6 Enter the **smallest** of line 3, 4, or 5 . . . .   **6**

7 Enter the amount from Form 1040, line 34 . . . .   **7**

8 Enter on line 8 the decimal amount shown below that applies to the amount on line 7

If line 7 is:			If line 7 is:		
Over	But not over	Decimal amount is	Over	But not over	Decimal amount is
$0—10,000		.30	$20,000—22,000		.24
10,000—12,000		.29	22,000—24,000		.23
12,000—14,000		.28	24,000—26,000		.22
14,000—16,000		.27	26,000—28,000		.21
16,000—18,000		.26	28,000—No limit		.20
18,000—20,000		.25			

8   ×.

9 Multiply **line 6** by the decimal amount on line 8. Enter the result here and on Form 1040, line 44. But if this amount is more than the amount on Form 1040, line 42, minus any amount on line 43, **or** you paid 2000 expenses in 2001, see the instructions for the amount to enter on line 44 . . . .   **9**

For Paperwork Reduction Act Notice, see page 3 of the instructions.   Cat. No. 11862M   Form **2441** (2001)

(continued)

138 THE TAX SIDE OF DIVORCE

FIGURE 11.2 Continued

Form 2441 (2001) Page **2**

Part III Dependent Care Benefits

10 Enter the total amount of **dependent care benefits** you received for 2001. This amount should be shown in box 10 of your W-2 form(s). **Do not** include amounts that were reported to you as wages in box 1 of Form(s) W-2 . . . . **10**

11 Enter the amount forfeited, if any. See the instructions **11**

12 Subtract line 11 from line 10 . . . . **12**

13 Enter the total amount of **qualified expenses** incurred in 2001 for the care of the **qualifying person(s)** . . . **13**

14 Enter the **smaller** of line 12 or 13 . . . . **14**

15 Enter your **earned income** **15**

16 If married filing a joint return, enter your spouse's earned income (if your spouse was a student or was disabled, see the instructions for line 5); if married filing a separate return, see the instructions for the amount to enter; **all others,** enter the amount from line 15 . . . . . **16**

17 Enter the **smallest** of line 14, 15, or 16 . . . . . . **17**

18 **Excluded benefits.** Enter here the **smaller** of the following:

  • The amount from line 17 or
  • $5,000 ($2,500 if married filing a separate return **and** you were required to enter your spouse's earned income on line 16). } **18**

19 **Taxable benefits.** Subtract line 18 from line 12. Also, include this amount on Form 1040, line 7. On the dotted line next to line 7, enter "DCB" **19**

To claim the child and dependent care credit, complete lines 20–24 below.

20 Enter $2,400 ($4,800 if two or more qualifying persons) **20**

21 Enter the amount from line 18 . . . . **21**

22 Subtract line 21 from line 20. If zero or less, **stop.** You cannot take the credit. **Exception.** If you paid 2000 expenses in 2001, see the instructions for line 9 . . . . **22**

23 Complete line 2 on the front of this form. **Do not** include in column (c) any benefits shown on line 18 above. Then, add the amounts in column (c) and enter the total here . . . **23**

24 Enter the **smaller** of line 22 or 23. Also, enter this amount on line 3 on the front of this form and complete lines 4–9 . . . . **24**

Form **2441** (2001)

First, only one credit can be taken per qualifying child. Thus both parents cannot take a credit for the same child. As a general rule, the parent who has custody for a longer period of time during the year is allowed to claim the credit relating to that child.

Second, in divorce or legal separation situations (or if you lived apart from your spouse during the last six months of the year) a parent may still be able to take the credit even without the dependency exemption for the child if the following five requirements are met:

1. You had custody of the child for a longer time during the year than the other parent.
2. One or both parents provide over half of the child's support.
3. One or both parents had custody of the child for more than half of the year.
4. The child was under the age of 13 or was disabled and could not care for him- or herself.
5. As a custodial parent you signed over the dependency exemption to your former spouse by signing IRS Form 8332.

Third, if you are married, you must file a joint return in order to qualify to take the credit. Having said that, if the following three items are met, you will be considered as being not married for purposes of claiming the credit.

1. You lived apart from your spouse during the last six months of the tax year.
2. The qualifying person lived in your home more than half of the year.
3. You provided over half the cost of keeping up your home.

For tax years beginning after 2002, the maximum amount of eligible employment-related expenses eligible for the dependent care credit increases from $2,400 to $3,000 if there is one qualifying individual and from $4,800 to $6,000 if there are two or more qualifying individuals. The applicable percentage also increases from 30% to 35%. Applying the math, you can see that the maximum credit that will be allowed after 2002 will be $1,050 for one child and $2,100 for more than one. The reduction in the applicable percentage will also be adjusted for tax years beginning after 2002. The reduction will still be such that the applicable percentage will not go below 20%, but the floor for the adjusted gross income will raise to $15,000. Thus, you will hit the 20% applicable percentage once your adjusted gross income goes over $43,000.

Adoption Credits

One of the comments we normally hear about adoption is the cost involved. Many people are not aware that, beginning in 1997 and further modified in 2001, those people who have recently adopted a child, are in the process of adopting a child, or are considering adopting a child can get assistance with the cost of adopting through the use of tax credits provided by the Internal Revenue Code.

The tax law was changed to give those adopting a child certain tax credits in order to offset the costs of adoption. Recently increased by the Tax Act of 2001, an adopting parent may now be eligible for up to $10,000 in credits for qualifying expenses paid or incurred.

Qualifying adoption expenses are those that are reasonable and necessary, which are directly related to and whose principal purpose is for the legal adoption of an eligible child. Such expenses include adoption fees, court costs, attorney fees, and traveling expenses while away from home. This also would include amounts spent for meals and lodging while away from home for purposes relating to an adoption. An eligible child must be under 18 years old or physically or mentally capable of caring for himself or herself. Additionally, after 2001 this will not apply to an adoption of a foreign child.

If the child to be adopted is one with special needs, the amount of the credit is $10,000 in the year such adoption is finalized regardless of whether the taxpayer has qualified adoption expenses. No credit is allowed with respect to the adoption of a special needs child if the adoption is not finalized. A child is considered a special needs child if he or she is a citizen or resident of the United States, and is the subject of a state determination that the child would most likely not be adopted unless assistance is provided.

Additionally, the same amounts which may have been paid or reimbursed by an adopting parent's employer for qualifying expenses may be excluded from the parent's gross income. Both a credit and an exclusion may be claimed for qualifying expenses, but one cannot claim both a credit and exclusion for the same expense. An adoption assistance program is a separate written plan of an employer that meets special requirements. Also, amounts that are paid or incurred under one's adoption assistance program for an employee's qualifying adoption expenses are not subject to income tax withholding. The amount paid for each employee for the year is reported in Box 13 of the employee's Form W-2.

Income Limitations

Like most other credits provided by the government, they are limited based on one's modified adjusted gross income. If the adoptive parents' modified adjusted gross income is less than $150,000, the full credit or exclusion may be taken. If it is between $150,000 and $190,000, the credit and exclusion may be reduced, and above $190,000, the credit and exclusion is eliminated. The credit also cannot be more than one's regular tax liability for that year and is allowed against the alternative minimum tax. If it is more than one's tax liability, the unused credit can be carried forward for the next five years or until used.

The timing of when the adoption credit can be taken depends on whether the eligible child is a citizen or resident of the United States at the time the adoption effort begins. For a child who is a U.S. citizen or resident the credit is taken as shown in Figure 11.3.

If the eligible child is not a U.S. citizen or resident, the taxpayer cannot take the adoption credit unless the adoption becomes final. For a foreign child, the credit is taken as shown in Figure 11.4.

In order to claim a credit or exclusion, Form 8839, Qualified Adoption Expenses, is to be filed with the adoptive parents' income tax returns. If the adoptive parents are married, they must file a joint return to take the adoption credit. Credit can be taken on a separate return if one is legally separated under a decree of divorce or separate maintenance, or if one lived apart from his or her spouse for the last six months of the tax year. Additionally, the person taking the credit must provide the eligible child's home for more than half the year, and must have paid more than half the cost of keeping up the home for the year. Additionally, the adopted child must have a Social Security number, or the IRS will issue a taxpayer identification number for the child.

FIGURE 11.3   Adoption Credit for a U.S. Citizen

Time when the expense(s) are paid	Time when the credit is taken
Any year before the year the adoption becomes final	The year after the year of the payment
The year the adoption becomes final	The year the adoption becomes final
Any year after the year the adoption becomes final	The year of the payment

FIGURE 11.4   Adoption Credit for a Foreign Citizen

Time when the expense (s) are paid	Time when the credit is taken
Any year before the year the adoption becomes final	The year the adoption becomes final
The year the adoption becomes final	The year the adoption becomes final
Any year after the year the adoption becomes final	The year of the payment

(Those provisions in the Economic Growth and Tax Relief Reconciliation Act of 2001 that extend the tax credit and exclusion from income for special needs adoptions regardless of whether the taxpayer has qualified adoption expenses are effective for tax years beginning after 2002.)

SECTION

III

THE VALUATION
PROCESS

CHAPTER

12

The Basics in Understanding the Valuation of the Closely-Held Business

From time to time, most attorneys who handle matrimonial cases are involved in cases where one of the assets is a business interest. The most factually and legally complex area of divorce law is business valuation, so an understanding of business valuation techniques is necessary for the practitioner engaging in matrimonial law. It is also the most confusing area for the spouse who is not involved in the business and the most controversial area for the business owner. In many cases involving a closely-held business, this is the most valuable asset of the entire estate. My goal in this section of the book is to introduce you to the concepts of business valuations and provide you with the knowledge to understand what is going on in your case and the questions to ask. Do not be afraid to question your attorney or the business valuator concerning the business and its fair market value. Make sure you understand the process and the ultimate product. This chapter should assist you when you read the valuation report prepared by your own expert or by your spouse's.

In the 1980s and 1990s huge strides were made in business valuation techniques due in large part to personal computers and the ability of business appraisers to develop intricate spreadsheets. These spreadsheets have allowed valuators to create models for valuing businesses which would have been virtually impossible before the advent of the personal computer. An additional reason for the progress in business valuation technique has been the mergers and acquisitions which occurred during this same period and provided a database to more accurately gauge the value of businesses based on actual transactions. Additionally, significant training for professionals in this area have been developed along with very active organizations. The ability to retrieve data in this technological age has also had a significant impact in getting relevant data. Moreover, case law regarding business valuation in divorce cases has become more complex for those states which require the business appraiser to differentiate enterprise goodwill from personal goodwill in valuations of closely held businesses.

Family law lawyers handling business valuation cases face an additional challenge in presenting these issues because many family law judges have very little of the accounting or financial theory background necessary to readily understand the testimony of the business appraisers. *Gitlin on Divorce: A Guide to Illinois Matrimonial Law* discussed this problem:

> A review of the case law dealing with valuations of professional practices and closely held corporations suggests that the lawyers involved in the trial of the case do not understand the concept of valuation, since the evidence of value is often unclear or inadequate. The courts of review have likewise not demonstrated an understanding of the process of evaluating professional practices and closely held corporations. (*Gitlin on Divorce*, Vol. 1, Sec. 8-13(E)(1), at 222.)

Therefore, a lawyer handling a business valuation issue in a matrimonial case has to be able to work effectively with the valuator to explain in a simplified fashion to the court the series of complex calculations at the heart of a business valuation. As discussed earlier, the financial expert or the business valuator can play dual roles especially if they are trained and specialized in the area of divorce. A lot of work and information obtained during the valuation process can be used in other areas of the divorce case, such as when recreating the spouse's true economic income from the company.

Hiring an Expert—Types of Business Appraisers, Professional Accreditation Criteria, and Standards of Business Valuation

Consulting (Consulting Experts) and Opinion Witnesses (Testifying Experts)

In general a consultant is retained in anticipation of litigation or preparation for trial but will not be called at trial. The identity, opinions, and work product of a consultant are discoverable only upon a showing of exceptional circumstances under which it is impracticable for the party seeking discovery to obtain facts or opinions on the same subject matter by other means.

It is important for the lawyer hiring the consulting expert to draft an engagement letter that specifically states in the scope section that the expert is being engaged as a consultant who is retained for preparation for trial, but who is not to be called as a witness at trial. The letter should also state that the expert will only be used as a testifying opinion witness if there is a separate engagement agreement to this effect. The engagement letter should be between the consultant and the lawyer or law firm.

In most states, an opinion witness (testifying expert) is a person who will offer any opinion testimony. Usually upon written interrogatory, the party must state:

- The subject matter on which the opinion witness is expected to testify

- The conclusions and opinions of the opinion witness and the bases therefor; and

- The qualifications of the opinion witness; and provide all reports of the opinion witness

Typically, the state's rules will require a party who is answering interrogatories to identify all witnesses including all opinion witnesses. It normally specifically mandates the disclosure of the reports of any opinion witnesses.

A party normally has a duty to seasonably supplement or amend any prior answer or response whenever new or additional information subsequently becomes known to that party. If a deposition of an opinion witness is taken, the witness at trial will usually be limited to the opinions expressed therein in addition to those opinions identified in answer to the interrogatories.

In terms of the timing for disclosure of opinion witness reports and related documents, each state may be different but most will have the judge conduct a case management conference with the attorneys where cut off dates will be discussed. For example, in Illinois all dates set for the disclosure of opinion witnesses and the completion of discovery shall be chosen to ensure that discovery will be completed not later than 60 days before the date on which the trial court reasonably anticipates the trial will commence.

Hiring and Payment of Experts

Selecting a business valuator/financial expert was discussed in Section I; however, when you look to engage such an expert, you will be given an engagement letter to sign. Please read it over carefully and ask the expert any questions you may have. The method of payment to the expert should be indicated in the expert's engagement letter. Most valuation experts require a retainer. Some may require payment for services rendered to date before releasing their valuation report. If you are the nonowner spouse and do not have sufficient funds available, ask your lawyer about filing an interim fee petition. The expert's engagement letter should be attached to the petition along with an affidavit from the expert defining the scope of services and minimal anticipated fees. It should be noted that the appraiser's retainer is just that, and funds to complete the assignment should be budgeted. A projected budget and total fee estimate should be brought to the court's attention as part of the interim fee petition so that funds will be available not only for payment of the initial retainer but for payment of the expert's additional fees needed to complete the assignment. Also, the interim fee petition should clearly set forth any specific assignments the expert will be performing in addition to the valuation so that the fee is supportable.

A good valuation expert, experienced with divorce cases, can serve many functions for divorce attorneys and their clients. Areas of assistance can include preparing for the deposition of the opposing expert; preparing for cross examination of the opposing expert; educating the attorney on the business and the fine points underlying the valuation; drafting of a comparison schedule using both experts' valuation reports which outline their differences; analyzing the economic value of perks taken by business owners; performing a cash flow analysis; and assisting the lawyer in structuring an appropriate settlement of the business valuation issue.

Certifications and Qualification of the Business Appraiser

Finding the right expert is important in preparing a business valuation case. The appraiser should be familiar with your state's divorce law and especially the distinction between enterprise and personal goodwill. A skilled appraiser should have good oral and written communication skills and be able to integrate quantitative and subjective data coherently. The appraiser should also have an understanding of financial and tax matters.

It appears that most states are relatively lenient in the issue of qualification of an expert to testify as to a business' value. Certified public accountants have many of the necessary tools required to render sound business valuations. However, this does not mean that a CPA is automatically qualified to perform a business valuation. In fact, the position of the American Institute for Certified Public Accountants (AICPA) is that specific specialized training is needed to be a professional/specialist in business valuations. Thus, there is a separate designation for those CPAs specializing in the area of business valuation called an ABV (Accredited Business Valuator).

Today there are many nationally recognized business valuation organizations that a business appraiser may join. To become certified under a particular organization, the appraiser usually needs to take an exam and submit samples of their valuation work product. These organizations are the American Institute for Certified Public Accountants (AICPA), the American Society of Appraisers (ASA), the Institute for Business Appraisers (IBA), and the National Association of Certified Valuation Analysts (NACVA).

In selecting a business appraiser, you may review certain online resources. The AICPA has an online directory of its members who are Accredited in Business Valuation (ABV) credential holders which can be found at www.aicpa.org. The list is organized by state and includes only the name, firm affiliation, and city of each ABV credential holder. The prerequisites for the ABV certification are that the member must be a member of the AICPA with a current CPA license. To obtain an ABV accreditation the applicant must be experienced in at least 10 business valuation engagements and pass a one-day examination. To maintain the accreditation, a member must complete 60 hours of related continuing professional education during the three-year period after obtaining the ABV accreditation.

The American Society of Appraisers has an online directory of its accredited members. The web address is www.appraisers.org. An accredited member does not have to be a certified public accountant but must have a college degree. Minimally, there is a day long exam. The applicant must also pass an ethics examination. The American Society of Appraisers is the only organization which has a separate ethics examination. To become an accredited member the expert must submit two valuation reports. There is also an experience requirement: the individual must have two years full-time or equivalent work. An accredited senior appraiser must have three years full-time or equivalent experience.

The third organization providing for accreditation of business appraisers is the Institute for Business Appraisers (IBA). It offers programs of interest to members whose business valuation activities are less than full-time or whose practice includes valuation of small to mid-size businesses. The IBA has an online directory of its members at *www.instbusapp.org*. A certified business appraiser does not need to be a certified public accountant. The prerequisite is four years of college or its equivalent. There is a 3.5 hour proctored examination to become a certified business appraiser (CBA). Similar to the American Society of Appraisers, to become a certified business appraiser, an individual must submit two business appraiser reports showing professional competence.

The fourth organization that provides accreditation for business appraisers is the National Association of Certified Valuation Analysts (NACVA). You may encounter two types of appraisers certified by NACVA: Accredited Valuation Analyst (AVA) and Certified Valuation Analyst (CVA). The NACVA web page address is *www.nacva.com*. Its online directory can be found at *www.nacva.com/DirectryCD*. To gain the AVA credential, an appraiser must have a business degree and must take a 30 to 50 hour, take home examination which includes one case study. To become a Certified Valuation Analyst an individual must be a CPA. The examination is a half day proctored exam which includes a case study. There is no requirement to submit actual reports to become a CVA.

Important Internal Revenue Service Revenue Rulings

Revenue Ruling 59-60

Revenue Rule 59-60 is the best known and most often used administrative ruling in the area of business valuation. The purpose of the revenue ruling is to give a general outline and review of the approach, methods, and factors to be considered in valuing shares of the capital stock of closely held corporations for estate and gift tax purposes. Although it was written over 40 years ago, it is cited by many family law decisions around the country.

Revenue Ruling 59-60 provides a definition for fair market value which is: ". . . the price at which the property would change hands between a willing buyer and willing seller, neither being under any compulsion to buy or sell and both having knowledge of relevant facts."

The ruling provides a solid basis for valuation. The business appraiser should consider it as the ruling itemizes and explains eight relevant factors to be considered in valuing a closely held business. The eight factors are:

1. The nature and history of the business since inception.
2. The economic outlook, in general, and the condition and outlook of the specific industry the subject company operates in.

3. The book value of the stock and the financial condition of the business.

4. The earnings capacity of the business.

5. The dividend-paying capacity of the business.

6. Whether or not the enterprise has goodwill or other intangible value.

7. Sales of stock and the size of the block of stock to be valued.

8. The market price of stocks of corporations engaged in the same or simi-lar line of business having their stocks actively traded in a free and open market, either on an exchange or over-the-counter.

In many states, when appraising a business in a divorce case, the appraiser needs to consider the effect of personal goodwill relating to the divorcing spouse. A similar issue is addressed in Revenue Ruling 59-60 relative to the loss of a key person in a small business. In both contexts, an adjustment must be made by the valuator. On this subject, Revenue Ruling 59-60 states:

The loss of the manager of a so-called "one-man" business may have a depressing effect upon the value of the stock of such business, particularly if there is a lack of trained personnel capable of succeeding to the man-agement of the enterprise. In valuing the stock of this type of business, therefore, the effect of the loss of the manager on the future expectancy of the business, and the absence of management-succession potentialities are pertinent factors to be taken into consideration. On the other hand, there may be factors which offset, in whole or in part, the loss of the manager's services. For instance, the nature of the business and of its assets may be such that they will not be impaired by the loss of the manager. Furthermore, the loss may be adequately covered by life insurance, or competent man-agement might be employed on the basis of the consideration paid for the former manager's services. These, or other offsetting factors, if found to exist, should be carefully weighed against the loss of the manager's ser-vices in valuing the stock of the enterprise.

Other Revenue Rulings

Three other rulings that the IRS has issued that directly affect the valuation of an interest in a business include:

1. *Revenue Ruling 68-609.* This revenue ruling addresses the formula method which was originally adopted in 1920 by an Appeals and Review Memorandum

of the U.S. Treasury Department. In 1920 the formula method was used to estimate the value of the goodwill that breweries and distilleries lost because of Prohibition. Since then, this method has been widely used in valuations including valuations in divorce cases. In 1968, the Internal Revenue Service addressed this method in Revenue Ruling 68-609 and ruled that ".... the 'formula' approach may be used for determining the fair market value of intangible assets of a business *only if there is no better basis therefore available.*" The application of this Revenue Ruling is discussed later in this book.

2. *Revenue Ruling 77-287.* This ruling discusses the value of restricted stock studies in determining marketability discounts.

3. *Revenue Ruling 93-12.* This ruling allows application of minority interest discounts to partial transfers even when a family owns overall control of a closely held business.

The significant portions of Revenue Rulings 59-60, 68-609, and 93-12 are included in Chapter 17.

Use of Financial Experts Generally

Standards as to Expert Opinions

Expert testimony is always at the core of business valuation cases. Because of the significant role the expert witness plays in a contested valuation case, it is crucial that the family law attorney is knowledgeable about the admissibility of this type of testimony. Though one will need to be familiar with state statutes and the local courts, it is important to consider the leading United States Supreme Court case addressing expert testimony which is *Daubert v. Merrell Dow Pharmaceuticals, Inc.*, 509 U.S. 579, 113 S. Ct. 2786, 125 L. Ed. 469 (1993). Before *Daubert* the standard for admission of expert testimony was the holding of the United States Supreme Court in *Frye v. United States*, 293 F. 1013, 1014 (D.C. Cir. 1923). *Frye* laid down the "general acceptance" rule: a scientific technique must be generally accepted within its field before it will be admissible as evidence.

Daubert replaced the *Frye* generally accepted rule with a standard of reliability. In *Daubert*, the plaintiffs argued that the *Frye* test was superceded by the adoption of the Federal Rules of Evidence (FRE). The U.S. Supreme Court agreed that FRE Rule 702 governs expert testimony. This rule states:

> If scientific, technical, or other specialized knowledge will assist the trier
> of fact to understand the evidence or to determine a fact in issue, a witness

qualified as an expert by knowledge, skill, experience, training, or education, may testify thereto in the form of an opinion or otherwise. (125 L.Ed.2d at 478)

Daubert addressed the application of FRE Rule 702 as it pertains to expert testimony regarding the hard sciences. *Daubert* set forth a two-prong analysis to determine whether to permit testimony as to scientific evidence: (1) Is the scientific reasoning the methodology underlying the theory reliable, and (2) Is the proposed evidence relevant to the facts of the case in which it is offered.

Daubert also laid down sub-rules for determining whether a theory or technique is reliable. In determining such reliability *Daubert* indicated that there were four general areas of inquiry as to what a trial court may consider in making this determination of reliability. First, there is the question of whether "it can be (and had been) tested." Second, the trial court should inquire whether the theory or technique has been subjected to peer review and publication. Third, in the case of a particular scientific technique, the court ordinarily should consider the known potential rate of error. The fourth test states:

[G]eneral acceptance can yet have a bearing on the inquiry. A reliability assessment does not require, although it does permit, explicit identification of a relevant scientific community and an express determination of a particular degree of acceptance within that community. [citation omitted.]

The *Daubert* opinion concludes:

To summarize: "general acceptance: is not a necessary precondition to the admissibility of scientific evidence under the Federal Rules of Evidence, but the Rules of Evidence—especially Rule 702—do assign to the trial judge the task of ensuring that an expert's testimony both rests on a reliable foundation and is relevant to the task at hand. Pertinent evidence based on scientifically valid principles will satisfy those demands."

The *Daubert* opinion makes it clear that the trial judge plays a vital gate-keeping function in determining whether scientific evidence will be accepted. This gate-keeping role requires the court to consider the reliability of the proffered scientific evidence as well as the relevance of the testimony to an individual case.

Three years after *Daubert*, *Joiner v. General Electric Co.*, 78 F.3d 524, 529-530 (11th Cir. 1996), addressed the *Daubert* standard, the court of appeals emphasized that *Daubert* is about "evidentiary reliability and relevancy" and under the first prong, evidentiary reliability, the trial court "must examine the reasoning or methodology underlying the expert opinion to determine whether it utilizes valid scientific methods and procedures." But judges should "be careful not to cross the line between deciding whether the expert's testimony is based on 'scientifically balanced principles' and deciding upon the correctness of the expert's conclusions."

The court in *Joiner* also narrowed the suggestions of *Daubert* and determined that "in evaluating whether a particular scientific theory or study is reliable," the following criteria should be considered: (1) its empirical reliability, (2) whether the study has been published or subject to peer review, (3) the known or potential rate of acceptable errors, and (4) whether the method is generally accepted in the scientific community.

Recently, the United States Supreme Court revisited *Daubert* in *Kumho Tire Co. v. Carmichael*, 526 U.S. 137, 119 S. Ct. 1167 (1999). *Kumho* held that its principles and the gate-keeping function assigned to the trial judge apply not only to testimony based upon scientific knowledge but to testimony based upon technical or other specialized knowledge. (119 S. Ct. at 1175 (1999))

When expert opinion testimony has been excluded on the basis of a *Daubert/ Kumho* challenge, often the reason is the unreliability of the underlying assumptions employed by the valuator. In *Target Market Publishing, Inc. v. ADVO, Inc.*, 136 F.3d 1139, 1142 (7th Cir. 1998), expert testimony was excluded because the valuator relied upon mere assumptions. The *Target Market Publishing* court of appeals commented that the expert's conclusion relied upon the "assumption that the publication could instantaneously achieve full penetration into dozens of geographic zones in which no sales efforts had even begun as of March 2, at which time the contract term was already well-half completed." The court of appeals ruled that the valuator's "report was not 'scientific' because it relied upon assumptions that were unrealistic . . . and divorced from the realities of the . . . venture."

In *The Cayuga Indian Nation of New York v. The Seneca-Cayuga Tribe of Oklahoma*, 83 F. Supp.2d 318 (N.D. N. Y. 2000), the value of ancestral Indian Nation tribal land was at issue. The federal district court conducted a seven day hearing as to the issue of admissibility of the expert opinion of three real estate appraisers. At the conclusion of the hearing, two of the experts' opinions were admitted into evidence and one was excluded.

The *Cayuga* valuator whose opinion was excluded used the sales comparison approach which the court found was acceptable. However, because the assumptions and data used by the valuator were unreliable, the court determined that the analysis suffered from a potentially significant rate of error. In *Cayuga*, the appellate court noted that it had serious concerns as to whether the comparison sales used were truly representative and complied with "established appraisal practices." The appellate court rejected what it called the "intuitive approach"—the valuator's method which was explained by him as having "a feeling of the values" from all the sales he reviewed. The testimony of the expert established that the sales data used by the valuator were not always accurate, there was not any indication that the sales were made at arms-length, and he failed to account for land mass adjustments. In rejecting the expert's valuation, the appellate court focused on the principles and methodology in determining the reliability and relevance of the expert. Thus, although the trial court may find that an expert is qualified to render an opinion of the value of a business, that factor standing alone does not necessarily mean that all of his testimony will be admissible following a specific *Daubert/Kumho* challenge.

Where the methods employed by the valuator are well accepted in the financial community, the court has the tendency to admit the expert opinion testimony.

Because expert testimony in business valuation cases would be one based upon technical or other specialized knowledge, it is clear that *Daubert* analysis may apply to business valuation cases, if your particular state court chose to adopt *Daubert*. The majority position in state courts follows the standards set forth in *Daubert/Kumho*.

Your lawyer handling your case needs to consider whether to challenge the valuation expert's testimony within the context of either *Frye* or the *Daubert* decision.

In summary, it appears that a trial court has broad discretion to determine whether a witness qualifies as an expert. To lay a foundation for expert testimony, a party must show that its expert has some special knowledge or experience in the area covered by the expert's opinion. Even if this is challenged, most judges are likely to allow the expert to testify and then consider the weight of the testimony.

General Authority for Court to Appoint Neutral Expert

My experience is that there has been a split among trial judges as to whether the trial court has the authority to employ its own business expert or other financial advisor. Again, a review of your particular state's law will dictate this area.

Under the Federal Rules of Evidence, "[t]he court may on its own motion or on the motion of any party enter an order to show cause why expert witnesses should not be appointed, and may request the parties to submit nominations. The court may appoint any expert witnesses agreed upon by the parties, and may appoint expert witnesses of its own selection. . . ."

While the court's appointment of its own expert is very frequent in custody cases because many states have a statutory provision specifically approving of the use of such experts, there is federal authority to support the proposition that a court on its own motion may appoint an expert of its own choosing. This proposition applies to business valuation cases. The Advisory Committee's note to Section 706 of FRE states:

> Generally speaking, the trial court can rely on the parties and the adversary system to reach the truth fairly by calling their own experts. However, it may occasionally occur that the experts are in such wild disagreement that the trial court might find it helpful and in furtherance of the search for truth to appoint an impartial expert. Other instances may arise, again infrequently, where the court might require technical assistance to sift through highly complex issues and unwieldy material, and where it might be useful to have that technical adviser testify." (Fed. R. Evid. 706 Advisory Committee's Note)

Undoubtedly, in business valuation cases, there may be cases where, because of extreme divergent views between the parties' own witnesses, the court may find it necessary to appoint its own expert witness in an attempt to reach some common ground.

Having talked about the court appointed expert, this does not preclude the parties to the divorce to agree to select one valuation expert to value the closely held business. There are many pluses for this, including the potential savings of significant expert fees. There is a big distinction between just having both sides agree to using one expert and one agreeing to stipulate to be bound by the valuation results determined by the jointly hired valuation expert. Unless there is a stipulation that the parties will be bound by the results of the jointly hired valuation expert, each party would still have the opportunity to engage their own expert.

Protective Orders

In many matrimonial cases, the parties' real battle is often not the trial of the case, but involves the discovery process in which the rights of third persons, who also have an interest in the business, have to be balanced against the need for discovery by a divorce litigant. In the business valuation context, a spouse often has interest in a closely held corporation. The corporation is a separate legal entity and will often claim that discovery requests are unduly onerous and that the nonbusiness owning spouse should not need copies of the actual documents upon which the financial statements of the business will be based. Not only the divorcing spouse may have a problem with his or her competitors seeing confidential information about the company. The best way to handle this is to request that both sides enter into confidentiality (protective) order. This order should incorporate not only the parties but their attorneys, experts, and consultants. The fact determination part of a trial seeks to ascertain truth. Discovery is a means of gathering facts so the truth may be ascertained. The danger of limiting discovery in order to protect privacy rights of non-parties is that there will not be ascertainment of the truth because there may be an informational vacuum on which the court rules on an issue.

A sample of a protective order and confidential agreement which might be used in a business valuation case is shown in Figures 12.1 and 12.2.

The Valuation Process

General Steps in the Valuation Process

The valuation professional must do more than simply apply a formula to a set of financial statements to arrive at a value. With the number of canned programs in the marketplace, the less skilled business appraiser falls prey to this shortfall. Computer programs can be useful, but remember the saying, garbage in— garbage out. An example of a case which involved an expert's over-reliance on a computer program was *Spillert v. Spillert*, 564 So. 2d 1146 (Fla. 1990). The court in *Spillert* commented:

> On cross-examination, the expert witness stated that the computer program he used was for service businesses, but that he had never evaluated a sole practitioner plastic surgeon and he was not aware that four plastic surgeons in Jacksonville had been unable to sell their practice.

It is important that if the expert uses a computer program, the expert is well-versed with the components of the program, has a full understanding of its formulas and calculations, and has properly analyzed the results provided from the program. In order to arrive at a reliable conclusion of value, the valuator must become involved in the tedious process of accumulating and analyzing

---

FIGURE 12.1   Protective Order

IN THE CIRCUIT COURT OF THE _____
JUDICIAL CIRCUIT, _____ COUNTY, SOME STATE IN THE USA

In Re the Marriage of	)	
	)	
Plaintiff,	)	
and	)	
	)	No.
Defendant.	)	

STIPULATED PROTECTIVE ORDER

Pursuant to the stipulation of the parties to this action and their respective undersigned attorneys, IT IS HEREBY ORDERED:

1. The _____ and her attorney have entered into a Confidentiality Agreement dated, _____, with _____, a copy of which is attached and incorporated herein.

2. Any documents, materials, or testimony designated as confidential in the Confidentiality Agreement shall not be disclosed to any third parties, other than as provided in the Confidentiality Agreement.

3. Nothing herein shall preclude any party from requesting the court to modify this Protective Order.

ENTER:

Judge

AGREED:

Plaintiff's Attorney

Defendant's Attorney

FIGURE 12.2   Confidentiality Agreement

CONFIDENTIALITY AGREEMENT (the "Agreement"), dated _____, 200__, by and among the company, _____, Inc., ("[Company]"); the non-business owning spouse, _____; and the nonbusiness owning spouse's attorney, _____:

WHEREAS, [Company] has been requested to provide certain documents and other material in connection with the divorce action entitled _____, Case No. _____, of the _____ Judicial Circuit, _____ County, (State) ("Action").

It is acknowledged by the parties to the Agreement that the documents and other material whose production by Company is sought in this action includes confidential and sensitive commercial, financial, and business information whose unauthorized dissemination would cause serious injury to [Company's] business; and

Plaintiff/Defendant engaged [Lawyer] to represent her in connection with the Action;

THEREFORE, in consideration of the foregoing and the agreements set forth herein, the parties agree as follows:

1. For purposes of the Agreement the term "[Company] Material" means any and all of the following: (i) documents, financials, projections, notes, agreements, or other material produced or delivered by [Company] or an affiliate thereof in the Action; (ii) testimony given in the Action by a member, agent, or employee of [Company] or an affiliate thereof testifying in his or her capacity as such, and the transcript of such testimony; (iii) information concerning [Company] or an affiliate thereof contained in any of the foregoing; (iv) testimony given in the Action by any witness in response to questions using, inquiring into, or referring to any of the foregoing, and the portion of the transcript of such witness's testimony recording such questions and testimony; and (v) documents prepared or delivered by a party to the Action, by counsel to a party to the Action, or by any person employed or retained by counsel to a party to the Action that incorporate any of the foregoing.

(continued)

FIGURE 12.2   Continued

2. [Nonbusiness Owning Spouse], [Lawyer] and persons to whom [Company] Material may be provided or disclosed pursuant to subparagraphs 3(d), 3(e), 3(f), or 3(g) of this Agreement shall not ever use [Company] Material for any purpose other than the conduct of the Action and preparation for the conduct of the Action, and shall not ever disclose, disseminate, distribute, broadcast, or publish the [Company] Material, by any means or in any form, except as permitted in paragraph 3 of the Agreement.

3. [Company] Material may be provided or disclosed by [Nonbusiness Owning Spouse] and/or [Lawyer] only to the following persons:

(a) the Court in the Action;

(b) the parties to the Action;

(c) counsel to the parties to the Action;

(d) those members of the support staff of [Lawyer] who are engaged in assisting [Lawyer] with the conduct of the Action or preparation therefor;

(e) the individuals other than the parties to the Action designated as deponents in the Action by agreement of the parties or by service of a deposition notice upon opposing counsel, and witnesses at any trial in the Action;

(f) independent third-parties retained by [Lawyer] for purposes of discovery in, preparation for, and/or any trial of, the Action (such as independent experts or consultants); and

(g) court reporters or stenographers transcribing proceedings in the Action.

4. With respect to any persons within a category described in subparagraphs 3(e), 3(f), or 3(g) above, whether a natural person or other entity (hereinafter referred to as a "Non-[Company] Third Party"), each such Non-[Company] Third Party to whom [Nonbusiness Owning Spouse] or [Lawyer] proposes to disclose [Company] Material shall be advised by [Nonbusiness Owning Spouse] or [Lawyer] of the provisions, and furnished with a copy, of the Agreement by [Nonbusiness Owning Spouse] or [Lawyer]. [Company] Material shall not be disclosed to any such Non-[Company] Third Party until the Non-[Company] Third Party has signed an acknowledgment that he or she has read this Agreement and agrees to be bound by it, and the original of such signed acknowledgment has been delivered to [Company].

FIGURE 12.2   Continued

---

5. The parties will request jointly that those portions of any trial of this Action, should such occur, at which [Company] Material will be the subject of examination, testimony, or argument be held in closed session, that the attending court reporter transcribe such proceedings separately under cover indicating that such transcript is to be filed under seal, and such transcripts shall be filed under seal, and that any trial exhibits that constitute [Company] Material be filed under seal.

6. The inadvertent production by [Company] of any privileged or otherwise protected materials shall not be deemed a waiver or impairment of any claim of privilege or protection, including but not limited to the attorney-client privilege and the protection afforded to work-product materials, or the subject matter therefor. Upon receiving notice from [Company] that materials have been inadvertently produced, [Nonbusiness Owning Spouse] and [Lawyer] shall return all such materials to [Company] within three working days of receipt of such notice, unless application is made to the Court in the Action within such period to challenge the claim of privilege. In the event such a challenge is made, the inadvertent production of the document shall not be deemed a waiver of the privilege.

7. Within thirty days after the termination of the Action, including all appeals, [Nonbusiness Owning Spouse] and [Lawyer] shall, at the option of [Company] return to [Company] or destroy all copies of [Company] Material, except for such [Company] Material [Lawyer] believes may be needed for purposes of possible continuing or ancillary proceeding, which documents may be retained by [Lawyer]. In the event [Lawyer] retains any [Company] Material, he shall take all steps reasonably necessary to protect the continuing confidentiality of all such [Company] Material in his possession.

IN WITNESS WHEREOF, the parties hereto have executed this Agreement as of the date first above written by their duly authorized representatives.

By: _____

Corporate President

Nonbusiness Owning Spouse

Nonbusiness Owning Spouse's Lawyer

---

vast amounts of quantitative data (e.g., financial statements) and qualitative data (e.g., competition, location, and so on).

The process of performing a business valuation is broken down into five general steps: (1) defining the assignment; (2) gathering the data; (3) analyzing the data and performing the valuation analysis; (4) using various methodologies to arrive at a conclusion of value (including applying discounts or premiums where applicable); and (5) writing the valuation report.

As the process begins, it is important that you and your attorney understand or at least be familiar with relevant valuation terminology. Appendix B provides a comprehensive list of the most common terms used by business appraisers and definitions of those terms. The terms have been obtained from a variety of sources including the American Society of Appraisers (ASA) and other recognized appraisal publications.

Defining the Assignment

In valuing a business, the appraiser must define what standard of value will be used. The appraiser must be familiar with the state statute for the particular state in which the client will be divorced in order to determine the applicable standard of value. In most states the standard of value is fair market value.

Very simply put, fair market value is the amount at which property would change hands between a hypothetical willing seller and a willing buyer when neither is acting under compulsion and when both have reasonable knowledge of the relevant facts. Clearly, this value may differ from the value the business has in relation to a particular buyer. Such a value has been termed a synergistic value, an investment value, or a strategic value, even though these terms are synonymous.

The appraisers must also understand what they are valuing. Is it important to know whether the appraiser is valuing a controlling interest or a minority interest in a closely held corporation. While in simplest terms a controlling interest is generally defined as one in which a shareholder has more than a 50 percent interest in a company, it is important to understand that control is not an all-or-nothing proposition. A shareholder may have the prerogatives of control despite not having a controlling interest in a company. Such prerogatives of control may include the ability to appoint management, ability to determine management compensation and perks, ability to develop a policy of the business, and so on.

Assume a divorce valuation case in which the wife has a 25% interest in a corporation and the husband has a 50% interest. Furthermore, it appears clear the husband will be awarded the entire marital interest in the corporation. The issue may be whether the appraiser is valuing a 75% interest or two separate interests (a 25% interest and a 50% interest). Some might suggest the valuator should appraise the interest of husband and wife collectively. It is further suggested that the valuator should consider these interests separately only if stock will continue to be held by each party individually. If the distribution of stock in a business is not clear (the determination of which party will be awarded the stock in a marital corporation), then the appraiser may consider completing two valuations, one based on valuing each holding individually and one valuing the marital interest of the stock as a block. Obviously, the issue should be addressed at the beginning of the assignment and the lawyer should determine what the state law dictates.

Gathering Data

Once the appraiser and lawyer have a clear understanding of the interest that is to be valued, the next step is to begin the process of gathering the data. The information needed will involve requesting standard information that is common to all business valuation engagements and also information that is unique to the specific company being valued and its industry. Normally, the business appraiser will provide the attorney or the property owner's spouse with a document and information request. If the attorney represents the nonproperty owner, the attorney will use the document request and incorporate it into a notice to produce. A sample document and information request is in Appendix C.

The general information requested will include:

- Financial statements for the last five years, as well as interim financial statements if the valuation is to be performed as of an interim date
- Detailed general ledgers and /or cash disbursement journals
- Income tax returns for the same five-year period
- Articles of incorporation or partnership agreement or operating agreement, depending on the type of entity being valued
- Listing of shareholders, partners, or members and ownership percentages
- Aging of accounts receivable
- Listing of investments
- Detailed list of all inventory adjusted to fair market value
- Detailed list of property and equipment with depreciation lapse schedules including any and all appraisals indicating their fair market value (A request for copies of insurance policies might also assist in this process.)
- Details of loans and other significant accounts payable

Other items typically requested are based on information obtained from the company's balance sheet. If the appraiser is looking at possibly using an asset-based valuation approach, the information detailed above may become crucial in the analysis. Even if the valuator considers an approach other than an asset-based valuation, these items may be important in determining if the company has any nonoperating assets and liabilities on its books, or whether the company has any excess working capital or working capital deficiencies.

Nonfinancial documents will normally also be requested to provide the appraiser with additional knowledge about the company, including its corporate structure, obligations, and various business agreements. These documents would include items such as: shareholder agreements, organizational charts, business plans, forecasts or projections, marketing materials, previous valuations, union agreements, stock transactions, insurance policies, information on litigation, and real estate and equipment appraisals.

A valuator may be useful in various aspects of a divorce case. For example, information obtained for purposes of normalizing the company's earnings may also be of use in determining the business-owner spouse's true economic income. Some of this information may be obtained through an on-site visit and the appraiser's discussion with management. If opposing counsel prohibits the appraiser from meeting with management personnel or refuses to provide information, the attorney will need to pursue other means, such as depositions or detailed interrogatories.

Initial Financial Analysis and On-Site Visit

It is necessary for the valuator to secure, review, and analyze as much historical financial and operational information as possible. This type of information acts as a building block for the valuator in gathering additional data, research, and in applying appropriate valuation methodology in the final preparation of the report. A thorough review of this information can point to the true historical performance of the company, trends in the operating business, and identify other issues for valuation analysis. In addition, this analysis will prepare the appraiser for one of the most important parts of the appraisal, the site visit.

One of the first steps in the appraiser's analysis is to prepare what are called common size financial statements. In this format the balance sheet is presented with each asset line item reported as a percentage of total assets and each liability and equity item reported as a percentage of their total. The income statement is also presented in a similar fashion with each category of income and expense reported as a percentage of net sales. This simple analysis highlights the relationship of the various account balances to one another and is also useful in spotting trends over the years. It also helps identify unusual or nonrecurring items and identifying differences from industry norms.

The appraiser should also look for trends in the company's annual sales growth, annual net income growth, gross margins, and operating expenses. Financial ratios are useful in performing this analysis. The computation of financial ratios is useful in comparing the subject company to other companies or industry statistics. A summary of the common ratios used by the appraiser are described in Appendix D. Identification of the trends of a business enables the appraiser to make further inquiries of management about the effect of those trends on future operations during the site visit.

A site visit is a key element of the appraisal process that cannot be ignored if the valuation is to be complete. During the site visit, the appraiser attempts to accomplish the following objectives:

- Tour the facilities and observe the operation of the business.

- Interview key management personnel to discuss the industry, the subject company's operations, and its outlook for the future.

- Present to management questions raised during the preliminary analysis phase of the valuation, review trends displayed during the analysis, and get management's feedback on those trends.

- Follow up on any missing information from the original request list.

Shannon P. Pratt, one of the most highly recognized persons in the business valuation field today, discusses the relative importance of site visits/management interviews in his book, *Valuing Small Businesses and Professional Practices* (New York: McGraw-Hill, 1998):

[F]or valuations subject to contrarian review (which most are), courts are becoming quite sensitive to the importance of site visits and management interviews. Many clients and attorneys dismiss or downplay the importance of a site visit and/or don't want to incur the interruption or the cost of the analyst's time for it. We prefer to make site visits and conduct management interviews. In our experience—as well as in many court cases—the site visit not only helps the analyst get a better perspective, it makes a difference in the analyst's credibility in the eyes of the court.

In addition to simply interviewing management, a tour of the company's facilities is also essential when valuing a business. The tour of the physical plant provides the appraiser with information that cannot be gleaned simply by looking at financial statements and other related financial information. The tour should provide the analyst with a better idea of the company's operations from a physical viewpoint. It permits an evaluation of the plant's physical adequacy and allows the appraiser to observe the efficiency of the location as well as the layout and condition of the facilities.

Remember that the judge or trier of fact will not have seen the company or have a feel of what your or your spouse's company is like. Dr. Pratt also commented on those cases where the intended user of the valuation report is unfamiliar with the business or has never seen the facilities in question. He indicates:

> If the analyst will need to communicate some description of the operations, facilities, or both to someone lacking the opportunity to visit the facilities, such as a judge in a court case, it may be desirable to take a set of pictures while on tour.

It is widely accepted in the valuation profession that a site visit/management interview is a very important part of the valuation process, and is, in fact, imperative if an appraiser is to perform a complete analysis of the operations of the company being appraised.

Completing the Financial Analysis and Normalizing the Earnings Stream

Once the site visit is complete, the appraiser should be in a position to complete the financial analysis. Based on the documents received, discussions with management, and the site visit, the appraiser determines what, if any, adjustments need to be made to the original financial statements provided. This process is known as normalizing the financial statements. Normalizing is a process of adjusting the financial information to take into account the following items:

- Nonrecurring items such as sales of fixed assets, lawsuit settlements, and casualty losses.

- Nonoperating items such as depreciation and related expenses for non-business real estate or personal property and investment income or expenses.

- Owner's discretionary expenses such as personal automobiles, insurance policies, travel, and other personal perks.

- Related party transactions which do not reflect market rates, such as leasing space from a building owned by the shareholder at above market rates.

- Compensation which does not reflect market rates.

By adjusting for these types of items, the appraiser portrays the business operations as they should be expected to look, under normal conditions on an ongoing basis, to a prospective buyer of the business. The appraiser must identify
what is being valued because the adjustments that the appraiser might consider
could be different depending on whether a control or minority interest is being
valued.

If the appraiser is valuing a controlling interest in a closely held corporation,
the issue of reasonable compensation must be addressed. The key is the ability
to distinguish between how much in dollar amounts is taken by the business
owner as reasonable compensation and what portion is the return on capital. In
other words, given the services that an owner provides, the appraiser examines
what is the reasonable amount that the business would expect to pay outside personnel to perform similar services.

Overcompensating the owner of a business will reduce the profitability of a
business. By normalizing the owner's income, the appraiser may lower the
owner's salary, which increases the profitability of the business, which in turn
may end up increasing the amount of the valuation. While this is a standard technique of business valuators in non-divorce cases, this presents problems in some
states with the concept of double dipping, in that the owner's income (without
a normalization adjustment) is counted once as income for the purpose of either
child support or maintenance and a second time for the purpose of determining
the value of the business.

Despite the double dipping argument, understanding the earnings stream of
the business excluding the earning capacity of the business-owning spouse is an
important part when dealing with the issue of personal goodwill. Thus, the valuator must assume the replacement of the business-owning spouse with another
person who would assume his or her duties. If this hypothetical person would
normally receive a lesser amount of compensation from the business without a
loss in business earnings, then there is a sound argument that the appraiser
should normalize the business owner's income and the amount of personal
goodwill is probably fairly limited. The issue of personal goodwill is discussed
later in this section.

In analyzing the reasonable compensation issue, the appraiser may need to
consider and present to the court many factors in justifying the compensation
adjustment, such as:

■ The appraiser must develop a full understanding of the operating entity.
   This includes the size of the company and the historical as well as the
   future growth plans of the company.

- The appraiser must consider the makeup of the management team. Determine who is included in officers' compensation and how much they are paid. The valuator should obtain a complete history of the various compensation levels.

- What are the job descriptions of the applicable officer(s)?

- What is the strength of the management team/officer group? Obtain the background of each member of the management team or officer group including their education, experience, time commitment (are they employed on a full-time or part-time basis), skills (what specialized skills do the individuals bring to the table)? How many hours do the individuals spend at their jobs, and how successful has the individual been at his/her particular job?

- How deep/diversified is the management, for example, is management distributed among a number of managers? Is management succession in place? What is the length of time various managers have been at their positions? What are the local employment conditions, especially regarding the ability to find and replace management personnel?

- What is the performance of the company before considering officers' compensation and how does it compare with the industry that they are in?

- What is typical compensation; how are officers compensated (salary versus bonus); what are the typical perks in the company's specific industry?

- What are the typical responsibilities for officers in that specific industry? (In some industries the officers / management team performs many functions.)

Once the appraiser fully understands the composition of the owner's officer/management team, the appraiser reviews the various databases and surveys which publish officers' compensation material.

Caution is required when using this data. The appraiser must not blindly apply the percentages provided from the various studies even when the compensation information is given as the mean, median, or broken down by quartiles as to the subject company's sales. The appraiser must consider the information about the officer/management team as discussed above and use common sense. The appraiser should consider whether he could reasonably expect to hire the applicable number of outside personnel for that amount of compensation considering the local employment conditions.

After all adjustments have been made, the appraiser must recompute the income taxes based on the normalized income.

CHAPTER

13

Business Valuation Approaches

General Introduction to Business Valuation Approaches

The previous chapter dealt with general concepts of evaluation. Now, however, we will discuss more complex matters dealing with the approaches and methods of valuing a business and the application of premiums and discounts drafted. There have been volumes written on the topic of business valuation approaches, premiums, and discounts. My goal is to have you simply grasp the key concepts so that you will understand what your business appraiser is doing as well as be in a position to ask questions of your appraiser or lawyer when reviewing your spouse's valuation report.

The appraiser considers the use of three approaches in valuing a closely-held business: the income approach, the market approach, and the asset-based or cost approach. Within each of these three approaches, the appraiser may use a number of different methods in determining the value of the business. The particular approach and method used by the appraiser depends on the facts and circumstances of the business interest being valued so the business appraiser must consider each approach and determine which are most appropriate.

The three business valuation approaches are:

1. *Income Approach.* The business is valued on the basis of the earning stream the business generates.

2. *Market Approach.* The business is valued based on references to other transactions, such as comparable sales.

3. *Asset Based "Cost" Approach.* The business is valued on the basis of its assets and liabilities.

Under each approach, the appraiser may use various methods in the valuation process. This summary lists common methods that you may come across:

1. Income Approach Methods.
   - *Discounted future earnings.* Under the discounting of future earnings method, the forecasted earning stream of the company is discounted back to a present value based on a rate of return known as a discount rate. This includes the capitalization of the terminal value as well.
   - *Capitalization of earnings.* Under the capitalizing method, a single period's economic earning stream is divided by a rate of return known as a capitalization rate.

2. Market Approach Methods.
   - Publicly Traded Guideline Company Method
   - Comparative Transaction Method (Mergers and Acquisition Method— Use of private transaction data bases)
   - Rules of Thumb/Industry Methods

3. Asset-Based Methods.
   - Adjusted Net Asset Value Method (Liquidation method)
   - *Excess Earnings Method.* This asset might be classified under an asset-based "cost" approach because it has added the values of the tangible and intangible assets. On the other hand, it also has features of an income approach because when using this method the valuator will consider the income stream of the business in determining the intangible value of the business and the evaluator will apply a capitalization rate to the excess earnings of the business.

Income Approach

The income approach is probably the most widely used approach in business valuation. It also may present the most problems for the court in differentiating between enterprise and personal goodwill. Under the income approach, the value of the business is based on the company's earnings, or the future earnings that the business is expected to produce. The company's earnings stream or future benefits are converted to a present value by either capitalizing the current benefits using an appropriate capitalization rate, or by discounting the future benefits using an appropriate discount rate. The capitalization of earnings method derives the company's value by looking at a single period of normalized earnings stream. The discounted future earnings method is derived by looking at the company's normalized earnings stream to be received over a number of years in the future. Using an income approach, there is a direct relationship between the amount of earnings or benefits the company will generate and its value. The determination of what is meant by earning stream is also important. Most valuations will use cash flow as the earning stream; however, it is possible to use net income, earnings before interest, taxes, depreciation, and amortization (EBITDA.) One must make sure that the discount rate or capitalization rate being used is appropriate for the earning stream that one is using.

The two primary methods used under the income approach are the discounted future earnings method and the capitalization of earnings method.

In the capitalization of earnings method, the appraiser is converting only a single number (a measure of earnings for a single period) to a value and has determined that historical returns of the business are indicative of future results and that the company's growth rate is stable and predictable. In the discounting of forecasted earnings method, the appraiser concludes that past results do not necessarily indicate future results and anticipates that the company will report earnings that vary significantly from year to year. Therefore, using the discount method the appraiser anticipates that the company has specific future earnings expectations, such as the expected growth of the company in the near term with growth slowing and leveling off in the future.

Under both methods, the appraiser needs to determine a normalized earnings stream. Usually, this is a cash flow earnings stream but there can be other types. The key is identifying the earning stream that the appraiser is using and matching the appropriate capitalization or discount rate for that particular income stream. For example, the appraiser does not apply the same discount rate to net cash flow and net income. Usually there must be an adjustment to the capitalization or discount rate to reflect the type of earnings stream that the appraiser is using.

Even though the income approach is widely accepted by business valuators, it may present problems in some states for divorce valuations. The lawyer handling a business valuation case needs to understand that the appraisal using an income approach results in a single value for the business which may include elements of personal goodwill. In looking at the future earnings stream of the company, the appraiser might assume that the continuing personal efforts of the business-owning spouse is a significant contributing factor in determining the future growth of the company and thus its future earnings stream. Because doing so may be contrary to state case law, the appraiser must make certain that the future earnings stream of the business does not take into consideration the earning potential and personal efforts of the business-owning spouse following the divorce.

Whenever the capitalization of earnings method is used, it is simply assumed that the expected state of affairs will continue indefinitely. While this method derives the company's value by looking at a single period of normalized earnings, long-term, sustainable growth may still be built into an appraiser's calculations using the capitalization method. In addition, the single period of normalized earnings stream used by the appraiser may already take into consideration earning potential of the spouse who owns the business.

Summary of Major Steps Using the Capitalization of Earnings Method or Discounted Future Earnings Method

Summary of major steps using the capitalization of earnings method:

1. Prepare a schedule of the normalized net income for the past five years. The period may be less depending on the circumstances, for example, if the company has only been in existence for three years, the current two years are more indicative of the future than the prior five years.

2. Determine the type of normalized earnings stream that will be used for the valuation. Typically, the appraiser will use a normalized cash flow earnings stream. If this is the case, generally the appraiser will start with normalized net income and add back depreciation, amortization, and subtract out both projected capital expenditures as well as changes in working capital. This will change if the appraiser uses a weighted average cost of capital for its capitalization rate [See discussion below]. In this case, the earnings stream may be called net cash flow to invested capital and the appraiser would add back any interest expense to arrive at cash flow before consideration of debt service. Also, as mentioned before, the appraiser needs to remember the tax effect of any adjustments to the earnings stream.

3. Determine the actual normalized earnings stream to be capitalized. This consists of earnings the company is expected to generate. Some appraisers valuate this by taking the most current year; taking an average of the

past several years, or forecasting the next year's results. After analyzing the historical earnings, the market, and the company's current situation the appraiser determines the appropriate method.

4. Calculate the appropriate capitalization rate to be used with the normalized earnings stream previously developed. The typical method used is the build-up method or the modified capital asset pricing model (CAPM) [See discussion below]. If the earnings stream is based on current or prior earnings the capitalization rate should be adjusted by dividing it by 1 plus the long-term growth rate.

5. Divide the normalized income base by the capitalization rate to obtain the indicated operating value of the company.

6. If the company has any nonoperating assets or excess assets they should be added to the operating value of the company. Nonoperating assets may be an owner's condominium or airplane that is not used in the business. Excess assets may be an excessive amount of cash maintained in the company over and above its business needs. In a divorce situation in which the owner has significant prerogatives of control, it is possible that such assets may be channels in which the business-owner spouse is concealing funds.

7. Apply the appropriate discount or premium. Identify whether the resulting indicated value represents a marketable minority interest or a marketable controlling interest. It is widely accepted that under the income approach the determination of minority or control is dictated by the earnings stream that is employed. If in normalizing the earnings stream, the appraiser makes those adjustments that only a controlling owner could make, the appraiser then develops an earnings stream which assumes a control value. If in normalizing the earnings stream, the appraiser does not make adjustments that the controlling owner could make, the appraiser develops an earnings stream that assumes a minority interest. Accordingly, the discounts and premiums applied must be consistent with the adjustment made during the normalization process.

Summary of Major Steps Using the Discount of Future Earnings Method

1. With input from management and research of industry standards compared with the subject company, the first step is to develop forecasted normalized earnings for a period of time, such as the next five years into the future. The projection should be based on the reasonableness of the time frame and is usually developed by management.

2. As described in the method above, determine the type of earnings stream that will be used in the valuation. Again, if it is cash flow, the normalized net income should be adjusted to add back depreciation and amortization and to deduct capital improvements as well as changes in working capital.

3. As described in the method above, a discount rate is determined.

4. A terminal value of the company as of the end of the forecasted period is estimated. This is usually calculated by taking the earnings stream as of the last period of the forecasted period and then capitalizing it in the same process as discussed above.

5. Using the discount rate that was previously calculated, the appraiser then calculates the present value of the forecasted normalized earnings stream which includes the terminal value of the company. The result is an indicated value of the company's operations.

6. As described in the method above, if the company has nonoperating assets or if excess assets were identified during the normalized process, they should be added to the operating value of the company.

7. Apply the appropriate discounts or premiums.

Determination of Capitalization/Discount Rate

You and the lawyer should conceptually understand the impact of the discount or capitalized rate on value. The discount or capitalization rate will be expressed as a percentage. In a vacuum, as the rate goes up, assuming no other changes in the facts or analysis, on a mathematical basis the value of the business goes down. A relatively small difference in the discount rate or capitalization rate chosen can have a significant impact on value. Accordingly, it is important for you and the lawyer involved in a case that has a business valuation to understand how the discount or capitalization rate is selected based on the two approaches that the appraiser will generally use.

Build-up Approach and Modified Capital Asset Pricing Model (CAPM) Generally

In the capitalization method, the appraiser divides next year's estimate of economic benefits (which could be based upon the immediate prior year, a simple average of prior years, a weighted average of prior years, etc.) by a capitalization rate. This capitalization rate equals the discount rate less the company's long-term sustainable growth of the company. Since a company's capitalization rate is derived from its discount rate, the appraiser must determine the discount rate before determining the capitalization rate. In developing a discount rate, appraisers generally use either the build-up approach or the modified capital asset pricing model (CAPM).

The Build-up Approach

The most common approach appraisers use to determine the discount rate for small closely-held businesses is the build-up approach. The build-up approach is based on the concept that the rate of return an investor would require to invest in a particular company is determined by starting with the risk-free rate and increasing the rate by an amount sufficient to compensate for all the identifiable risk factors associated with that company. The appraiser simply adds these various percentage amounts together to determine the discount rate. The following summarizes the discount rate components under the build-up approach:

The equation is expressed as follows:

$$Re = Rf + (Rm - Rf) + S + C$$

where
Re = Cost of equity capital
Rf = Risk-free rate of return
$(Rm - Rf)$ = Market equity risk premium
S = Small company risk premium
C = Company specific risk premium

1. *Risk Free Rate of Return.* The appraiser determines the risk-free rate of return as of the valuation date. This is the rate of return that an investor could obtain from a relatively risk-free investment. It is generally accepted that an appraiser can use the rate on a long-term U.S. Treasury bond, such as the 20-year U.S. Treasury bond yield.

2. *Equity Risk Premium.* The appraiser adds to the risk-free rate an equity risk premium. The equity risk premium represents the additional return an investor would require based on the perceived risk of ownership in a publicly traded company as compared to the return on U.S. Treasury bonds. The addition of the risk-free rate and the equity risk premium produces an average market return for a large publicly traded company. Since closely-held companies being valued in divorce cases are much smaller than large publicly traded companies, further adjustments must be made.

3. *Size Premium.* The valuator next adds a risk premium for size. This assumes that an investor requires an additional return for investing in small companies rather than large ones because of the additional risk. Ibbotson

Associates has been publishing the Stocks, Bonds, Bills, and Inflation (SBBI) edition annually for 24 years. This yearbook is an outgrowth of Professor Ibbotson's 1976 study analyzing long-term returns of principle asset classes in the domestic economy. Beginning in 1999, a special valuation edition was published (and still is today) specifically for the business valuation community. Within this book, size premiums for ten size groupings are reported. The sizes are determined by market capitalization. Returns are adjusted so that the reported premium reflects returns not associated with the stock's betas.

Studies have provided strong evidence that the degree of risk and the corresponding cost of capital increases as the size of the company decreases. Ibbotson Associates have broken down the size of all companies on the New York Stock Exchange (NYSE) into deciles based on the market value of common equity. The excess returns over the basic equity risk premium increase dramatically with decreasing size. For example, mid-cap stock which would have a size of approximately $1.0 billion to $4.0 billion, have a small stock premium of 0.6%. Low-cap stock ranges from $200 million to $800 million and has a premium of 1.1%. The smallest category, micro-cap stock ranges from $1 million up to $200 million and carries a premium of 2.6%. As previously mentioned these were broken down further into ten deciles. Recently Ibbotson broke out the very smallest of the micro-caps and they demonstrate a very high size premium of 8.4%.

Another study done by Roger Grabowski and David King of PricewaterhouseCoopers, known as the "PricewaterhouseCoopers Risk Premium Report 2000," took the size concept a step further. On top of Ibbotson's deciles, they added seven more measures of size. Also, they broke down the size groups into 25 portfolios, each representing four percentage points of the companies on the NYSE as measured by each of their eight size criteria. What they found is that the size effect is significant regardless of what measure of size is used and secondly, the size effect continues to increase through the smallest size categories, with a significant jump in its effect for the smallest four percent of stocks.

4. *Company Specific Risk.* Finally, the appraiser adds an additional premium for the return an investor would require to account for particular risks associated with the company being valued. This specific company risk number will generally be a positive number assuming greater risk for the companies set forth in step 3 above. Some factors the appraiser considers in developing this premium include the depth of company management,

the company's competitive position, and a number of other subjective factors. The specific company risk premium is the most subjective factor used in the build-up approach.

Beyond the scope of this book, Ibbotson has begun to track risk by industry groups in their latest publication.

Modified Capital Asset Pricing Model

The formula under the Modified Capital Asset Pricing Model (CAPM) is very similar to the build-up approach except that it considers beta. Beta simply measures the variance between stock price of a single company and a broad index of stocks, such as the S&P 500. If a company or industry group has a beta less than 1.0 it indicates that the returns of that group tend to go up less than the market when the market goes up and tend to go down less than the market when the market goes down. If a company's beta is greater than 1.0, its returns would tend to go up more than the market when the market is up and down more than the market when the market goes down. Securities with betas greater than 1.0 are characterized as aggressive securities and are more risky than the market as a whole. Thus, beta can be characterized as a sort of volatility index. The formula for modified CAPM considers beta as well as the same factors in the build-up approach: the risk-free rate, an equity risk premium, a small company risk premium, and a specific company risk adjustment.

The equation to be used in the Modified CAPM calculation is expressed as follows:

$$Re = Rf + B\,(Rm - Rf) + S + C$$

where

Re = Cost of equity capital
Rf = Risk-free rate of return
B = Industry beta coefficient
$(Rm - Rf)$ = Market equity risk premium
S = Small company risk premium
C = Company specific risk premium

While beta is readily available for publicly traded companies, the appraiser must estimate it for privately held companies. Doing so is a laborious task which is not required when using the build-up approach. It is done by referring to proxy companies which are substantially similar to the company being appraised. In a recent tax court case, the court indicated that generally, the capital asset pricing model should not be used by the appraiser of a closely-held business unless the company is a candidate to go public or a candidate for acquisition by a public company. (Estate of Klauss v. Commissioner, T.C. Memo 2000-191 (June 27, 2000)). The essential problem with use of the CAPM model to value a closely-held corporation is that the beta to be applied must be estimated from comparable publicly traded companies and often there are not comparable public companies when valuing a relatively very small closely-held business.

Under both the build-up approach and CAPM approach the discount rate derived is generally assumed to be a rate to be applied to a net cash flow earnings stream. If the earnings stream being used is one other than net cash flow, the discount rate needs to be adjusted further.

Determination of the Capitalization Rate from the Discount Rate

Once the appraiser has calculated the discount rate, to determine the capitalization rate, the valuator simply subtracts the company's long-term growth rate from the discount rate. The capitalization rate that results from this calculation should appropriately be applied to the following year's income or earnings stream. Thus, if the appraiser is using the current year's earnings stream or an average of prior years' earnings, an adjustment to the capitalization rate is needed. The appraiser does this by dividing the capitalization rate by one plus the long-term growth rate.

Debt Inclusive Method (Valuing Company's Equity) vs. Debt Free Method (Valuing Company's Total Invested Capital)

The preceding analysis assumes the appraiser is valuing only the company's equity (e.g., the stock of a corporation). This is known as the debt inclusive method or direct equity method.

Alternatively, the expert could value the total invested capital (both the equity and the interest bearing debt). This is known as the total invested capital or debt free method. In a controlling equity valuation, the appraiser examines the capitalization structure of companies in its industry. This is because only a controlling owner has the ability to change the company's capital structure. By valuing a company's invested capital, the appraiser considers the effects of debt on the company's valuation. The formula to compute the weighted average cost of capital is as follows:

$$[(\text{Cost of Equity} * \text{Equity \%}) + (\text{After Tax Cost of Debt} * \text{Debt \%})]$$

The following example illustrates why it is important for the valuator to consider assessing the total invested capital of a business. Assume there are two companies, company A and company E. Each company has $100 cash as its only asset and each company earns $25. Company A's capital structure consists of $50 in interest-bearing debt and $50 in equity capital while company E's structure consists of $100 in equity capital (i.e., there is no interest-bearing debt). Also assume that debt payment is $10. Company A's return on the money invested (equity) is 30% ($15/$50) while company E's return on equity is 25% ($25/$100). While any investor should be interested in a company's return on equity, it should be kept in mind that only a controlling investor has the ability to alter the subject company's capital structure. Therefore, when valuing a closely-held company under the fair market value standard of value, the appraiser should consider the company's capital structure, notwithstanding the fact that no change in the existing business is likely to occur as a result of a divorce when there is a valuation of a controlling interest.

If the appraiser is using the total invested capital method of valuation, a rate of return associated with investing in both the equity and the debt capital of the business must be determined. There is an averaging of each of these components of the business' capitalization. This average is not a simple average. Instead, the discount rate is the weighted average of the cost of each of the components in the business' capital structure. This is called the weighted average cost of capital (WACC). In order to develop a discount rate under WACC, the appraiser needs to determine the cost of equity capital, the cost of debt capital, the proportion of equity in the capital structure, and the proportion of debt in the capital structure.

First, the appraiser determines that the cost of the company's debt which is usually based on the current interest rates on the company's current interest-bearing debt. The debt cost is then adjusted for taxes.

Next, the appraiser determines the weight to be applied to the debt and equity (the proportion of debt and equity in the capital structure of the business.) The weights that are applied to the cost of debt and the cost of equity are based on whether or not the appraiser is valuing a controlling interest or minority interest. When appraising a minority interest where the buyer cannot control the capital structure of the company, a WACC based on the company's actual weight of debt and equity is used. If the appraiser is valuing a controlling interest where the potential buyer would also have control over the capital structure, the appraiser may use WACC based on the debt and equity cost and weights of capital that are typical in the industry, that is a hypothetical capital structure discussed above.

Third, the appraiser determines the cost of equity capital. Typically, this is the discount rate that the appraiser has calculated previously for the return to the equity holder. After applying the respective weights to the costs of debt and the cost of equity, the appraiser finally adds the weighted cost of equity and debt together for the determination of the WACC. The WACC must be applied to an earnings stream that has been adjusted for the cost of the debt. For example, interest expense is added back to determine the net cash flow to invested capital. The appraiser looks to determine the earnings stream that is available to both the debt holders and equity holders (the total invested capital of the business).

Using the WACC method, once the appraiser determines the value for the total invested capital of the company (which includes the company's interest-bearing debt), the appraiser then subtracts out the amount of this debt to arrive at the value of the equity of the company.

CHAPTER

14

Market Approach

Introduction

A market approach is a general way of determining a value of a business interest using one or more methods that compare the company to similar business interests that have been sold. Market transactions in businesses, business ownership interests, or securities can provide objective data for developing value measures to apply in business valuations. Such value measures are frequently derived from guideline companies. Guideline companies are companies that provide a reasonable basis for comparison to the relative investment characteristics of the company being valued.

Transactions entered into in a free and open market can provide the clearest indication of what value the market places on a particular type of business. However, the key to using this method is the ability to obtain financial data for companies that are comparable to the company being valued. The key is comparability because, unfortunately, businesses are not interchangeable assets.

First, the appraiser examines transactions involving the stock of the company being valued. However, it is important to review these types of transactions carefully to determine if they were an arm's-length transaction, as opposed to simply a transfer of shares to related or friendly parties. The next place to look for transactions is the marketplace that consists of both publicly traded companies as well as private transactions.

Guideline Publicly Traded Company Method

There is an enormous amount of data from the transactions in publicly traded companies. Under this method, which is referred to as the "guideline method," the appraiser is looking to compare pricing multiples of the free-market transactions to the company being appraised. Pricing multiples usually consist of the following: Price/Net Earnings; Price/Pretax Earnings; Price/Cash Flow; Price/Sales; Price/Dividends; and Price/Book Value. The appraiser needs to decide which multiple is applicable for the type of entity being valued. For example, Price/Net Earnings is appropriate when the company has relatively high income compared to depreciation and depreciation represents actual physical wear and tear; Price/Cash Flow is appropriate when the company has low income due to depreciation and depreciation represents low physical, functional, and/or economic obsolescence; Price/Sales would be appropriate when the company being appraised is homogeneous to the guideline companies selected in terms of operating expenses, such as service companies and lastly, Price/Book Value would be appropriate if the company has significant tangible assets. Factors to be considered in selecting comparable companies include percentage of revenues derived from sales of similar products or services, comparable markets, size of the companies, comparable growth prospects, and risks.

In searching for guideline companies to compare with the company being valued, the appraiser tries to determine from the owners or management who their direct competitors are. There are also a number of sources that compile names and data regarding companies. Whatever sources are used to identify potential guideline companies, the appraiser must use both quantitative and qualitative analysis in the selection. In looking at quantitative factors, the appraiser is looking for size, growth, liquidity, profitability, turnover, and leverage. One of the major factors is size. Larger companies tend to operate differently than smaller privately held companies and thus do not necessarily make good guideline companies. An appraiser would look at the quantitative factors because he or she would have a difficult time trying to make meaningful comparisons between a company producing strong earnings and a company which is 1/100th the size with marginal earnings or operating losses. The same type of problem will exist in comparing a company that is well capitalized with little debt to a company that is highly leveraged and undercapitalized.

When we talk about qualitative factors, the appraiser needs to look at: management depth, diversity of operations and product, geographic diversity, market position and market share, supplier or customer dependence, and the lack of access to capital markets. The appraiser looks for a guideline company whose revenues are from activities similar to the company being appraised. A large public company may have sales from diversified activities where the risk and markets would be different from the company being appraised. An example of looking at qualitative factors when selecting guideline companies would be comparing the company being appraised, which has only one location versus a public company that has many locations spread across the country or internationally. A company like this tends to experience less sales volatility and therefore is subject to less risk. Less risk in turn means a lower return is required and a potentially higher price multiple, thus the companies may not be comparable.

Revenue Rule 59-60, commenting on the use of the guideline company method, states:

> In selecting corporations for comparative purposes, care should be taken to use only comparable companies. Although the only restrictive requirement as to comparable corporations specified in the statute is that their lines of business be the same or similar, yet it is obvious that consideration must be given to other relevant factors in order that the most valid comparison possible will be obtained.

Determining whether or not a particular public company should be considered as being comparable depends on a number of factors including capital structure, credit status, depth of management personnel experience, the nature of competition, and the maturity of the business. As I mentioned previously, one of the significant factors for comparability is size. Larger companies tend to operate differently than smaller privately-held companies and as a result do not necessarily make good guideline companies. In many valuations the company is so unique that it is difficult to find a set of guideline companies. Once the appraiser has selected a set of guideline companies, the following procedures are performed in developing a set of multiples to use in valuing the closely-held company:

1. Accumulate financial, operating, and market data about the guideline companies that have been selected. Financial and operating data can be obtained from the companies' annual reports and 10Q's. Information on the companies' market prices can be obtained on the Internet or simply by looking in the *Wall Street Journal*.

2. The financial statements of the guideline companies need to be adjusted to remove extraordinary items to make them comparable to the company being appraised.

3. Determine the appropriate multiples to use as discussed above. As listed earlier, these multiples might be Price/Earnings, Price/EBITDA or Price/EBIT, Price/Gross Revenue, Price/Cash Flow, or Price/Book Value.

4. Determine the period of earnings to be used. Again, information available and other factors will assist in this decision to select either: latest 12 months, last fiscal year, average of X# of years, or weighted average of X# of years.

5. Compute the applicable valuation multiples for each guideline company. The appraiser needs to remember to use the market prices for each guideline company as of the valuation date or as close as possible.

After calculating all of the relevant multiples for the guideline companies selected, the next step is to develop a single multiple to be applied to the earnings or revenues of the company being appraised.

Since the appraiser uses market information from the sale of minority interests when using the guideline publicly traded company method, the indicated value that is realized is a marketable, minority indicated value. Therefore, in valuing an interest in a closely-held company for a divorce valuation, a premium might be added if the appraiser is valuing a controlling interest. On the other hand, the appraiser must also discount the guideline publicly traded indicated value due to the lack of marketability of the closely-held business interest. These premiums and discounts are discussed in Chapter 16.

Private Transactions—The Comparative Transaction Method

In addition to using publicly traded companies, private transactions may also be analyzed to determine the value of a company. The appraiser may review various databases in order to find comparable companies that are not publicly traded. This may be called the comparative transaction method. The significant difference between the use of the market for guideline companies and the use of private transactions for guideline companies is that the guideline publicly traded companies involve minority interest transactions of fully marketable securities. Generally, private transactions provide data about transfers of controlling interests and the transfers may include the entire capital structure of the business, not just the equity of the business.

Using a market approach based on private transactions, experts often rely on market valuation multiples, such as pricing/earnings ratios or price/sales ratios, from sales of comparable businesses or practices that included a covenant not to compete or an employment agreement. This overstates the value of the business or practice without the participation or restrictions on the business owner. The expert avoids this problem by subtracting from the total consideration paid in the comparable transaction, the value of the covenant not to compete or the employment agreement and recomputes the valuation multiples without those agreements. This may be difficult to obtain from some of the databases available.

Three other sources of smaller private company transactions include the following databases:

1. *Bizcomps.*[1] This database provides sales statistics for thousands of closely-held business transactions based on the Standard Industrial Classification (SIC) and business type.

2. *Pratt's Stats.*[2] This is the newest of the three databases used. This database goes into more detail in presenting financial information about the company being acquired as well as the terms of the deal. The database presents up to seven valuation benchmarks from which to analyze the transactions. The benchmarks include price to net sales, price to net income, price to gross cash flow, price to earnings before taxes (EBT), price to earnings before interest and taxes (EBIT), price to earnings before interest, taxes, depreciation and amortization (EBITDA), and price to discretionary earnings.

3. *The Institute of Business Appraisers (IBA).*[3] This source also compiles a database of sales transactions for closely-held businesses, similar to Bizcomps. It provides valuation benchmarks based on sales price to gross revenue and also sales price to earnings before owner's compensation, interest, and taxes. The indications of value derived from this database generally represent the fair market value of a company's operating assets, exclusive of cash, accounts receivable, and real estate.

Rules of Thumb/Industry Method

Often parties in divorce cases will have heard of rules of thumb applicable to a particular industry. If rules of thumb in a particular industry are widely disseminated and referenced in the industry, they should not be completely ignored. On the other hand, rules of thumb or industry methods should be used only as a starting point in the valuation process or as what is known as a sanity check in the appraisal process. The typical rule of thumb is a valuation formula that is usually developed by interpretation of market transactions. The market transactions convert into rule of thumb multiples by computing the actual transaction price as a multiple of net revenue or owners' cash flow. Specific industry trade associations sometimes develop their own rules of thumb or industry formulas as a method for valuing a company in a specific industry.

Rules of thumb or industry methods should be used only as a starting point in the valuation process or as a sanity check. The value that the appraiser develops using the rule of thumb should be tested against other methods and only accepted if clearly supported by these other methods. The thing to remember is that rules of thumb or industry methods are not substitutes for careful consideration of other appropriate valuation methods that are applicable to the entity being appraised.

Sources of these formulas can be found through Internet searches, from trade associations, or from the books listed in the chapter endnotes.

Notes

[1] *Bizcomps.* John Wiley & Sons, Inc., 1997

[2] *Pratt's Stats.* Business Valuation Resources, fourth quarter 1997

[3] *Market Comparison Data.* The Institute of Business Appraisers, Inc.

The Cost Approach

An asset-based approach is a general way of determining a value indication of a business' assets or equity interest using one or more methods based directly on the value of the assets of the business less liabilities. The theoretical basis for this approach is the principle of substitution. The premise is that a potential buyer of a business would not pay more than the amount necessary to replace each of the business assets owned by the entity with ones of equal utility, less any liabilities to which the entity is obligated.

The problem with the cost approach to valuing many businesses is that the value of a business interest, in many instances is not due the value of the underlying assets of the business themselves but is dependent on the value of the earnings stream that is expected to be derived from the business assets. Thus, this approach is usually more appropriate for valuing businesses such as holding companies or investment companies, real estate partnerships, and start-up companies. This approach is also used when there is an insufficient earnings stream of the business or when liquidation of the business may be contemplated. It is not appropriate for entities that are profitable operating companies with intangible assets that are not contemplating liquidation.

Net Asset Value Method

Under the net asset value method, the company's assets and liabilities are individually adjusted to their fair market value in order to determine the company's equity value. In analyzing the balance sheet, all necessary adjustments to account for missing assets and liabilities must be determined. For example, if the company maintains its books and records on a cash basis of accounting, the appraiser must calculate and record the trade receivables and payables. Although this discussion has focused on the tangible assets of a company, it is also important to recognize and identify intangible assets. Any goodwill on the balance sheet from a prior acquisition should be eliminated. However, other intangible assets such as patents, copyrights, and bargain leases should be valued. It is also important to identify and value contingent liabilities.

After the assets and liabilities are recorded on the balance sheet, the appraiser must value each of the assets. Items such as cash or marketable securities may be valued by researching published closing prices as of the date of the valuation. However, unless qualified, the business appraiser should not act as a real estate or machinery and equipment appraiser. The business appraiser usually requests a real estate appraiser (MAI) to perform a complete valuation of all of the company's real estate holdings. There are also appraisers who are specially trained and certified to value the fair market value of machinery and equipment. Accounts receivable must also be analyzed. The appraiser should look at the company's aging of accounts receivable. Based on the aging taken in conjunction with a review of the historical collection results and discussions with management, the appraiser adjusts the balance of the accounts receivable to the estimated fair market value. You may need to review your state's divorce case law when it comes to accounts receivable and whether they are to be treated as an asset. For example, Illinois case law generally holds that accounts receivable may be considered in valuing a business.

In valuing the intangible assets of the business, the methods that can be used are the discrete method (valuing each asset of the business individually) and the collective method. In the discrete method, each of the individual intangible assets (or individual category of intangible assets) of the business or professional practice is separately identified and valued. In valuing intangibles collectively, the aggregate intangible value of the business or professional practice, from whatever source, is analyzed and quantified. The discrete method of valuation is much more costly to perform. It will value items separately, such as a trained and assembled workforce in place, a trade name, client records, a favorable lease-hold interest, just to name a few.

An issue often raised is how individual assets should be appraised. This is usually dictated by the premise of value that is selected. The premise of values that is typically considered in valuing individual assets includes fair market value (in continued use or as part of a going concern) or orderly liquidation value.

Under the premise of fair market value in continued use, it is assumed the assets are sold as a mass assemblage and as part of an income-producing company where the business earnings support the value. The American Society of Appraisers (ASA) define orderly liquidation value as the gross amount expressed in terms of money which could be typically realized from a sale, as of a specific date, given a reasonable period of time to find a purchaser(s), with the seller being compelled to sell on an as is-where is basis. It is assumed that the assets are to be sold piecemeal, not as part of a mass assemblage.

Excess Earnings Method

Under the cost approach, there is a method referred to as either the capitalized excess earnings method, the excess earnings method, the treasury method, or the formula approach which is discussed briefly with regards to Revenue Rule 68-609. This method was designed as a procedure to determine the fair market value of a company's intangible assets by capitalizing all earnings beyond a fair return on its tangible assets. The Revenue Ruling which sets forth the steps in the excess earnings method is discussed here. While the steps appear straightforward, the naive use and the overuse of this method has been criticized by the IRS as well as various learned treatises. The ruling itself states that, "[T]he "formula" approach may be used for determining the fair market value of intangible assets of a business only if there is no better basis therefor available." This method is sometimes referred to as the method of last resort.

Although use of the excess earnings method is not encouraged, the following is a brief summary of the procedures for this method:

1. The appraiser estimates the fair market value of each identified asset of the company. Because the valuation is based in significant part on valuing identified assets, this method is considered an asset-based method of valuation. Next, the valuator determines the reasonable rate of return to be applied to the net tangible assets. A significant problem with this valuation method is that there is no objective means of establishing this rate of return. Different types of assets have different risks. For example, cash has very little risk and has a rate close to the risk-free rate. Obviously, inventory and machinery and equipment are riskier and require a higher rate of return. Next, the dollar amount of the total return on the tangible assets is calculated by adding the rate of returns for each asset or group of assets. Some appraisers merely determine the weighted average rate of return and apply

the rate to the total tangible assets. In effect, this is the first capitalization rate that the appraiser must determine when using this method.

2. The appraiser next takes the dollar amount calculated as the total return on the tangible assets in step one and subtracts it from the company's normalized earnings stream. The result of this is the calculation of the excess earnings amount—the earnings attributable to the intangible assets of the company.

3. Next, the appraiser must determine the appropriate capitalization rate to apply to the excess earnings. This is the second capitalization rate that the appraiser must use when using this method. Problems may occur here. This rate applies to the intangible assets of the company which are the riskiest and thus should yield the highest rate of return. This rate should be significantly higher than the capitalization rate computed under the income approach for the equity of the company because the rate of return computed under the income approach relates to the entire company, including the tangible assets of the company. While there is empirical data supporting the use of the capitalization rates under an income approach there is no such data supporting the use of essentially two separate capitalization rates under the excess earnings method (one rate applied under step 1 and the second rate applied under step 3).

4. The appraiser next calculates the intangible value of the business by dividing the excess earnings by the capitalization rate developed for the excess earnings.

5. Finally, the appraiser determines the value of the company by adding together the fair market value of the company's net tangible assets determined in step 1 and the value of the intangible assets of the company as calculated in the previous step.

16

Discounts and Premiums

A nother aspect of the business valuation process for the matrimonial lawyer to understand is the issue of discounts and premiums. Common types of valuation discounts or premiums are control premiums, discounts for lack of control (minority interest discounts), marketability discounts, and key-person discounts.

Before applying any discount or premium, the appraiser must look carefully at the methodology used as well as the type of value to be determined. For example, if the appraiser uses the income approach, the assumptions used in developing the earnings stream determine whether or not the indicated value is a minority or controlling value. If in developing this earnings stream, the appraiser makes all of the modifications that a controlling shareholder would be able to make, then the indicated value would result in a control value. On the other hand, if these adjustments were not considered, the earnings stream and ultimate indicated value may represent a minority value.

The same analysis applies under each approach used by the appraiser. Under the market approach, the comparative data that the appraiser uses determines the type of preliminary value. For example, if the appraiser uses data from merger and acquisition data, the resulting value usually represents a control value. If the appraiser uses multiples from publicly traded companies' minority shares, the resulting value usually represents a minority interest value. Under the cost approach, the indicated or preliminary value is usually a control value.

Control Premiums and Minority Discounts

If the valuator is appraising a control value and the indicated or preliminary value determined is a minority value, a control premium is applied to the indicated value. Conversely, if the appraiser is valuing a minority interest and the preliminary value is a control value, then a minority discount must be applied to the preliminary value. The same analysis applies in determining whether to apply a lack of marketability discount.

In determining the extent of a discount or premium, the degree of attributes of a controlling shareholder as compared to a minority shareholder must be understood. The controlling shareholder has certain prerogatives of control and can set corporate policy, appoint management, determine compensation for management, determine perks of management, acquire or liquidate corporate assets, and declare and pay dividends. Interested buyers are usually willing to pay a premium for these rights. Minority stock interests in a closely-held business are usually worth much less than the proportionate share of the business to which it attaches. In other words, the pieces of the pie added together probably will not equal the value of the whole pie, as the whole pie is worth more than its individual pieces.

There are many factors in determining the level of the discount or premium. The degree of control that the shareholder possesses to perform some of the items mentioned above is important. The prerogatives of control the minority shareholder possesses must also be considered. Sometimes, the degree of control is dictated by such factors as contractual restrictions, industry or governmental regulations, state laws, distribution of the ownership of the company, size of the company, depth of management, or the size of the block of stock that is being valued.

Once the economic implications associated with the rights are identified, the appraiser can then determine the appropriate magnitude of a control premium or a minority interest discount in the valuation process. The size of the minority discount or control premium may vary with the facts and circumstances of the specific company being valued.

The economic implications associated with the rights should be identified, and should determine the appropriate magnitude of a control premium or a minority interest discount.

A number of studies have attempted to examine the range of premiums buyers would be willing to pay for a controlling interest in a company. One source of data on control premiums has been presented in *Mergerstat Review* compiled by Houlihan, Lokey, Howard, & Zukin (HLHZ). This study provides historical summaries of the average and medium premiums paid for control and certain noncontrol blocks of common shares. These premiums are measured in percentages as the difference between the acquisition price and the price of the freely traded public shares five days before the announcement of the acquisition. For example, the average premium for 1995 was 44.7%, while the median was 35%. Over the last 10 years the median premium paid ranged from 29% to 35% and averaged 31.4%.

Another study, the HLHZ control premium study, also provides data on premiums paid in the cash purchase of control interests and value observed at various intervals prior to takeover. They looked at the premiums paid in relation to the market price one day, one week, one month, and two months prior to takeover. The premiums are also categorized by size of company, industry of the target company, exchange of target company (NYSE, AMEX, etc.), date, and tender offer versus leveraged buyout. The premiums in this study were slightly higher than *Mergerstat Review's* study.

The impact of lack of control (minority discount) can also be measured through the above studies. The appraiser can calculate the inverse of a control premium to determine the discount for lack of control (minority discount). In order to calculate the minority discount from the control premium (CP), the following formula is applied:

$$\text{Minority Discount} = CP/(1 + CP)$$

Thus, if the appraiser translates the *Mergerstat* control premiums for the last 10 years, the range of the implied minority discount would be from 21.7% to 25.9%. The HLHZ study shows a higher discount.

Lack of Marketability Discounts

The concept of lack of marketability discounts refers to the liquidity of the interest in the company being appraised (i.e., the ease and speed at which it can be sold). An ownership interest in a business is worth significantly more if it is readily marketable because owners prefer to own liquid investments. The minority shareholder in a closely-held company does not have the same market access as a holder of a interest in a publicly traded company. The challenge to the business appraiser of a privately held company then is to quantify the effect of lack of marketability in terms of its impact on the value of the company.

The effect of a lack of marketability on the value of financial assets has been analyzed and commented on by many learned treatises and long been recognized by the courts. These studies can be broken down into two major groupings: those dealing with restricted securities and those dealing with initial public offerings.

Restricted Stock Studies

A restricted stock is also known as a letter stock. Restricted stock is identical to freely traded stock of a public company except it is restricted from trading on the open market for a certain period. The duration of the period of restriction varies but usually the restrictions will lapse within 24 months. Since marketability is the only difference between restricted stock and freely traded stock, studies of such stocks are often used to measure the lack of marketability discount to be applied to the valuation of a closely-held corporation. Because the short time period in which the restrictions on such stock expire, shares of closely-held stock would be expected to require a higher marketability discount compared to the restricted stock of a publicly traded company.

The Securities and Exchange Commission's "Institutional Investor Study" was a major study which analyzed discounts associated with restricted shares of publicly traded companies. Generally, the SEC concluded that the differences between the prices paid for the restricted shares and their publicly traded counterparts were a function of the sales and earnings of the issuing corporation, the trading market for the stock, and resale constraints applicable to the restricted securities. In 1977, the Internal Revenue Service issued Revenue Ruling 77-287, "Valuation of Securities Restricted from Immediate Resale." This ruling and its conclusions were based on the SEC's study and recognized that a marketability discount was associated with shares that did not have immediate access to an active public market.

Studies of marketability discounts based on restricted stock studies are summarized in Figure 16.1.

In reviewing the restricted stock studies, there is an extreme range of discounts in the studies from very small discounts to a 91% discount. The only restricted stock study to address a correlation between the size of the discount and the attributes of the business was the recent Pratt study. The conclusions from this study were that small companies generally have larger marketability discounts than do larger companies. Similarly, companies with lower net incomes had higher marketability discounts. This is likely due to the increased risk related to small companies.

Initial Public Offering Studies

Before the 1980s virtually all of the research directed at quantifying lack of marketability discounts was based on the restricted stock studies. Generally, it

FIGURE 16.1   Marketability Discounts Summary

Study	Years	Average Discount
SEC Institutional	1966–1969	25.8%
Milton Gelman	1968–1970	33%
Robert Trout	1968–1972	33.5%
Robert Moroney	1969–1972	35.6%
J. Michael Maher	1969–1973	35.4%
Standard Research Consultants	1978–1982	45.0% (median)
FMV Opinions, Inc.	1979–1992	23.0%
Management Planning, Inc.	1980–1995	27.7%
Willamette Management Assoc.	1981–1984	31.2% (median)
William Silber	1981–1998	33.8%
Pratt	1991–1995	23.0%

was acknowledged that the lack of marketability discounts should be greater for closely-held companies compared to companies in which the ability to trade stock was limited for a certain time period. There are now two studies of private transactions before an initial public offering.

In a study by John Emory, the results of which were published in "The Value of Marketability as Illustrated in Initial Public Offerings of Common Stock" (*Business Valuation News*, December 1996) and recently further updated, he analyzed 130 initial public offerings to determine the relationship between the price at which the stock was initially offered to the public and the price at which private sales were transacted within five months before the initial public offering. The results of this study showed that the private buyers paid, on average, 43% less than the price at which the stock later appeared on the market. The private sale prices reflected a range of discounts from 3% to 83%, with the median being 43%. In an earlier study covering the 18 months prior to June 30, 1981, Emory found the average discount was 60% and the median was 66%. The decrease in the 1986 study may be attributed to record highs in the stock market and a more active initial public offering market.

Willamette Management Associates conducted a series of fourteen studies comparing private stock transactions to later public offerings. The studies covered the years 1975 through 1993. The median discount for private transaction Price/Earnings (P/E) multiples compared to public offering P/E multiples ranged from a low of 31.8% to a high of 73.1%.

The results of these studies are critical to the determination of an appropriate marketability discount because the share prices analyzed reflected the buyer's ability to gain access to a public market within a readily foreseeable, well-defined period of time ranging from a few months to a few years. These studies support the assumption that the fair market value of minority interests of closely-held companies should sell at significant discounts from their publicly traded counterparts. Minority shareholders in privately held companies do not enjoy as favorable an investment. Their shares have no immediate or predictable access to a public market, and the value of those shares suffers accordingly. The average marketability discount determined from the studies ranged from 25% to 45%.

Tax Court Cases

The majority of United States Tax Court cases which have addressed this point have allowed a marketability discount. In a recent case, *Mandelbaum v. Commissioner*, T.C. Memo 1995-255, Judge Laro provided some keen insight as to various factors the court should consider in establishing a marketability discount. The *Mandelbaum* court stated:

> When determining the value of unlisted stock by reference to listed stock, a discount from the listed price is typically warranted in order to reflect the unlisted stock's lack of marketability. Such a discount, commonly known as a "lack of marketability" discount (or, more succinctly, a "marketability discount"), reflects the absence of a recognized market for closely-held stock and accounts for the fact that closely held stock is generally not readily transferrable. A marketability discount also reflects the fact that a buyer may have to incur subsequent expense to register the unlisted stock for public sale. [Citation omitted.]

Factors the tax court considered in applying a 30% marketability discount were the financial statement analysis, the company's dividend policy, the nature of the company, the company's management, amount of control in the shares being valued, restrictions on the transferability of the shares, the holding period of the stock, the company's redemption policy, the costs of going public, and the general attractiveness of the company.

Marketability Discount on Controlling Interests

Although controlling shareholders can force registration to provide marketability, small closely-held companies rarely, if ever, contemplate a public offering. Without market access, an investor's ability to control the timing of potential gains, to avoid losses, and to minimize the opportunity costs associated with the inability to direct funds to a more promising investment is severely impaired. The challenge to the appraiser of a private company then is to quantify the effect of marketability, or lack thereof, in terms of its impact on the value of the company even when dealing with a control interest.

Although the previously discussed studies did not address controlling interests, they do tell us that even a temporary lack of marketability can be largely negative. When valuing a controlling interest in a privately held going concern, the risk of being locked-in is present and should be recognized.

In the case of *Estate of Woodbury G. Andrews*, 79 T.C. 938 (1982), Judge Whitaker, in his opinion, states:

> Even controlling shares in a nonpublic corporation suffer from lack of marketability because of the absence of a ready private placement market and the fact that flotation costs would have to be incurred if the corporation were to publicly offer its stock.

Discount for Lack of Voting Rights

This discount may be in addition to the discount for lack of control and lack of marketability. Of the studies performed, they have consistently found that the incremental difference in value between voting and nonvoting shares was not great when all other things are equal. The percentage discounts are in the range of 1% to 3%. However, the appraiser should realize that the importance of one's voting rights in a public company may be much less important than in a closely-held company.

On the reverse side of this is a premium to consider for the ownership of the swing vote. A swing vote is when someone who has a minority ownership but if acquired by another shareholder would create a control position. There is no empirical data on the quantification of this premium.

Key-Person Discounts

In addition to the discounts discussed above, there are other discounts that should be considered, such as a key-person discount. The ASA defines a key person as an individual whose contribution to a business is so significant that there is a certainty that present earnings levels would be adversely affected by the company losing that individual. This discount applies more to small service-oriented businesses but can have an impact on the value of larger businesses.

The key-person discount is taken if the business appraiser expects a reduction in the value of the subject company because of the loss of services of an individual who is actively involved and key to the company's operations. The person must play a significant role in the management of the company and possess talents or information that are not easily replaced or that require a significant investment on the part of the company in order to replace that person. Revenue Ruling 59-60 clearly addresses this point in its ruling with the following:

> . . . . The loss of the manager of a so-called 'one man' business may have a depressing effect upon the value of the stock of such business, particularly if there is a lack of trained personnel capable of succeeding to management of the enterprise. In valuing the stock of this type of business, therefore, the effect of the loss of the manager on the future expectancy of the business, and the absence of management succession potentialities are pertinent factors to be taken into consideration. On the other hand, there may be factors which offset, in whole or in part, the loss of the manager's services.

In developing a key-person discount the appraiser attempts to calculate the effect on earnings; research the replaceability of the key person without material adverse effects on the company's profit level; and determine the level of key-person life insurance that the company has. Assuming that the company is the beneficiary, key-person life insurance may be important if the amount of the death benefit is enough to help the company recover from a loss of a key person.

The appraiser must be careful not to double count with this discount, as the factors discussed above concerning the key-person discount may have already been taken into account in developing the discount rate used under the same income approach. If these factors were already taken into consideration in developing the discount rate a separate key-person discount should not be taken.

Blockage Discount

A blockage discount is usually taken when a large number of shares of a publicly traded company are valued, the disposition of which would require a significant period of time under normal trading conditions. The size of the block relative to the trading volume has a direct impact as to the size of the discount to take.

Personal Goodwill Discounts

We have now concluded the discussion of the more technical aspects of business valuation. The next issue that needs to be addressed in a divorce setting is the concept of goodwill. A number of states mandate a distinction between enterprise versus personal goodwill, especially if the court is addressing a small, closely-held business, which may be a professional practice. This distinction has been given various names by the various court decisions. Personal goodwill may be called professional goodwill. Enterprise goodwill may also be referred to as practice goodwill. This discussion will use the terms personal and enterprise goodwill in making this distinction.

So what is this concept of goodwill? *Blacks Law Dictionary*, 5th Edition, defines goodwill as ". . . the ability of the business to generate income in excess of a normal rate of assets due to superior managerial skills, market position, new product technology, etc. In the purchase of a business, goodwill represents the difference between the purchase price and the value of the net assets." Some courts have followed this definition, while others are more specific. For example, in the Kansas Supreme Court case of *Powell v. Powell*, 231 Kan. 456, 648 P.2d 218 (1982) the court defined goodwill as: ". . . the chief elements of goodwill are continuity of place and continuity of time. Goodwill is that advantage which is acquired by an establishment in consequence of the general public's continued patronage of the place because of its reputation; it is the probability that old customers will return to the old place."

So the key is this piece of value that the company or the individual has created which causes its customers to return to the business and generate a value which is greater than its tangible assets. For purposes of divorce, it is critical that we breakdown the makeup of this concept of goodwill even further into two classifications: professional (personal) goodwill and practice (enterprise) goodwill.

Professional or personal goodwill is based on the individual's personal reputation, experience, training, and ability which creates the customer to return to the business or practice. Having said this, it is possible that even personal goodwill can be transferred if the individual assists with the transfer, usually through the professional providing a transition period. The problem in divorce is that to do this would require the professional to provide personal efforts to the business after the period of the divorce. Thus, in a professional practice, personal goodwill is usually dependent upon the professional. The argument is that the value of the practice or company does not exist absent the individual. A simple check list that one can follow for professional or personal goodwill is as follows:

☐ Is the value inseparable from the actions, skill, the expertise and reputation of the practitioner?

☐ Is the value of the company other than its hard assets that cannot be transferred?

☐ The economic benefits of the practice or company to be transferred can only be realized through the performance of post-divorce services of the professional.

☐ Is the revenue or the ability to acquire future income tied directly to the effort of the individual?

☐ Is the ability of the entity to attract referrals separate and apart from the persona of the professional?

The main argument in dealing with personal goodwill cases is that it should be considered as a factor in analyzing the professional's income and thus included in the consideration of maintenance (alimony) and child support. If one is to include it in the valuation of the practice or company as well, many courts believe that this would be what is referred to as "double dipping" or duplicative.

Practice or enterprise goodwill relates more to the practice or company's reputation and its ability as an institution to attract and hold business even with a change of ownership. The major factor here is that the continuation of the client relationships are not dependent on a single professional or owner, thus, the customers of the entity will stay with the practice or company even upon the change of its ownership. The key is whether the goodwill can be sold or transferred independent of the professional, if it is not marketable or cannot be sold it does not have value.

In determining the valuation of goodwill, many methods can be utilized as discussed throughout this book. However, the determination of value and the methods to be used are based on the individual facts and circumstances of the particular case. In fact, there is no one right way, or a set formula for determining the value of goodwill. The IRS itself states in the famous Revenue Ruling 59-60, ". . . A sound valuation will be based upon all the relevant facts, but the elements of common sense, informed judgement, and reasonableness must enter into the process of weighting those facts and determining their aggregate significance."

Though many will use the concept of goodwill as going concern value, they are different. Going concern value is an asset-based operational concept. This is the value of the work force and physical components in place and operating in unison that creates income and value. In essence, one could acquire the operating business, including its tangible assets, without incurring the cost and time to assemble it.

It is also important to mention at this time, that one should understand that goodwill is just one type of intangible asset of a business or practice. Too many times we jump the gun and automatically conclude that the value of a practice such as a medical or dental practice is all personal goodwill thus the value is only its tangible assets, including its accounts receivable. However, many a professional practice or company, may have other transferable intangible assets that have value other than just goodwill such as: location of the business or practice, client records, telephone number of the business, work force, set protocol, trade name, patents, intellectual property, and the administrative facilities of the business or practice, to name a few. This argument was supported in an Illinois Appellate court decision [*Suzanne Head v. Henry Head*, 652 N.W. 2d. 1246 (Ill. App. 1 Dist., 1995)] where the court stated, ". . . enterprise goodwill cannot be premised upon the income potential of the professional. . . ." To the extent that evidence of goodwill did not include future earning potential, the court was required to consider it as part of the valuation of the practice, ". . . like other reviewing courts which have faced this issue, we acknowledge that on appropriate proof, enterprise goodwill may be susceptible of valuation. . . ." The trial court reasoned that this value might arise from or be based in part, upon:

- Location of the practice
- The transferable affiliation of the practice
- The administrative facilities of the practice
- Patient/client list

When we value these intangibles we can look to value these under a discrete method (individually) or on a collective method. Under a discrete method each of the individual intangible assets of the practice or company are specifically identified and valued separately. Some times the various intangible assets are grouped into categories of intangible assets and are valued by group. Under either way, once the intangible assets are valued, they are then added to fair market value of the net tangible assets of the practice or company to determine the value of the practice or company as a whole.

This is different than under the collective manner. Under this method, all of the intangible assets, from whatever source, are analyzed and ultimately valued in the aggregate. Thus under this method the individual intangible assets are not broken out but rather it is sufficient to identify that intangible asset value exists and what the total amount of the value is. Under this method, it is not uncommon to refer to this generically as goodwill of the business.

The discrete method of valuing the intangible assets of a practice or company is much more costly to perform than under the collective method. Thus, for many smaller practices or companies the collective method is typically used in valuing the intangible assets.

Generally, states follow several approaches to the issue of personal goodwill.

The first approach distinguishes personal versus enterprise goodwill in valuation of all business interests and does not make an explicit distinction between whether the business is a professional business or a nonprofessional business. This is spelled out cleanly in a 1999 Indiana case [*Yoon v. Yoon*, 711 N.E.2d 1265 (Ind.Sup.Ct. 1999)] as follows:

> . . . before including the goodwill of a self-employed business or professional practice in a marital estate, a court must decide that the goodwill is attributable to the business as opposed to the owner as an individual. If attributable to the individual, it is not a divisible asset and is properly considered only as future earning capacity that may affect the relative property division . . . some ownership interests in a professional practice are properly viewed as divisible property even if goodwill is a component of their value. Otherwise stated, even a professional practice can have an enterprise goodwill component to its value."

> As further shown in a Illinois Supreme Court case [In re *Marriage of Helen Talty v. William F. Talty*, G62 N.E.2d 330 (Ill. 1995)] that dealt with an auto dealership, the court stated that ". . . to the extent that goodwill inheres in the business, existing independently of one's personal efforts, and will outlast one's involvement with the enterprise, it should be considered an asset of the business, and hence, of the marriage.

The second approach is similar to the first but distinguishes between professional and nonprofessional goodwill. Under each of these approaches, case law generally does not allow the court to consider in the valuation an implied covenant not to compete.

One will need to be careful, as a Maryland appellate court stated in *Prahinski v. Prahinski*, 75 Md. App 113, 540 A.2d 833 (1988), ". . . The fact that such a noncompetition clause was as essential factor in the expert's valuation sub judice clearly establishes that what the expert referred to as goodwill was in reality the business owner's reputation."

A third approach takes the position that value must be established without dependence on the net income of the professional but will allow consideration of continuity of practice, that is, the cases may assume that the owner will enter a covenant not to compete in valuing the subject business. However, one needs to be careful under the fair market value standard of value not to overvalue the business or practice based on this position.

A fourth approach states that professional goodwill is a marital asset subject to distribution in the divorce. Very few states take this position.

It is imperative that you review the issue of goodwill with your attorney and that the attorney and business valuation have a clear understanding of your state's law and the court's position on dealing with personal goodwill.

17

Effect of Purchase Price, Buy-Sell Agreements, and Key-Person Insurance Upon Valuation

A buy-sell agreement is not necessarily based on the fair market value of the business. A buy-sell agreement is simply an agreement between friendly parties to address the smooth transition of ownership due to the business owner's termination of employment, death, or sale of the individual's business interest.

Rule 9-2(d)(i) of the USPAP addresses buy-sell agreements. It states:

In developing a business or intangible asset appraisal, an appraiser must identify: The business enterprises, assets, or equity to be valued: and (i) identify any buy-sell agreements, investment letter stock restrictions, restrictive corporate charter or partnership agreement clauses, and any similar features or factors that may have an influence on value.

Typically, the threshold issue in divorce cases involving valuation of an owning spouse's interest in a professional corporation is whether there is a buy-out agreement, and if so, how much consideration the court should attach to the valuation of the buy-out agreement. Here again, it is imperative that your attorney be well versed in the case law in your particular state as it relates to the issue.

Common Business Valuation Mistakes in Divorce Cases

Under the various approaches to valuations there are numerous common mistakes that occur, such as applying the wrong cap rate to the type of earning stream being used. This section lists some of the specific mistakes that I have seen during the divorce process, as opposed to mistakes specific to the mechanics of valuation.

Failure to Hire an Expert With Experience in Divorce Valuations

Hiring an expert with a significant history in cases involving valuations in divorce cases is critical, especially considering the case law from the various states regarding personal and enterprise goodwill.

Failure to Account for Personal Goodwill

This involves the concept of replacing the business owner spouse with another person who would be paid a reasonable executive salary. The issue as to goodwill and its distinction between personal and enterprise goodwill is critical and must be addressed within the valuation.

Failure in relying on Rules of Thumb or averaging of Valuation Methods

It is an error to use rules of thumb as a primary valuation method without considering each valuation method. However, it may equally be an error of the valuator to simply use an average of multiple valuation approaches without a convincing rationale for doing so. So often this is the problem when you hire an inexperienced valuator who simply uses a computer program without understanding the process. It is also important to draw the judge's attention as to what level should be placed on rules of thumb so that the judge puts it in perspective, as well.

Failure to Fully Disclose Expert's Opinion or Failure to Provide Disclosure of Reports in Time for Each Expert to Comment Upon Others' Report

Often, experts will not include in the report backup documentation, such as reference materials. Such information should include industry studies, charts, graphs, and additional calculations to support the expert's written valuations. Care should be taken to work with the expert in providing full documentation in support of the expert's opinions. The lawyer handling the business valuation case should also provide a copy of the opposing expert's report to his or her own expert so that it can be reviewed and criticized. Keep in mind, that unless the opinions critical of the opposing expert's report are disclosed (either at the discovery deposition of the expert or in the expert's report—including any supplemental report) then the testimony may be barred. Also, remember to use your own expert (1) to educate you and your attorney about the opposing expert's report, and (2) in preparation of your attorney for depositions and cross examination of the opposing expert.

Failure of Parties or Court to Set Same Valuation Date

If your state supports the proposition that the proper date of valuation is the date as near to the date of the dissolution of marriage as is possible, your expert's opinion may be rejected by the court if it is too remote in time.

Failure to Have Expert Perform On-Site Valuation

The failure of the expert to conduct an on-site interview can lead to a number of mistakes. Short-cutting the valuation process by eliminating the site visit does not give the valuator hands-on experience of seeing what is being valued. The fact that you are the nonproperty owner is not an excuse.

Failure to Properly Consider all Perks of the Business

Common perks in divorce case valuations of closely-held businesses include payments of car expenses, country club memberships, vacation expenses, furniture and other items not used in the business, payments to relatives for salaries above and beyond work performed, and payment for expense accounts. All of these perks have to be considered to determine the actual earnings of the business as well as the true economic income of the spouse.

Failure to Properly Determine and Value Inventory and Machinery and Equipment

Mistakes commonly occur because of the failure of the expert to conduct an on-site interview and the failure to properly determine and value inventory. The lawyer handling the business valuation case should remember that the inventory on the books and records of the business may not be accurate. There may be an element of divorce planning and it is possible that the spouse who owns the business may underestimate the amount or the value of the inventory. Thus, in any case where there is substantial inventory, the amount and the value of the inventory should be properly determined as well as the true value of the machinery and equipment. Use an expert in the valuation of machinery and equipment when needed.

18

Revenue Rulings

Rev. Rul. 59-60, 1959-1 C.B. 237

Sec. 1. Purpose

The purpose of this revenue ruling is to outline and review in general the approach, methods, and factors to be considered in valuing shares of the capital stock of closely-held corporations for estate tax and gift tax purposes. The methods discussed herein will apply likewise to the valuation of corporate stocks on which market quotations are either unavailable or are of such scarcity that they do not reflect the fair market value.

Sec. 2. Background and Definitions

.01 All valuations must be made in accordance with the applicable provisions of the Internal Revenue Code of 1954 and the Federal Estate Tax and Gift Tax Regulations. Sections 2031(a), 2032, and 2512(a) of the 1954 Code (sections 811 and 1005 of the 1939 Code) require that the property to be included in the gross estate, or made the subject of a gift, shall be taxed on the basis of the value of the property at the time of death of the decedent, the alternate date if so elected, or the date of gift.

.02 Section 20.2031-1(b) of the Estate Tax Regulations (Section 81.10 of the Estate Tax Regulations 105) and Section 25.2512-1 of the Gift Tax Regulations (Section 86.19 of Gift Tax Regulations 108) define fair market value, in effect, as the price at which the property would change hands between a willing buyer and a willing seller when the former is not under any compulsion to buy and the latter is not under any compulsion to sell, both parties having reasonable knowledge of relevant facts. Court decisions frequently state in addition that the hypothetical buyer and seller are assumed to be able, as well as willing, to trade and to be well informed about the property and the market for such property.

.03 Closely-held corporations are those corporations the shares of which are owned by a relatively limited number of stockholders. Often the entire stock issue is held by one family. The result of this situation is that little, if any, trading in the shares takes place. There is, therefore, no established market for the stock and such sales as occur at irregular intervals seldom reflect all of the elements of a representative transaction as defined by the term "fair market value."

Sec. 3. Approach to Valuation

.01 A determination of fair market value, being a question of fact, will depend upon the circumstances in each case. No formula can be devised that will be generally applicable to the multitude of different valuation issues arising in estate and gift tax cases. Often, an appraiser will find wide differences of opinion as to the fair market value of a particular stock. In resolving such differences, he or she should maintain a reasonable attitude in recognition of the fact that valuation is not an exact science. A sound valuation will be based upon all the relevant facts, but the elements of common sense, informed judgment, and reasonableness must enter into the process of weighing those facts and determining their aggregate significance.

.02 The fair market value of specific shares of stock will vary as general economic conditions change from normal to boom or depression, that is, according to the degree of optimism or pessimism with which the investing public regards the future at the required date of appraisal. Uncertainty as to the stability or continuity of the future income from a property decreases its value by increasing the risk of loss of earnings and value in the future. The value of shares of stock of a company with very uncertain future prospects is highly speculative. The appraiser must exercise judgment as to the degree of risk attaching to the business of the corporation which issued the stock, but that judgment must be related to all of the other factors affecting value.

.03 Valuation of securities is, in essence, a prophesy as to the future and must be based on facts available at the required date of appraisal. As a generalization, the prices of stocks which are traded in volume in a free and active market by informed persons best reflect the consensus of the investing public as to what the future holds for the corporations and industries represented. When a stock is closely-held, is traded infrequently, or is traded in an erratic market, some other measure of value must be used. In many instances, the next best measure may be found in the prices at which the stocks of companies engaged in the same or a similar line of business are selling in a free and open market.

Sec. 4. Factors to Consider

.01 It is advisable to emphasize that in the valuation of the stock of closely-held corporations or the stock of corporations where market quotations are either lacking or too scarce to be recognized, all available financial data, as well as all relevant factors affecting the fair market value, should be considered. The following factors, although not all-inclusive, are fundamental and require careful analysis in each case:

(a) The nature of the business and the history of the enterprise from its inception

(b) The economic outlook in general and the condition and outlook of the specific industry in particular

(c) The book value of the stock and the financial condition of the business.

(d) The earning capacity of the company

(e) The dividend-paying capacity

(f) Whether or not the enterprise has goodwill or other intangible value

(g) Sales of the stock and the size of the block of stock to be valued

(h) The market price of stocks of corporations engaged in the same or a similar line of business having their stocks actively traded in a free and open market, either on an exchange or over-the-counter

.02 The following is a brief discussion of each of the foregoing factors:

(a) The history of a corporate enterprise will show its past stability or instability, its growth or lack of growth, the diversity or lack of diversity of its operations, and other facts needed to form an opinion of the degree of risk involved in the business. For an enterprise which changed its form of organization but carried on the same or closely similar operations of its predecessor, the history of the former enterprise should be considered. The detail to be considered should increase with approach to the required date of appraisal, since recent events are of greatest help in predicting the future; but a study of gross and net income, and of dividends covering a long prior period, is highly desirable. The history to be studied should include, but need not be limited to, the nature of the business, its products or services, its operating and investment assets, capital structure, plant facilities, sales records, and management, all of which should be considered as of the date of the appraisal, with due regard for recent significant changes. Events of the past that are unlikely to recur in the future should be discounted, since value has a close relation to future expectancy.

(b) A sound appraisal of a closely-held stock must consider current and prospective economic conditions as of the date of appraisal, both in the national economy and in the industry or industries with which the corporation is allied. It is important to know that the company is more or less successful than its competitors in the same industry, or that it is maintaining a stable position with respect to competitors. Equal or even greater significance may attach to the ability of the industry with which the company is allied to compete with other industries. Prospective competition which has not been a factor in prior years should be given careful attention. For example, high profits due to the novelty of its product and the lack of competition often lead to increasing competition. The public's appraisal of the future prospects of competitive industries or of competitors within an industry may be indicated by price trends in the markets for commodities and for securities.

The loss of the manager of a so-called one-man business may have a depressing effect upon the value of the stock of such business, particularly if there is a lack of trained personnel capable of succeeding to the management of the enterprise. In valuing the stock of this type of business, therefore, the effect of the loss of the manager on the future expectancy of the business and the absence of management-succession potentialities are pertinent factors to be taken into consideration. On the other hand, there may be factors which offset, in whole or in part, the loss of the manager's services. For instance, the nature of the business and of its assets may be such that they will not be impaired by the loss of the manager. Furthermore, the loss may be adequately covered by life insurance, or competent management might be employed on the basis of the consideration paid for the former manager's services. These, or other offsetting factors, if found to exist, should be carefully weighed against the loss of the manager's services in valuing the stock of the enterprise.

(c) Balance sheets should be obtained, preferably in the form of comparative annual statements for two or more years immediately preceding the date of appraisal, together with a balance sheet at the end of the month preceding that date, if corporate accounting will permit. Any balance sheet descriptions that are not self-explanatory, and balance sheet items comprehending diverse assets or liabilities, should be clarified in essential detail by supporting supplemental schedules. These statements usually will disclose to the appraiser: (1) liquid position (ratio of current assets to current liabilities), (2) gross and net book value of principal classes of fixed assets, (3) working capital, (4) long-term indebtedness; (5) capital structure, and (6) net worth. Consideration also should be given to any assets not essential to the operation of the business, such as investments in securities, real estate, etc. In general, such nonoperating assets will command a lower rate of return than do the operating assets, although in exceptional cases the reverse may be true. In computing the book value per share of stock, assets of the investment type should be revalued on the basis of their market price and the book value adjusted accordingly. Comparison of the company's balance sheets over several years may reveal, among other facts, such developments as the acquisition of additional production facilities or subsidiary companies, improvement in financial position, and details as to recapitalizations and other changes in the capital structure of the corporation. If the corporation has more than one class of stock outstanding, the charter or certificate of incorporation should be examined to ascertain the explicit rights and privileges of the various stock issues including: (1) voting powers, (2) preference as to dividends, and (3) preference as to assets in the event of liquidation.

(d) Detailed profit-and-loss statements should be obtained and considered for a representative period immediately prior to the required date of appraisal, preferably five or more years. Such statements should show (1) gross income by principal items; (2) principal deductions from gross income including major prior items of operating expenses, interest and other expense on each item of long-term debt, depreciation and depletion if such deductions are made, officers' salaries in total if they appear to be reasonable or in detail if they seem to be excessive, contributions (whether or not deductible for tax purposes) that the nature of its business and its community position require the corporation to make, and taxes by principal items, including income and excess profits taxes; (3) net income available for dividends; (4) rates and amounts of dividends paid on each class of stock; (5) remaining amount carried to surplus; and (6) adjustments to, and reconciliation with, surplus as stated on the balance sheet. With profit-and-loss statements of this character available, the appraiser should be able to separate recurrent from nonrecurrent items of income and expense, to distinguish between operating income and investment income, and to ascertain whether or not any line of business in which the company is engaged is operated consistently at a loss and might be abandoned with benefit to the company. The percentage of earnings retained for business expansion should be noted when dividend-paying capacity is considered. Potential future income is a major factor in many valuations of closely-held stocks, and all information concerning past income which will be helpful in predicting the future should be secured. Prior earnings records usually are the most reliable guide as to the future expectancy, but resorting to arbitrary five-or-ten-year averages without regard to current trends or future prospects will not produce a realistic valuation. If, for instance, a record of progressively increasing or decreasing net income is found, then greater weight may be accorded the most recent years' profits in estimating earning power. It will be helpful, in judging risk and the extent to which a business is a marginal operator, to consider deductions from income and net income in terms of percentage of sales. Major categories of cost and expense to be so analyzed include the consumption of raw materials and supplies in the case of manufacturers, processors, and fabricators; the cost of purchased merchandise in the case of merchants; utility services; insurance; taxes; depletion or depreciation; and interest.

(e) Primary consideration should be given to the dividend-paying capacity of the company rather than to dividends actually paid in the past. Recognition must be given to the necessity of retaining a reasonable portion of profits in a company to meet competition. Dividend-paying capacity is a factor that must be considered in an appraisal, but dividends actually paid in the past may not have any relation to dividend-paying capacity. Specifically, the dividends paid by a closely-held family company may be measured by the income needs of the stockholders or by their desire to avoid taxes on dividend receipts, instead of by the ability of the company to pay dividends. Where an actual or effective controlling interest in a corporation is to be valued, the dividend factor is not a material element, since the payment of such dividends is discretionary with the controlling stockholders. The individual or group in control can substitute salaries and bonuses for dividends, thus reducing net income and understating the dividend-paying capacity of the company. It follows, therefore, that dividends are less reliable criteria of fair market value than other applicable factors.

(f) In the final analysis, goodwill is based upon earning capacity. The presence of goodwill and its value, therefore, rests upon the excess of net earnings over and above a fair return on the net tangible assets. While the element of goodwill may be based primarily on earnings, such factors as the prestige and renown of the business, the ownership of a trade or brand name, and a record of successful operation over a prolonged period in a particular locality also may furnish support for the inclusion of intangible value. In some instances it may not be possible to make a separate appraisal of the tangible and intangible assets of the business. The enterprise has a value as an entity. Whatever intangible value there is, which is supportable by the facts, may be measured by the amount by which the appraised value of the tangible assets exceeds the net book value of such assets.

(g) Sales of stock of a closely-held corporation should be carefully investigated to determine whether they represent transactions at arm's length. Forced or distress sales do not ordinarily reflect fair market value nor do isolated sales in small amounts necessarily control as the measure of value. This is especially true in the valuation of a controlling interest in a corporation. Since, in the case of closely-held stocks, no prevailing market prices are available, there is no basis for making an adjustment for blockage. It follows, therefore, that such stocks should be valued upon a consideration of all the evidence affecting the fair market value. The size of the block of stock itself is a relevant factor to be considered. Although it is true that a minority interest in an unlisted corporation's stock is more difficult to sell than a similar block of listed stock, it is equally true that control of a corporation, either actual or in effect, representing as it does an added element of value, may justify a higher value for a specific block of stock.

(h) Section 2031(b) of the code states, in effect, that in valuing unlisted securities the value of stock or securities of corporations engaged in the same or a similar line of business which are listed on an exchange should be taken into consideration along with all other factors. An important consideration is that the corporations to be used for comparisons have capital stocks which are actively traded by the public. In accordance with Section 2031(b), stocks listed on an exchange are to be considered first. However, if sufficient comparable companies whose stocks are listed on an exchange cannot be found, other comparable companies which have stocks actively traded in an the over-the-counter market also may be used. The essential factor is that whether the stocks are sold on an exchange or over-the-counter there is evidence of an active, free public market for the stock as of the valuation date. In selecting corporations for comparative purposes, care should be taken to use only comparable companies. Although the only restrictive requirement as to comparable corporations specified in the statute is that their lines of business be the same or similar, yet it is obvious that consideration must be given to other relevant factors in order that the most valid comparison possible will be obtained. For illustration, a corporation having one or more issues of preferred stock, bonds, or debentures in addition to its common stock should not be considered to be directly comparable to one having only common stock outstanding. In like manner, a company with a declining business and decreasing markets is not comparable to one with a record of current progress and market expansion.

Sec. 5. Weight to Be Accorded Various Factors

The valuation of closely-held corporate stock entails the consideration of all relevant factors as stated in Section 4. Depending upon the circumstances in each case, certain factors may carry more weight than others because of the nature of the company's business. To illustrate:

(a) Earnings may be the most important criterion of value in some cases, whereas asset value will receive primary consideration in others. In general, the appraiser will accord primary consideration to earnings when valuing stocks of companies which sell products or services to the public; conversely, in the investment or holding type of company, the appraiser may accord the greatest weight to the assets underlying the security to be valued.

(b) The value of the stock of a closely-held investment or real estate holding company, whether or not family owned, is closely related to the value of the assets underlying the stock. For companies of this type the appraiser should determine the fair market values of the assets of the company. Operating expenses of such a company and the cost of liquidating it, if any, merit consideration when appraising the relative values of the stock and the underlying assets. The market values of the underlying assets give due weight to potential earnings and dividends of the particular items of property underlying the stock, capitalized at rates deemed proper by the investing public at the date of appraisal. A current appraisal by the investing public should be superior to the retrospective opinion of an individual. For these reasons, adjusted net worth should be accorded greater weight in valuing the stock of a closely-held investment or real estate holding company, whether or not family owned, than any of the other customary yardsticks of appraisal, such as earnings and dividend paying capacity.

Sec. 6. Capitalization Rates

In the application of certain fundamental valuation factors, such as earnings and dividends, it is necessary to capitalize the average or current results at some appropriate rate. A determination of the proper capitalization rate presents one of the most difficult problems in valuation. That there is no ready or simple solution will become apparent by a cursory check of the rates of return and dividend yields in terms of the selling prices of corporate shares listed on the major exchanges of the country. Wide variations will be found even for companies in the same industry. Moreover, the ratio will fluctuate from year to year depending upon economic conditions. Thus, no standard tables of capitalization rates applicable to closely-held corporations can be formulated. Among the more important factors to be taken into consideration in deciding upon a capitalization rate in a particular case are: (1) the nature of the business, (2) the risk involved, and (3) the stability or irregularity of earnings.

Sec. 7. Average of Factors

Because valuations cannot be made on the basis of a prescribed formula, there is no means whereby the various applicable factors in a particular case can be assigned mathematical weights in deriving the fair market value. For this reason, no useful purpose is served by taking an average of several factors (for example, book value, capitalized earnings, and capitalized dividends) and basing the valuation on the result. Such a process excludes active consideration of other pertinent factors, and the end result cannot be supported by a realistic application of the significant facts in the case except by mere chance.

Sec. 8. Restrictive Agreements

Frequently, in the valuation of closely-held stock for estate and gift tax purposes, it will be found that the stock is subject to an agreement restricting its sale or transfer. Where shares of stock were acquired by a decedent subject to an option reserved by the issuing corporation to repurchase at a certain price, the option price is usually accepted as the fair market value for estate tax purposes. See Rev. Rul. 54-76, C.B. 1954-1, 194. However, in such case the option price is not determinative of fair market value for gift tax purposes. Where the option, or buy and sell agreement, is the result of voluntary action by the stockholders and is binding during the life as well as at the death of the stockholders, such agreement may or may not, depending upon the circumstances of each case, fix the value for estate tax purposes. However, such agreement is a factor to be considered, with other relevant factors, in determining fair market value. Where the stockholder is free to dispose of his shares during life and the option is to become effective only upon his death, the fair market value is not limited to the option price. It is always necessary to consider the relationship of the parties, the relative number of shares held by the decedent, and other material facts, to determine whether the agreement represents a bona fide business arrangement or is a device to pass the decedent's shares to the natural objects of his bounty for less than an adequate and full consideration in money or money's worth. In this connection see Rev. Rul. 157 C.B. 1953-2, 255, and Rev. Rul. 189, C.B. 1953-2, 294.

Rev. Rul. 68-609, 1968-2 C.B. 327

The purpose of this revenue ruling is to update and restate, under the current statute and regulations, the currently outstanding portions of A.R.M. 34, C.B. 2, 31 (1920), A.R.M. 68, C.B. 3, 43 (1920), and O.D. 937, C.B. 4, 43 (1921).

The question presented is whether the formula approach, the capitalization of earnings in excess of a fair rate of return on net tangible assets, may be used to determine the fair market value of the intangible assets of a business.

The formula approach may be stated as follows:

A percentage return on the average annual value of the tangible assets used in a business is determined, using a period of years (preferably not less than five) immediately prior to the valuation date. The amount of the percentage return on tangible assets, thus determined, is deducted from the average earnings of the business for such period and the remainder, if any, is considered to be the amount of the average annual earnings from the intangible assets of the business for the period. This amount (considered as the average annual earnings from intangibles), capitalized at a percentage of, say, 15 to 20%, is the value of the intangible assets of the business determined under the formula approach.

The percentage of return on the average annual value of the tangible assets used should be the percentage prevailing in the industry involved at the date of valuation, or (when the industry percentage is not available) a percentage of 8 to 10% may be used.

The 8% rate of return and the 15% rate of capitalization are applied to tangibles and intangibles, respectively, of businesses with a small risk factor and stable and regular earnings; the 10% rate of return and 20% rate of capitalization are applied to businesses in which the hazards of business are relatively high.

The preceding rates are used as examples and are not appropriate in all cases. In applying the formula approach, the average earnings period and the capitalization rates are dependent upon the facts pertinent thereto in each case.

The past earnings to which the formula is applied should fairly reflect the probable future earnings. Ordinarily, the period should not be less than five years, and abnormal years, whether above or below the average, should be eliminated. If the business is a sole proprietorship or partnership, there should be deducted from the earnings of the business a reasonable amount for services performed by the owner or partners engaged in the business. [Citation Omitted.] Further, only the tangible assets entering into net worth, including accounts and bills receivable in excess of accounts and bills payable, are used for determining earnings on the tangible assets. Factors that influence the capitalization rate include (1) the nature of the business, (2) the risk involved, and (3) the stability or irregularity of earnings.

The formula approach should not be used if there is better evidence available from which the value of intangibles can be determined. If the assets of a going business are sold upon the basis of a rate of capitalization that can be substantiated as being realistic, though not within the range of figures indicated here as the ones ordinarily to be adopted, the same rate of capitalization should be used in determining the value of intangibles.

Accordingly, the formula approach may be used for determining the fair market value of intangible assets of a business only if there is no better basis therefore available.

See also Rev. Rul. 59-60, C.B. 1959-1, 237, as modified by Rev. Rul. 65-193, C.B. 1965-2, 370, which sets forth the proper approach to use in the valuation of closely-held corporate stocks for estate and gift tax purposes. The general approach, methods, and factors, outlined in Rev. Rul. 59-60, as modified, are equally applicable to valuations of corporate stocks for income and other tax purposes as well as for estate and gift tax purposes. They apply also to problems involving the determination of the fair market value of business interests of any type, including partnerships and proprietorships, and of intangible assets for all tax purposes.

A.R.M. 34, A.R.M. 68, and O.D. 937 are superseded, since the positions set forth therein are restated to the extent applicable under current law in this revenue ruling. Rev. Rul. 65-192, C.B. 1965-2, 259, which contained restatements of A.R.M. 34 and A.R.M. 68, is also superseded.

Rev. Rul. 93-12 might be considered and brought up to the courts if each of the spouses has an ownership interest in a marital corporation and there are minority discount issues or control premium issues.

Rev. Rul. 93-12, 1993-1

Issue

If a donor transfers shares in a corporation to each of the donor's children, is the factor of corporate control in the family to be considered in valuing each transferred interest, for purposes of Section 2512 of the Internal Revenue Code?

Facts

P owned all of the single outstanding class of stock of X corporation. P transferred all of P's shares by making simultaneous gifts of 20% of the shares to each of P's five children, A, B, C, D, and E.

Law and analysis

Section 2512(a) of the Code provides that the value of the property at the date of the gift shall be considered the amount of the gift.

Section 25.2512-1 of the Gift Tax Regulations provides that, if a gift is made in property, its value at the date of the gift shall be considered the amount of the gift. The value of the property is the price at which the property would change hands between a willing buyer and a willing seller, neither being under any compulsion to buy or to sell, and both having reasonable knowledge of relevant facts.

Section 25.2512-2(a) of the regulations provides that the value of stocks and bonds is the fair market value per share or bond on the date of the gift. Section 25.2512-2(f) provides that the degree of control of the business represented by the block of stock to be valued is among the factors to be considered in valuing stock where there are no sales prices or bona fide bids or asked prices.

Rev. Rul. 81-253, 1981-1 C.B. 187, holds that, ordinarily, no minority shareholder discount is allowed with respect to transfers of shares of stock between family members if, based upon a composite of the family members' interests at the time of the transfer, control (either majority voting control or de facto control through family relationships) of the corporation exists in the family unit. The ruling also states that the Service will not follow the decision of the Fifth Circuit in *Estate of Bright v. United States*, 658 F.2d 999 (5th Cir. 1981).

In *Bright,* the decedent's undivided community property interest in shares of stock, together with the corresponding undivided community property interest of the decedent's surviving spouse, constituted a control block of 55% of the shares of a corporation. The court held that, because the community-held shares were subject to a right of partition, the decedent's own interest was equivalent to 27.5% of the outstanding shares and, therefore, should be valued as a minority interest, even though the shares were to be held by the decedent's surviving spouse as trustee of a testamentary trust. See also, *Propstra v. United States,* 680 F.2d 1248 (9th Cir. 1982). In addition, *Estate of Andrews v. Commissioner,* 79 T.C. 938 (1982), and *Estate of Lee v. Commissioner,* 69 T.C. 860 (1978), *nonacq.,* 1980-2 C.B. 2, held that the corporation shares owned by other family members cannot be attributed to an individual family member for determining whether the individual family member's shares should be valued as the controlling interest of the corporation.

After further consideration of the position taken in Rev. Rul. 81-253, and in light of the cases noted above, the Service has concluded that, in the case of a corporation with a single class of stock, notwithstanding the family relationship of the donor, the donee, and other shareholders, the shares of other family members will not be aggregated with the transferred shares to determine whether the transferred shares should be valued as part of a controlling interest. In the present case, the minority interests transferred to A, B, C, D, and E should be valued for gift tax purposes without regard to the family relationship of the parties.

Holding

If a donor transfers shares in a corporation to each of the donor's children, the factor of corporate control in the family is not considered in valuing each transferred interest for purposes of Section 2512 of the Code. For estate and gift tax valuation purposes, the Service will follow *Bright, Propstra, Andrews,* and *Lee* in not assuming that all voting power held by family members may be aggregated for purposes of determining whether the transferred shares should be valued as part of a controlling interest. Consequently, a minority discount will not be disallowed solely because a transferred interest, when aggregated with interests held by family members, would be a part of a controlling interest. This would be the case whether the donor held 100% or some lesser percentage of the stock immediately before the gift.

Effect on other documents

Rev. Rul. 81-253 is revoked. Acquiescence is substituted for the nonacquiescence in issue one of *Lee,* 1980-2 C.B. 2.

Stock Options

T he area of stock options is complex but can be a valuable, often missed, marital asset. With the current environment of start-up companies and dot.com companies, it is not uncommon for management as well as general employees to receive some form of a stock option as a part of their compensation package. The divorce attorney needs to be aware of this asset and the following is a summary of terms and concepts to be aware of in this complex area.[1]

Stock Options Defined

A stock option is a right or privilege from a corporation to an employee that entitles them to the option of purchasing stock from the corporation at a later date for a specified price. There are two types of stock options: statutory stock option (qualified) and nonstatutory stock option (nonqualified). The purchaser is usually called the holder and the seller is called the writer. The most significant distinction between the two types of stock options is the different tax treatment applied when the options are granted or exercised.

Qualified Stock Options

A qualified stock option can be either an incentive stock option (ISO) or part of an employee stock purchase plan. An option is only a statutory option if it is not transferable by the individual to whom it is granted and is exercisable during their lifetime only by the individual. The main determination of whether or not an option can be classified as qualified or statutory is if it follows the rules laid out in Section 422 and 423 of the Internal Revenue Code. If any of the requirements are not met, it is considered to be a nonqualified option.

Incentive Stock Options

The first type of statutory stock options, also known as qualified stock options, is an incentive stock option (ISO). An option can only qualify as an ISO if all requirements set forth in the Internal Revenue Code Section 422 are met. Under an ISO, an employee must have the option to receive shares of the employer under a plan that includes the aggregate number of shares, which may be issued and the employees must be eligible to receive the options and be approved by the stockholders of the corporation. The options must be granted within ten years from the date the plan is adopted or approved, whichever is earlier. An ISO must be exercised within ten years from the date it is granted.

The option price may not be less than the fair market value of the stock at the time the option is granted, thus there will be no income at the time of grant. Further, the option is not transferable other than by will and is exercisable only during the individual's lifetime. The option may not be granted to an individual who owns more than ten percent of the total combined voting power of all classes of stock of the employer. Once the stock has been purchased, it cannot be sold within two years from the date the option was granted or within one year from the date the option was exercised and the stock was purchased, whichever is later.

Employee Stock Purchase Plans

The second type of statutory or qualified stock options is employee stock purchase plans. These are stock option plans approved by shareholders that give corporate employees the option to purchase shares of their employer's stock or the stock of a parent or subsidiary corporation. Similar to ISOs, an employee stock option plan must also fall under an Internal Revenue Code, Section 423, to qualify as a statutory stock option and receive preferable tax treatment.

The stock purchased under the option may not be sold within two years from the grant of the option and one year after the shares are transferred. The employee must remain an employee of the corporation during the option period. If the employee does leave the corporation, they have three months from the time they leave to exercise the option. No employee who has more than five percent of the voting power of the parent or subsidiary corporation can be granted an employee stock purchase plan. Another requirement is that all full-time employees must be included in the plan, with exceptions for employees with less than two years of employment, highly compensated employees, part-time employees, and seasonal employees. However, the plan may be tied to compensation and it also may limit the amount of stock an employee can buy.

The option price may not be less than the lesser of the fair market value at the time the option is exercised or 85% of the fair market value at the time the option is granted. Exercise date cannot exceed the latter of 27 months from the date the option is granted or five years from the date the option is granted if the option price is not less than 85% of the fair market value at the date exercised. A limit of $25,000 worth of stock is set for the maximum amount an employee can buy per year at the time the option is granted. The option is not transferable except by will and distribution.

Nonqualified Stock Options

A stock option plan can also be nonstatutory, or nonqualified. If an option is granted to an employee or independent contractor (or beneficiary of) in connection with the performance of services and if the option does not meet the specific statutory requirements set forth in the Internal Revenue Code Sections (421-424), the option would qualify as a nonstatutory stock option. Non-qualified stock options encompass all options that do not specifically fall under the Internal Revenue Code sections dealing with qualified stock options. IRC Section 83 will deal with this situation.

The basis an individual has in a nonstatutory stock option plan is determined by the amount that was paid for the option plus any amounts included in the individual's income as compensation. In most cases, the option has to be given as payment for services, therefore the amount paid for the option is zero. Thus, the basis of such an option would be the option's fair market value when granted.

The holding period for a nonstatutory stock option begins the date the option was granted. Thereafter, if it is subsequently sold, the general holding period rules for determining short- and long-term capital gain or loss apply. If the options have been exercised, the holding period will begin the day after the options are exercised. General holding period rules then apply.

Vested and Unvested

Compensation is only recognized as income if the property becomes substantially vested. Property becomes substantially vested when it is either not subject to a substantial risk of forfeiture or it is transferable. Property is substantially nonvested when it is subject to a substantial risk of forfeiture and nontransferable.

Property that is subject to a substantial risk of forfeiture and nontransferable will not be taxable until the property becomes transferable or free of substantial risk of forfeiture or both. The amount of income to be recognized at that time is equal to the excess of the fair market value of the property over any amount paid for the property.

Property is subject to substantial risk of forfeiture when the rights to full enjoyment of the property transferred are conditioned upon the future performance of substantial services by an individual. Substantial services can be determined by the regularity of such services, the time spent performing them, and whether the individual has the right to decline performing such services without forfeiture. Property can also be subject to a substantial risk of forfeiture if the transferee's rights in the property are conditioned on the occurrence of a condition related to the purpose of the transfer. The risk of forfeiture is substantial if the condition is not satisfied. Stock, when conditioned on a successful underwriting or ascertaining specified earnings has a substantial risk of forfeiture. The following terms are often used and you and your attorney should be familiar with their meanings.

- *Granting.* The granting of a stock option refers to the date or time when the corporation completes the action constituting an offer of stock for sale to an employee under the terms and conditions of the option.

- *Exercise.* The act of acceptance by the optionee of the offer to sell an option. For example, the time of exercise is the time when there is a sale or a contract to sell between the corporation and the employee.

- *Option price.* Also referred to as the strike price, this is the amount of consideration, in money or other property, (pursuant to the terms of the option) that must be given up to purchase the stock under the option. This is also referred to as exercise price.

- *Option period.* This is the time frame during which the options can be granted.

- *Intrinsic value.* The difference at any point in time between the option's market price and the price at which they were granted.

- *Expiration date.* The last date the holder can exercise his right.

- *Warrant.* A long-term call option issued by a company, rather than a third party.

Tax Treatment of Stock Options

The tax treatment of stock options can be very complicated. The following is just a basic overview in a simplistic manner. Whenever dealing with compensation issues such as stock options, I recommend referring to a tax specialist to review the entire plan and the facts pertaining to your specific case as the tax consequences could be significant.

Qualified Incentive Stock Options

As previously mentioned, no income is recorded by the holder at the time the options are granted or at the time they are exercised if rules are followed, therefore income is recognized when the options are exercised and the shares obtained are subsequently sold. Depending on when the employee sells the shares purchased under an ISO the tax consequences vary. The employee's basis in the stock is the amount paid for the stock when the option was exercised, plus any amount that was paid for the option. If the employee sells the shares before the required period, any gain on the sale is treated as ordinary income or compensation. If the stock has been held for the required period, the employee recognizes a capital gain (or loss) in the amount of the difference between what was paid for the shares and what he sold them for. The gain is recognized during the year in which the stock is sold. The difference between the types of income (gain) to be recognized is the rate at which the gain is to be taxed. The maximum tax rate for individuals on capital gains is 20%; the maximum for ordinary income could be as high as 39.6%, though under the new tax rates under the 2001 Tax Act this would be reduced to 36%.

Qualified Employee Stock Purchase Plans

The tax treatment of this type of statutory stock option plan is dependent on the option price. When the option price is between 85% and 100% of the fair market value of the stock on the date the option is granted and either the holding period requirements have been met or the option holder's death occurred, a portion of that shall be included as compensation to the shareholder. The amount to be included as ordinary income is the lesser of (1) the excess of the fair market value of the share at the time of the disposition or death over the amount paid for the share under the option or (2) the excess of the fair market value of the shares at the time the option was granted over the option price. The balance of any gain shall be treated as capital gain.

Nonqualified Stock Options

If the option has a readily ascertainable fair market value at the time the option is granted, the option is taxable to the optionee at the grant date. An option that is not actively traded on an established market can have a readily ascertainable market value only if all of the following are true: the option is not transferable, the option must be exercised immediately and completely when it is granted, there can be no condition or restriction on the option which would affect its fair market value, and the fair market value of the option privilege must be readily ascertainable. At the grant date the optionee has compensation equal to the fair market value of the option, less any amount paid by the optionee for the option.

An option is not treated as income if there is a substantial risk of forfeiture. An option is subject to a substantial risk of forfeiture if the options are given to an employee with a restriction on the ability to exercise the options. The restriction delays the employee's ability to benefit from the options. Restrictions are typically conditioned upon the future performance of substantial service from the employee. Once the condition or restriction has been met, the employee can recognize compensation from the options.

IRC Section 83 is applicable when there is an ascertainable fair market value. However, a nonqualified stock option may have another taxable option under IRC Section 83 which allows the employee to include in his income as compensation, the stock option upon the issuance of the grant by the company in accordance with Section 83(b). An employee can make an election under Section 83(b) that allows the employee to include the fair market value of the stock on the day the employee receives the stock option in their income as additional compensation.

If the election under 83(b) is made within 30 days of receiving the stock option, then for tax purposes, the employee will have a tax basis in the stock equal to the stock's value on the date the option was received. Any future gain on subsequent sale of the stock acquired will be reported as capital gain with the holding period beginning on the date the option was received. Consequently, if the stock price falls after the date of a Section 83(b) election is made, a capital loss will occur and for tax purposes, the amount of capital loss allowed is limited to $3,000 per year. The option receives capital gain or loss treatment with the period, long-term versus short-term, determined under general holding period rules.

IRS Ruling

The IRS in Revenue Ruling 98-21 ruled that the transfer to a family member, for no consideration, of a nonstatutory stock option is a completed gift under Section 2511 on the latter of transfer or the time when the donee's right to exercise the option is no longer conditioned on the performance of services by the transferor. The IRS explained that the gift tax applies to a transfer of property by way of gift, but that certain rights such as nonvested pension rights are not considered property.

The IRS explained that generally a gift is complete when the donor has parted with dominion and control over the property as to leave the donor no power to change its disposition whether for the donor's own benefit or for the benefit of another. In this case, however, the IRS observed the non-statutory stock option is conditioned on the performance of additional services by the employee. If the employee fails to perform the services, the option cannot be exercised. Therefore, the IRS reasoned that before the employee performs the services, the rights that the employee possesses in the stock option have not become enforceable property rights susceptible to transfer for federal gift tax purposes. The IRS concluded that the employee can make a gift of stock options to a family member for federal gift tax purposes only after the employee has completed the additional required services because only upon completion of the services does the right to exercise the option become binding and enforceable.

The IRS also ruled that in the event the option were to become exercisable in stages, each portion of the option that becomes exercisable at a different time is treated as a separate option for the purposes of gift taxes.

Valuation Issues

As mentioned earlier, intrinsic value is defined as the difference between the stock's value and the exercise price. This portion of the option value can never be less than zero since the holder of the option has no liability or obligation to buy the stock. In looking forward, the value of the option is the present value of the expected difference between the price of the stock at the date of expiration of the option and the option's exercise price.

The fair market value of an option is influenced by many factors. Most of the option valuation models incorporate a variety of parameters. The following is a general list of factors that option valuations are generally considered sensitive to:

- Time to expiration
- Degree of leverage
- Growth rate of stock value
- Volatility of the stock value
- Dividends paid by the underlying stock
- Interest rates
- Potential dilution from exercised options
- Degree of liquidity of the stock

The IRS in Revenue Ruling 98-34 sets forth a methodology to value certain compensatory stock options for gift, estate, and generation-skipping transfer tax purposes. This methodology applies only to the transfer tax valuation of non-publicly traded compensatory stock options on stock that, on the valuation date, is publicly traded on an established securities market. The ruling provides that taxpayers relying on this ruling may use an option pricing model that takes into account, on the valuation date, specific factors that are similar to those established by the FASB in the Statement of Financial Accounting Standards No. 123 (FAS 123), and that the IRS will treat the value as properly determined if these requirements are met.

Generally following FAS 123, 98-34 provides that taxpayers may determine the value of compensatory stock options for transfer tax purposes by using a generally recognized option pricing model, such as the Black-Scholes or a binomial pricing model, that takes into account certain factors related to option pricing.

These factors include the exercise price of the option, the expected life of the option, the current trading price of the underlying stock, the expected volatility of the underlying stock, expected dividends on the underlying stock, and the risk-free interest rate over the remaining option term. The ruling states that on the valuation date, the taxpayer must use either the expected life of the option or the computed maximum remaining term of the option. It details how to determine the expected life of the option. It also details under what conditions the taxpayer must use the maximum remaining term on the option as opposed to the expected life. In addition, the ruling also sets out requirements for determining certain factors regarding stock volatility, expected dividends, and the correct discount rates to be used for use in the valuation in order to comply with FAS 123.

Valuation Approaches

Numerous methods for determining the value of stock options exist. Determining which method is best depends on the information available and marketability factors. There is no one best model, however, the Black-Scholes Model is the most widely recognized and most frequently used model. The information below describes Black-Scholes as well as other valuation approaches.

Black-Scholes Option Pricing Model

The Black-Scholes is basically a mathematical extension of the binomial pricing model, based on the assumption that it is possible to set up a perfectly hedged position consisting of long and short positions in a stock and option.

The assumptions underlying the model are rather restrictive and it is important to be aware of them in order to avoid a misapplication of the model. Your attorney needs to address these assumptions as they will have a direct impact on the value of the options. The assumptions are:

- The short-term interest rate is known and is constant through time.
- The stock price follows a random walk in continuous time with a variance rate proportional to the square of the stock price.
- The distribution of possible stock prices at the end of any finite interval is lognormal.
- The variance of the rate of return on the stock is constant.
- The stock pays no dividends and makes no other distributions.
- The option can be exercised only at maturity.
- There are no commission or other transaction costs in buying or selling the stock or option.
- It is possible to borrow any fraction of the price of a security at the short-term interest rate.
- A seller who does not own a security (short seller) will simply accept the price of the security from the buyer and will agree to settle with the buyer on some future date by paying him an amount equal to the price of the security on that date. While the short sale is outstanding, the short seller will have the use of, or interest on, the proceeds of the sale.
- The tax rate is identical for all transactions and all market participants.

The equation for the model is shown here:

$$\text{Option Value} = S * N(d_1) - Ee^{-rt} * N(d_2)$$

where   S = stock price
  E = exercise (strike) price
  N(d) = value of the cumulative normal distribution at the given point
  $d_1 = [\ln(S/E) + (r + .5 \text{ VAR})t]/SD * \text{sqrt}(t)$
  $d_2 = d_1 - (SD * \text{sqrt}(t))$
  ln = natural logarithm
    r = short term riskless rate (continuously compounded)
    t = time to expiration in years
    e = base of natural logarithms
  VAR = variance of returns
  SD = standard deviation
  sqrt = square root

The primary limitation is that the model only allows for the valuation of options that can only be exercised at maturity. The second major limitation is that the model does not allow for the payment of dividends. There have been subsequent adjustments made to the model that attempt to take these factors into consideration. The practical problem is that there are many assumptions necessary for its derivation. In a litigated matter, due to the degree of assumptions needed, it could tend to a large variation in value among experts.

Binomial Option Pricing Model

The binomial option pricing model allows for the valuation of stock options by allowing the stock price to increase and decrease over time, possibly at different rates. It is based on a binomial probability distribution in which there are only two outcomes, or states.

The model can be extended for use in multiple periods and also allow for different levels of appreciation or depreciation of the stock price. The model must impose some finite limits in order to make a valuation possible, but it does become more realistic as the model is extended over several periods. The model does fail to take into consideration expected future stock price or investors' feelings about risk in determining the option's price. Other available models do take these factors into consideration.

Shelton Model

The Shelton model, developed in 1967 by John Shelton, is simplistic. This model relies on the accuracy of the stock markets to forecast a reasonable price for the options. Due to the volatility of the markets, the results from this model will vary greatly, possibly on a daily basis, making this model only beneficial for a very specific point of time.

Noreen-Wolfson Model

In 1981, Eric Noreen and Mark Wolfson adapted the Black-Scholes model for use in valuing executive options. They made two basic changes in the assumptions. First, the Noreen-Wolfson model allows for dividends and assumes they are paid continuously. Second, the model considers the dilution that would take place upon exercise of the option.

While the pitfalls of this model are similar to the Black-Scholes Model, Noreen-Wolfson allows more flexibility by modifying the assumptions regarding dividends and possible dilution upon exercising options.

How to Handle Option Issues in Dissolution of Marriage Cases

In order to distribute stock options in a dissolution of marriage case, an attorney must obtain a stock option history or summary. From the information contained therein, the attorney must ascertain the following:

- The number of stock options which have been granted to the employee
- The strike/exercise price of each option
- The current market price of the stock of which the employee has an option (This is easily ascertainable if the stock is publicly traded, and if the stock is not publicly traded, the stock option is known as a warrant.)
- Whether the stock options are vested or unvested
  - *Vested Stock Options.* Vested stock options are either accrued and matured which means they are vested in the owner and are currently exercisable; or, they are accrued and not matured, meaning that the stock options are vested in the owner, but not yet exercisable. The vested and matured and the vested and unmatured stock options are usually unqualified and the unvested stock options are usually qualified stock options. This difference is important in order to determine the tax consequences as previously discussed herein;
  - *Unvested Stock Options.* Unvested stock options are contingent upon certain future events before they will become exercisable. These future events may include continued employment, which may be considered a condition precedent to the stock option becoming exercisable; or, that the employee not terminate his employment prior to a certain date. Some unvested stock options may be divested if a condition subsequently occurs prior to the stock option becoming exercisable.
- The exercise date of all stock options
- Whether the grant of the stock option was for compensation for past services or as an incentive for future services

After an attorney has obtained the above information concerning the stock options, the next issue is whether or not the stock options are considered marital or nonmarital property. It would seem stock options are similar in many respects to retirement benefits in that they are provided to the employee as additional compensation. Vested and matured, as well as vested and unmatured stock options are similar to vested retirement benefits in that at the time of their grant, they are vested in the employee and are not subject to defeasance. Similarly, retirement benefits are provided by reason of past performance by the employee, and vested stock options provided to the employee for past performance. Stock options are in the nature of a contract right provided by reason of employment, and subject to the terms of the specific stock option plan.

If options are granted during the marriage they would appear to be marital property and it would appear that vested matured stock options which were granted to a spouse during the marriage, are marital property and can be valued as of the date of the dissolution of the marriage. Further, courts in some states may have the power to order the spouse to sell the marital assets, which should include the exercise of stock options, in order to accomplish the division of marital property. The court may also be able to order an in-kind division of the vested and matured stock options or immediately offset the value of the stock options with other marital property, if the value is easily ascertainable.

Vested unmatured stock options, if granted to a spouse during the marriage, would likewise appear to be marital property, but are a little more difficult to divide in that they are not exercisable by the employee's spouse until certain events occur, usually the passage of a specific time. Vested and unmatured stock options are not subject to defeasance. Since these stock options are not matured and cannot be exercised until a future date, they may be difficult to value at the time of the dissolution of marriage. The reserve jurisdiction approach should then be applied by the court in order to provide the division of the proceeds from the stock options as, if and when the stock options are actually exercised.

The division or allocation of unvested stock options is much more difficult than vested matured and vested unmatured stock options. Unvested stock options are often granted by the employer for past employment being deferred compensation or as an incentive to enhance the employee's future performance. At the time of the granting of an unvested stock option, it usually has little, if any, value which can be ascertained. For the employee to realize the benefit of the stock option, the employee must continue to work and meet whatever other conditions are required by the stock option plan. If the employee can only meet these conditions after the Judgment of Dissolution of Marriage, the argument may be that the granting of the unvested stock options is really nonmarital property because the value is unascertainable at the time of the Judgment of Dissolution of Marriage and only appreciates in value after the Judgment of Dissolution of Marriage by reason of the performance of the divorced employee. The manner in which states classify stock options varies. Indiana has held ". . . we have consistently held that only property in which the party has a vested interest at the time of dissolution may be divided as a marital asset" Han v. Han, 655 N.E. 2d 566, Indiana Court of Appeals, 1995. It has been argued in other jurisdictions that if the court divides unvested options as property, it is overlooking and not recognizing that unvested stock options are compensation for post-dissolution of marriage employment efforts. Whether unvested stock options are marital property, nonmarital property, or income paid for future employment efforts is the question that your attorney will need to address.

Most matrimonial courts have provided little direction with reference to categorizing unvested stock options and have failed to clarify the manner in which they should be divided and apportioned between the parties. Courts, like those in Illinois, have indicated that stock options have no value until they are exercised, and are neither nonmarital property nor marital property, but are the separate property of the party being granted the options until such time as they are exercised. I believe that in order to define the marital fraction which should be employed in the allocation of unvested stock options, the attorney must ascertain whether the grant of the stock options was for compensation for past services or whether they were granted as an incentive for future services. If the services were performed during the marriage to obtain the stock options and they are in the form of deferred compensation, they should be divided as marital property when exercised. If they are in the form of incentives for future services and are to be performed after the Judgment of dissolution of marriage, it would appear to be more in the nature of earnings acquired after the Dissolution of the Marriage and the stock options should be more equitably allocated in favor of the grantee.

Several states have discussed the use of a time rule to equitably divide unvested stock options which will become exercisable after the Dissolution of Marriage. When the stock options are characterized as deferred compensation having been earned from the commencement of employment through the date of the Judgment of the Dissolution of Marriage, a formula may be employed to define a marital fraction. The fraction would have as the numerator the number of months worked during the marriage by the grantee for the grantor employer, and the numerator being the months worked by the grantee for the grantor employer to the date the stock options are exercisable. This marital fraction would then be multiplied by the number of stock options to be exercised and then multiplied by percentage award to the nongrantee spouse. See *Marriage of Hug*, 154 CA 3d 780 (1984).

If stock options are characterized as being provided as incentives for future services to be performed after the granting of the option, then one would use as the numerator the months worked for the grantor from the date of the option grant to the date of the Judgment of Dissolution and the denominator would be the number of months worked from the option grant to the date that it is exercisable. See *Marriage of Nelson*, 177CA 3d 150 (1986) and *In the Matter of the Marriage of Powell*, 147 Or. App. 17, 934p. P 2d 612, (1997). This method only divides the option between the parties during periods in which marital efforts are used to enhance the unvested option, being from the date of the grant to the date of the Judgment of Dissolution of Marriage. This formula does not include the appreciation to the stock options after the Judgment of Dissolution of Marriage which may be attributable to the later efforts of the grantee and the actual compensation for services performed after the Judgment of Dissolution of Marriage.

If you can value the stock options at the time of the Judgment of Dissolution of Marriage, it would appear to be marital property subject to immediate allocation.

The failure to provide a valuation of unvested stock options to the court by an attorney is not unusual, but rather the norm. Although there are several recognized valuation approaches for stock options which were previously mentioned, they are rarely implemented because of their cost and the number assumptions used. The cost of an expert to value stock options could be extremely expensive as compared to the benefits which may be received from such valuation. Each of the valuation processes which an expert could employ contain numerous assumptions which must be made in order to reach a stated value of the options. If a valuation is even obtained, its credibility and reliability could be diminished by any effective cross examination which would point out that the basis of the valuation contains numerous assumptions.

It is strongly recommended that in cases involving the allocation and division of unvested stock options that the attorneys actively work to negotiate and agree on the division of the unvested stock options rather than allowing a court to allocate the options after they are exercisable. It appears that the courts, without an agreement of the parties, will retain jurisdiction to allocate the unvested stock options at the time they become exercisable and will most likely leave the discretion in the grantee of the stock options to determine the time when they are actually exercised. The court may immediately allocate the unvested stock options at the time of Judgment of Dissolution of Marriage which will be implemented at the time the stock options become exercisable, based upon a marital fraction. It is unclear how the courts will define marital fraction. It is important that a non-grantee spouse has the ability to direct when his or her portion of the exercisable stock options are actually exercised in order to avoid taxes. It is important to both parties that the purpose of the grant of the unvested stock options be ascertained in order to provide more equitable allocation of the unvested stock options. If the purpose of the grant of the stock options was for deferred compensation for employment during the marriage, the Court should employ the first marital fraction discussed, and if the purpose of the grant of stock options was incentives for future services, then one should use the second fraction as the definition of marital fraction.

Sample Language for Marital Settlement Agreements for the Allocation of Stock Options

Both parties acknowledge that the Plaintiff, by reason of his employment with the NOAH BOAT Company, has been granted certain stock options during the marriage of the parties and the stock options are listed as follows:

(provide a complete description of the options)

1. Options A are vested and matured
2. Options B are vested and not matured
3. Options C are unvested stock options

Both parties agree and acknowledge that in the above options from stock, the NOAH BOAT Company were provided to the Husband by reason of his employment, or purchased prior to the execution of this Agreement, shall be considered marital property and will be divided between the parties at the time the options are exercised. Any Court of competent jurisdiction which this Marital Settlement Agreement is approved, shall retain jurisdiction over the parties and the subject matter in order to enforce the distribution and allocation of the stock, or net proceeds from same, from the exercise of the stock options as described below:

A. As to options A above, when they are exercised, the Wife shall receive fifty percent (50%) of the stock options or net proceeds from same, after the payment of all taxes and brokerage fees incurred as a result of the exercise of the options. The taxes shall include Federal, State, FICA, and Medicare taxes incurred by the Husband in connection with the exercise of the aforesaid stock options. The stock or the remaining net proceeds of the stock options shall be immediately divided equally between the parties.

(If the options were a form of deferred compensation)

B. As to option B above, when they are exercised, the Wife is awarded a portion of the stock options or net proceeds from same, after the payment of all taxes and brokerage fees incurred as a result of the exercise of the options. The Wife's portion shall be calculated on the basis of fifty percent (50%) of the product of the "marital fraction," where the numerator equals the number of months from the date of the grantee's employment with the grantor of the options, to the date of the Judgment of Dissolution of Marriage and the denominator equals the number of months from the date of grantee's employment with the grantor of the options, to the date that the options are exercisable, multiplied by the exercised stock options.

(options are an incentive for future services)

C. As to options C, when they are exercised, the Wife is awarded a portion of the stock options or net proceeds from same, thereof after the payment of all taxes and brokerage fees incurred as a result of the exercise of the options. The Wife's portion shall be calculated on the basis of fifty percent (50%) of the product of the "marital fraction," where the numerator equals the number of months from the date the option was granted to the date of dissolution of marriage, and the denominator equals the number of months from the date of the option grant to the date the option is exercisable, multiplied by the exercised stock options.

The Husband may exercise his portion of the stock options as he deems appropriate with notice as provided herein. The Wife shall have the absolute right to require the Husband to exercise stock options which are exercisable in a quantity and amount equal to the portion she is entitled as set forth hereinabove with respect to each option. Prior to the exercise of each option, the Wife shall have the right to advance the monies necessary to exercise her portion of the options when she intends to retain the purchased stock as her sole property, rather than immediately selling the stock and receiving the net proceeds. The monies to be advanced shall include an amount equal to the strike/exercise price, brokerage costs, and an amount equal to the grantee's effective tax rate applied to the gain on the exercise stock options. In that event, the Husband shall exercise the stock options and immediately transfer the shares of stock to the Wife in the amount set forth hereinabove.

In the event the Wife does not wish to retain the stock acquired from the exercise of the stock options, but merely intends to exercise the stock options and sell the stock, then it shall be the Husband's sole obligation to provide the funds necessary to purchase the stock and pay the taxes and associated brokerage fees for the transaction, if required.

The Husband shall exercise all stock options, including those in which the Wife has an interest as provided herein, prior to their expiration date. The Husband agrees to take all reasonable actions necessary to exercise these options in such a manner to maximize the value thereof. The Husband shall give the Wife at least 30 days written advance notice of his intent to exercise any of the stock options and the price at which he intends to complete the exercise. This notice shall include the number of units or stocks to be acquired, the estimated per unit market value and the per-unit exercise price. Accompanying this written notice, the Husband shall provide the Wife with all reasonable and necessary information and documentation to allow the Wife to determine the reasonable market value of the option units. The Wife shall have no interest in any options granted to the Husband by reason of his employment with the ABC Corporation after the date of the Judgment of Dissolution of Marriage which incorporates this Marital Settlement Agreement or makes reference thereto. Husband shall retain as his sole property, without claim by the wife, all stock options described above which are not otherwise allocated to the wife herein.

Notes

[1]Exerpts taken from presentation by William J. Stogsdill, Jr. and Bruce L. Richman, CPA, CVA, ABV presented to the Illinois State Bar Association, June 2000. William Stogsdill, Jr. is a leading divorce attorney who practices in Wheaton, Illinois.

Uniform Standards of Professional Appraisal Practice and Business Valuation Standards of ASA

Importance of USPAP Generally

The American Standards Board of the Appraisal Foundation promulgated the Uniform Standards of Professional Appraisal Practice (USPAP). These standards apply to any appraiser including an appraisal of real estate, personal property, intangible assets, and business interests. An updated version of the USPAP is published annually, generally in November. The appraisal foundation placed the current version online at www.appraisalfoundation.org/uspap2000/toc.htm. Standards 9 and 10 of the USPAP address business valuations. The 2000 version of these standards are provided in this appendix.

The American Society of Appraisers mandates compliance with USPAP for appraisals prepared by its members. The Institute for Business Appraisers generally endorses USPAP but compliance is not mandatory for its members. Additionally, USPAP is not binding on members of AICPA or NACVA.

The ASA has also issued "Principles of Appraisal Practice and Code of Ethics." This code is designed to provide guidance to appraisers generally and to provide a structure for regulating conduct of members of the ASA through disciplinary actions. The eight covered topics relate to all types of appraisals and are:

1. Introduction, which describes the definition of Appraisal Practice and the purpose of promulgating the Principles of Appraisal Practice and Code of Ethics
2. Objectives of appraisal work
3. Appraiser's primary duty and responsibility
4. Appraiser's obligation to his client
5. Appraiser's obligation to other appraisers and to the society
6. Appraisal methods and practices
7. Unethical and unprofessional appraisal practices
8. Appraisal reports

These standards apply to both business valuations and other types of valuations and are general in nature. An example of the standards applicable to divorce valuations is standard 4.3 which states:

When an appraiser is engaged by one of the parties in controversy, it is unethical for the appraiser to suppress any facts, data, or opinions which are adverse to the case his client is trying to establish; or to over-emphasize any facts, data, or opinions which are favorable to his client's case; or in any other particulars to become an advocate. It is the appraiser's obligation to present the data, analysis, and value without bias, regardless of the effect of such unbiased presentation on his client's case.

Business Valuation Standards Promulgated by the ASA Business Valuation Committee

While USPAP addresses ethical issues and generally addresses the process of business valuation, the American Society of Appraisers recognized that the USPAP did not comprehensively outline the factors that should be considered in a business appraisal. Accordingly, the American Society of Appraisers Business Valuation Committee developed business valuation standards that every member must follow in a business valuation.

Currently, there are eight Standards. Additionally, there is one Statement on Business Valuation Standards and one Advisory Opinion. The standards represent the minimal criteria that must be present in a business valuation. Every appraiser who is a member of the ASA must adhere to the various standards. Additionally, because these standards are generic in treatment of generally accepted valuation theory and practice, a business appraiser who is not a member of the ASA may find it hard to justify reasons that the standards should be ignored. In the unlikely event that an ASA appraiser has good cause to depart from the Standards, the appraiser must state the specific reasons for the departure in the report.

The standards are:

BVS-I	General Requirements for Developing a Business Valuation
BVS-II	Financial Statement Adjustments
BVS-III	Asset Based Approach to Business Valuation
BVS-IV	Income Approach to Business Valuation
BVS-V	Market Approach to Business Valuation
BVS-VI	Reaching a Conclusion as to Value
BVS-VII	Valuation Discounts and Premiums
BVS-VIII	Comprehensive, Written Business Valuation Report Definitions
SBVS-I	The Guideline Company Valuation Method

In addition there is Advisory Opinion No. 1, Financial Consultation and Advisory Services, which provides procedural guidelines.

Reading Material on Business Valuation

There are several articles, studies, and books prepared on the subject of business valuation. Some are relied upon more than others by the valuation community, though one is not necessarily authoritatively better than another. Two of the better-known books are Shannon Pratt's *Valuing a Business: The Analysis and Appraisal of Closely Held Companies* (New York: McGraw-Hill, 2000) and *Valuing Small Business and Professional Practices* (New York: McGraw-Hill,

1988). Other good resources include, but are not limited to: *Guide to Business Valuations* (Practitioners Publishing Company), *Valuing a Business* (Ray Miles), AICPA's *Conducting a Valuation of a Closely Held Business* (Gary Trugman).

Business Valuation Standards of USPAP 2000

Standard 9 and 10 Business Appraisal, Development

In developing a business or intangible asset appraisal, an appraiser must identify the problem to be solved and the scope of work necessary to solve the problem, and correctly complete the research and analysis steps necessary to produce a credible appraisal.

Comment: Standard 9 is directed toward the substantive aspects of developing a competent business or intangible asset appraisal. The requirements of Standard 9 apply when the specific purpose of an assignment is to develop an appraisal of a business or intangible asset.

Standards Rule 9-1

In developing a business or intangible asset appraisal, an appraiser must:

a. be aware of, understand, and correctly employ those recognized methods and procedures that are necessary to produce a credible appraisal

   Comment: Changes and developments in the economy and in investment theory have a substantial impact on the business appraisal profession. Important changes in the financial arena, securities regulation, tax law, and major new court decisions may result in corresponding changes in business appraisal practice.

b. not commit a substantial error of omission or commission that significantly affects an appraisal

   Comment: In performing appraisal services an appraiser must be certain that the gathering of factual information is conducted in a manner that is sufficiently diligent, given the scope of work as identified according to Standards Rule 9-2(e), to reasonably ensure that the data that would have a material or significant effect on the resulting opinions or conclusions are identified and, where necessary, analyzed. Further, an appraiser must use sufficient care in analyzing such data to avoid errors that would significantly affect his or her opinions and conclusions.

c. not render appraisal services in a careless or negligent manner, such as by making a series of errors that, although individually might not significantly affect the results of an appraisal, in the aggregate affect the credibility of those results

Comment: Perfection is impossible to attain and competence does not require perfection. However, an appraiser must not render appraisal services in a careless or negligent manner. This rule requires an appraiser to use diligence and care.

Standards Rule 9-2

In developing a business or intangible asset appraisal, an appraiser must identify:

a. the client and any other intended users of the appraisal and the client's intended use of the appraiser's opinions and conclusions

Comment: An appraiser must not allow a client's objectives or intended use of the appraisal to cause an analysis to be biased.

b. the purpose of the assignment, including the standard of value (definition) to be developed

c. the effective date of the appraisal

d. the business enterprises, assets, or equity to be valued, and

i. identify any buy-sell agreements, investment letter stock restrictions, restrictive corporate charter or partnership agreement clauses, and any similar features or factors that may have an influence on value

ii. ascertain the extent to which the interests contain elements of ownership control

Comment: Special attention should be paid to the attributes of the interest being appraised including the rights and benefits of ownership. The elements of control in a given situation may be affected by law, distribution of ownership interests, contractual relationships, and many other factors. As a consequence, the degree of control or lack of it depends on a broad variety of facts and circumstances which must be evaluated in the specific situation.

Equity interests in a business enterprise are not necessarily worth the pro rata share of the business enterprise value as a whole. Conversely, the value of the business enterprise is not necessarily a direct mathematical extension of the value of the fractional interests.

e. the scope of work that will be necessary to complete the assignment

Comment: The scope of work is acceptable when it is consistent with the expectations of participants in the market for the same or similar appraisal services; and what the appraiser's peers' actions would be in performing the same or a similar business valuation assignment in compliance with USPAP. [Footnote omitted.]

An appraiser must have sound reasons in support of the scope of work decision, and be prepared to support the decision to exclude any information or procedure that would appear to be relevant to the client, an intended user, or the appraiser's peers in the same or a similar assignment. (See the Departure Rule.)

An appraiser must not allow assignment conditions to limit the extent of research or analysis to such a degree that the resulting opinions and conclusions developed in an assignment are not credible in the context of the intended use of the appraisal.

f. any extraordinary assumptions necessary in the assignment; and

Comment: An extraordinary assumption may be used in an appraisal only if: it is required to properly develop credible opinions and conclusions, the appraiser has a reasonable basis for the extraordinary assumption, use of the extraordinary assumption results in a credible analysis, and the appraiser complies with the disclosure requirements set forth in USPAP for extraordinary assumptions.

g. any hypothetical conditions necessary in the assignment

Comment: A hypothetical condition may be used in an appraisal only if use of the hypothetical condition is clearly required for legal purposes, for purposes of reasonable analysis, or for purposes of comparison; use of the hypothetical condition results in a credible analysis; and the appraiser complies with the disclosure requirements set forth in USPAP for hypothetical conditions.

Standards Rule 9-3

In developing a business or intangible asset appraisal relating to an equity interest with the ability to cause liquidation of the enterprise, an appraiser must investigate the possibility that the business enterprise may have a higher value by liquidation of all or part of the enterprise than by continued operation as is. If liquidation of all or part of the enterprise is the indicated basis of valuation, an appraisal of any real estate or personal property to be liquidated may be appropriate.

> *Comment:* This rule requires the appraiser to recognize that continued operation of a business is not always the best premise of value as liquidation of all or part of the enterprise may result in a higher value. However, this typically applies only when the business equity being appraised is in a position to cause liquidation. If liquidation of all or part of the enterprise is the appropriate premise of value, competency in the appraisal of assets such as real estate (Standard 1) and tangible personal property (Standard 7) may be required to complete the business valuation assignment.

Standards Rule 9-4

In developing a business or intangible asset appraisal, an appraiser must collect and analyze all information pertinent to the appraisal problem, given the scope of work identified in accordance with Standards Rule 9-2(e).

a. An appraiser must develop value opinion(s) and conclusion(s) by use of one or more approaches that apply to the specific appraisal assignment

> *Comment:* This rule requires the appraiser to use all relevant approaches for which sufficient reliable data are available. However, it does not mean that the appraiser must use all approaches in order to comply with the rule if certain approaches are not applicable.

b. include in the analyses, when relevant, data regarding

   i. the nature and history of the business

   ii. financial and economic conditions affecting the business enterprise, its industry, and general economy

   iii. past results, current operations, and future prospects of the business enterprise

   iv. past sales of capital stock or other ownership interests in the business enterprise being appraised

   v. sales of similar businesses or capital stock of publicly held similar businesses

   vi. prices, terms, and conditions affecting past sales of similar business equity

   vii. economic benefit of intangible assets

> *Comment:* This rule directs the appraiser to study the prospective and retrospective aspects of the business enterprise and to study it in terms of the economic and industry environment within which it operates. Further, sales of securities of the business itself or similar businesses for which sufficient information is available should also be considered.

Standards Rule 9-5

In developing a business or intangible asset appraisal, an appraiser must reconcile the indications of value resulting from the various approaches to arrive at the value conclusion.

> *Comment:* The appraiser must evaluate the relative reliability of the various indications of value. The appraiser must consider the quality and quantity of data leading to each of the indications of value. The value conclusion is the result of the appraiser's judgment and not necessarily the result of a mathematical process.

Standard 10 Business Appraisal, Reporting

In reporting the results of a business or intangible asset appraisal, an appraiser must communicate each analysis, opinion, and conclusion in a manner that is not misleading.

> *Comment:* Standard 10 addresses the content and level of information required in a report that communicates the results of a business or intangible asset appraisal developed under Standard 9. Standard 10 does not dictate the form, format, or style of business or intangible asset appraisal reports, which are functions of the needs of users and providers of appraisal services. The substantive content of a report determines its compliance.

Standards Rule 10-1

Each written or oral business or intangible asset appraisal report must

  a. clearly and accurately set forth the appraisal in a manner that will not be misleading

  b. contain sufficient information to enable the intended user(s) to understand it. Any specific limiting conditions concerning information should be noted

c. clearly and accurately disclose any extraordinary assumption or hypothetical condition that directly affects the appraisal and indicate its impact
on value

Comment: This requirement calls for a clear and accurate disclosure of
any extraordinary assumptions or hypothetical conditions that directly
affect an analysis, opinion, or conclusion. Examples might include items
such as the execution of a pending agreement, atypical financing, infusion
of additional working capital or making other capital additions, or compliance with regulatory authority rules. The report should indicate whether
the extraordinary assumption or hypothetical condition has a positive,
negative, or neutral impact on value.

Standards Rule 10-2

Each written business valuation or intangible asset appraisal report must be
prepared in accordance with one of the following options and prominently state
which option is used: Appraisal Report or Restricted Use Appraisal Report.

Comment: When the intended users include parties other than the client,
an appraisal report must be provided. When the only intended user is the
client, a restricted use appraisal report may be provided. The essential difference between these options is in the content and level of information
provided. An appraiser may use any other label in addition to, but not in
place of, the label set forth in this Standard for the type of report provided.
The report content and level of information requirements set forth in this
Standard are minimums for both types of report. An appraiser must ensure
that any intended user of the appraisal is not misled and that the report
complies with the applicable content requirements set forth in this Standards Rule. A party receiving a copy of an appraisal report does not
become an intended user of the appraisal unless the client identifies such
party as an intended user as part of the assignment.

a. The content of an Appraisal Report must be consistent with the intended
use of the appraisal and, at a minimum

i. state the identity of the client and any intended users, by name or type

Comment: An appraiser must use care when identifying the client to ensure
a clear understanding and to avoid violations of the Confidentiality section
of the ethics rule. In those rare instances where the client wishes to remain

anonymous, an appraiser must still document the identity of the client in the workfile, but may omit the client's identity in the report.

    ii. state the intended use of the appraisal

   iii. summarize information sufficient to identify the business or intangible asset appraised

Comment: The identification information must include property characteristics relevant to the assignment.

   iv. state as relevant to the assignment, the extent to which the business interest or the interest in the intangible asset appraised contains elements of ownership control, including the basis for that determination

    v. state the purpose of the appraisal, including the standard of value (definition) and its source

Comment: Stating the standard of value requires the definition itself and any comments needed to clearly indicate to the reader how the definition is being applied.

   vi. state the effective date of the appraisal and the date of the report

Comment: The effective date of the appraisal establishes the context for the value opinion, while the date of the report indicates whether the perspective of the appraiser on the market or property use conditions as of the effective date of the appraisal was prospective, current, or retrospective.

  vii. summarize sufficient information to disclose to the client and any intended users of the appraisal and the scope of work used to develop the appraisal

Comment: This requirement is to ensure that the client and intended users whose expected reliance on an appraisal may be affected by the extent of the appraiser's investigation are properly informed and are not misled as to the scope of work. The appraiser has the burden of proof to support the scope of work decision and the level of information included in a report.

  viii. state all assumptions, hypothetical conditions, and limiting conditions that affected the analyses, opinions, and conclusions

Comment: Typical or ordinary assumptions and limiting conditions may be grouped together in an identified section of the report. An extraordinary assumption or hypothetical condition must be disclosed in conjunction with statements of each opinion or conclusion that was affected.

ix. summarize the information analyzed, the appraisal procedures followed, and the reasoning that supports the analyses, opinions, and conclusions

Comment: The appraiser must attempt to determine that the information provided is sufficient for the client and intended users to adequately understand the rationale for the opinion and conclusions.

x. state and explain any permitted departures from specific requirements of Standard 9, and the reason for excluding any of the usual valuation approaches

Comment: An appraisal report must include sufficient information to indicate that the appraiser complied with the requirements of Standard 9, including any permitted departures from the specific requirements. The amount of detail required will vary with the significance of the information to the appraisal. When the departure rule is invoked, the assignment is deemed to be a limited appraisal. Use of the term limited appraisal makes clear that the assignment involved something less than or different from the work that could have and would have been completed if departure had not been invoked. The report of a limited appraisal must contain a prominent section that clearly identifies the extent of the appraisal process performed and the departures taken.

xi. include a signed certification in accordance with Standards Rule 10-3

b. The content of a Restricted Use Appraisal Report must be for client use only and consistent with the intended use of the appraisal and, at a minimum:

i. state the identity of the client

Comment: An appraiser must use care when identifying the client to ensure a clear understanding and to avoid violations of the Confidentiality section of the Ethics Rule.

ii. state the intended use of the appraisal

Comment: The intended use of the appraisal must be client use only.

iii. state information sufficient to identify the business or intangible asset appraised

Comment: The identification information must include property characteristics relevant to the assignment.

iv. state as relevant to the assignment, the extent to which the business interest or the interest in the intangible asset appraised contains elements of ownership control, including the basis for that determination

vi. state the purpose of the appraisal, including the standard of value (definition) and its source

vii. state the effective date of the appraisal and the date of the report

Comment: The effective date of the appraisal establishes the context for the value opinion, while the date of the report indicates whether the perspective of the appraiser on the market or property use conditions as of the effective date of the appraisal was prospective, current, or retrospective.

vii. state the extent of the process of collecting, confirming, and reporting data or refer to an assignment agreement retained in the appraiser's workfile, which describes the scope of work to be performed

viii. state all assumptions, hypothetical conditions, and limiting conditions that affect the analyses, opinions, and conclusions

Comment: Typical or ordinary assumptions and limiting conditions may be grouped together in an identified section of the report. An extraordinary assumption or hypothetical condition must be disclosed in conjunction with statements of each opinion or conclusion that was affected.

ix. state the appraisal procedures followed, and the value opinion(s) and conclusion(s), and reference the workfile

Comment: An appraiser must maintain a specific, coherent workfile in support of a restricted use appraisal report. The contents of the workfile must be sufficient for the appraiser to produce an appraisal report. The file must be available for inspection by the client (or the client's representatives, such as those engaged to complete an appraisal review), such third parties as may be authorized by due process of law, and a duly authorized professional peer review committee.

x. state and explain any permitted departures from applicable specific requirements of Standard 9; state the exclusion of any of the usual valuation approaches; and state a prominent use restriction that limits use of the report to the client and warns that the appraiser's opinions and conclusions set forth in the report cannot be understood properly without additional information in the appraiser's workfile

Comment: When the Departure Rule is invoked, the assignment is deemed to be a limited appraisal. Use of the term limited appraisal makes it clear that the assignment involved something less than or different from the work that could have and would have been completed if departure had not been invoked. The report of a limited appraisal must contain a prominent section that clearly identifies the extent of the appraisal process performed and the departures taken. The restricted use appraisal report is for client use only. Before entering into an agreement, the appraiser should establish with the client the situations where this type of report is to be used, and should ensure that the client understands the restricted utility of the restricted use appraisal report.

    xi. include a signed certification in accordance with Standards Rule 10-3

Standards Rule 10-3

Each written business or intangible asset appraisal report must contain a signed certification that is similar in content to the following:

I certify that, to the best of my knowledge and belief:

- The statements of fact contained in this report are true and correct.

- The reported analyses, opinions, and conclusions are limited only by the reported assumptions and limiting conditions, and are my personal, impartial, and unbiased professional analyses, opinions, and conclusions.

- I have no (or the specified) present or prospective interest in the property that is the subject of this report, and I have no (or the specified) personal interest with respect to the parties involved.

- I have no bias with respect to the property that is the subject of this report or to the parties involved with this assignment.

- My engagement in this assignment was not contingent upon developing or reporting predetermined results.

- My compensation for completing this assignment is not contingent upon the development or reporting of a predetermined value or direction in value that favors the cause of the client, the amount of the value opinion, the attainment of a stipulated result, or the occurrence of a subsequent event directly related to the intended use of this appraisal.

- My analyses, opinions, and conclusions were developed, and this report has been prepared, in conformity with the *Uniform Standards of Professional Appraisal Practice.*

- No one provided significant professional assistance to the person signing this report. (If there are exceptions, the name of each and the significant professional assistance must be stated.)

Standards Rule 10-4

An oral business or intangible asset appraisal report must, at a minimum, address the substantive matters set forth in Standards Rule 10-2(a).

> *Comment:* See Record Keeping in the Ethics Rule for corresponding requirements.

Standards Rule 10-5

An appraiser who signs a business or intangible asset appraisal report prepared by another, even under the label appraisal reviewer, must accept full responsibility for the contents of the report.

> *Comment:* This requirement is directed to the employer or supervisor signing the report of an employee or subcontractor. The employer or supervisor signing the report is as responsible as the individual preparing the appraisal for the content and conclusions of the appraisal and the report. Using a conditional label next to the signature of the employer or supervisor or signing a form report on the line over the words appraisal reviewer does not exempt that individual from adherence to these Standards.

APPENDIX
C

Information and Documents Requested for Sample Company

[Note: This is an initial document request and is general. Once the documents are received and reviewed a follow-up detail document request is usually issued.]

A. Financial Statements

1. Annual financial statements for the years ended December 31, 1996–2000: balance sheets, statements of operations and shareholders' equity, statements of cash flows and footnotes for each period.

2. Copies of detailed general ledgers for the fiscal years ending December 31, 1996–2000.

3. Income tax returns for the last five years.

4. List of subsidiary and/or financial interests in other companies including relevant financial statements.

B. Other Financial Data

1. Detailed fixed asset listing (This list should provide date of acquisition, cost, current physical condition, etc.) and depreciation schedules, including any appraisals with respect to the fair market value of fixed assets.

2. Aging of accounts receivable as of December 31, 2000.

3. Aged accounts payable listing as of December 31, 2000.

4. Copies of all notes payable and interest bearing debt, including lines of credit and other financing, as of December 31, 2000. Include:
   - Date of Indebtedness
   - Repayment Terms and Interest Rate
   - Holder of Indebtedness

6. A detailed inventory listing of all items at cost and fair market value as of December 31, 2000.

7. Detailed listing of revenues broken down by product line or process on an annual basis for the last five years.

8. Any other existing contracts (employment agreements, covenants not to compete, supplier and franchise agreements, royalty agreements, equipment and/or capital leases or rental contracts, loan agreements, labor contracts, employee benefit and profit sharing plans, etc.).

9. Compensation schedule for officers, including all benefits and personal expenses ("Perks") for the last five years (include copies of all W-2s and form 1099s).

10. Provide an accounting of all pension and profit sharing plans, including a summary of the ending balances of all participant accounts as of December 31, 2000, and the amount of annual matching or profit sharing contributions allocated to shareholders for each of the last five years.

11. Schedule of insurance in force (key-man life, property, casualty, and liability).

12. Schedules of Cost of Sales and Operating expenses, if not detailed on the income statements for the fiscal years ended December 31, 1996-2000.

13. Copies of any budgets or projections prepared by management or other parties.

C. Company and Other Documents Relating to Rights of Owner

1. Articles of incorporation and corporate minutes for the last five years.

2. Copies of all current offers for purchase of the company. This would include a list of transactions currently being discussed or proposed.

3. Copies of all valuations prepared or performed with respect to the company, or individual assets.

4. Copies of the most current existing buy/sell agreements, options to purchase stock, rights of refusal, or other documents attesting to the ownership rights of the interest being valued.

D. Other Information

1. Brief history, including details of any changes in ownership and/or bona fide offers received.

2. Brief description of business, including position relative to competition and any factors that make the business unique.

3. Organization chart and list of all employees and position at the company.

4. Information on related-party transactions, including leases and related party purchases.

5. Marketing literature (catalogs, brochures, advertisements, etc.).

6. List of competitors, broken down by location, including the relative size, and any other relevant factors.

7. List of locations where licensed to do business.

8. List of states and/or countries in which the company operates.

9. List of key personnel with age, position, compensation, length of service, and prior experience.

10. Current resumes of management personnel.

11. Name and telephone number of trade associations to which the company belongs or would be eligible for membership.

12. Any existing indicators of asset values, including insurance property and casualty policies and any appraisals that have been done.

13. List of patents, copyrights, trademarks, and other intangible assets.

14. Any contingent or unrecorded liabilities (pending lawsuit, compliance requirements, warranty or other product liability, etc.).

15. Any regulatory filings or correspondence.

16. Breakdown of suppliers of the company's raw materials for the last five years.

17. Breakdown of sales by customer, at least for the top ten customers, for the last five years.

18. Current resumes of key personnel.

19. Copies of all leases.

20. Any agreements and documentation pertaining to amount due from officer/shareholder on balance sheet as of December 31, 1999.

21. Copy of business plan.

22. List of stockholders and their percentage of ownership as of December 31, 1999.

Summary of Common Ratios Used By Business Appraisers

Financial statement ratios fall into four general categories: (1) liquidity ratios, (2) activity ratios, (3) leverage ratios, and (4) profitability ratios. It is suggested that these ratios be calculated over a number of years to spot trends and to also compare them to industry standards.

Liquidity Ratios

Liquidity ratios are used to indicate the extent to which a company may have either inadequate or excessive working capital. There are two primary liquidity ratios: (1) the current ratio, and (2) the acid test ratio. The current ratio is defined as current assets divided by current liabilities. It is a commonly used liquidity ratio. The acid test (quick ratio) is more conservative because it considers only assets that can be readily liquidated. It is defined as total cash, cash equivalents, and accounts receivable divided by current liabilities.

Activity Ratios

Activity ratios measure how efficiently assets of a business are being used. The primary activity ratios are accounts receivable turnover, which estimates the average collection period for credit sales; inventory turnover, which indicates the average number of days to sell inventory; and asset turnover (sales divided by total assets which shows how efficiently the company's assets are producing sales; and sales to net fixed assets, which indicate the efficiency that fixed assets are producing sales).

- $$\text{Inventory Turnover} = \frac{\text{Average Inventory} \times 365 \text{ Days}}{\text{Cost of Goods Sold}}$$

- $$\text{Sales to Net Fixed Assets} = \frac{\text{Net Sales}}{\text{Property, Plant, and Equipment}}$$

- Accounts Receivable Turnover =
$$\frac{\text{Average Accounts Receivable} \times 365 \text{ Days}}{\text{Net Credit Sales}}$$

- $$\text{Asset Turnover} = \frac{\text{Net Sales}}{\text{Total Assets}}$$

Leverage Ratios

Leverage ratios measure the level of leverage of a business. The primary leverage ratios are the equity ratio (owner's equity as a percent of total assets) and the long-term debt to equity ratio. The long-term debt to total equity ratio indicates the extent of debt financing used to fund company assets. These ratios help indicate the risk of a business. As a general rule, the lower the equity relative to the total assets and to the long-term debt, the greater the degree of risk of the business. These ratios may also indicate borrowing power since ratios well below industry average may indicate unused borrowing power. There is also a ratio times interest earned that indicates the ability of the company and its operations to remove interest charges on the debt.

- $$\text{Long-Term Debt to Equity Ratio} = \frac{\text{Long-Term Debt}}{\text{Stockholder Equity}}$$

- $$\text{Times Interest Earned} = \frac{\text{Earnings before Interest and Taxes}}{\text{Interest Expense}}$$

Profitability Ratios

There are two categories of profitability ratios: (1) income statement profitability ratios, and (2) rates of return ratios. Income statement profitability ratios are usually expressed as a percentage of sales. For example, the gross profit margin of a business is defined as the gross profit divided by net sales. Common rates of return ratios include pretax earnings/sales, pretax earnings/total equity, and pretax earnings/total assets.

The measure of profitability used in profitability ratios may include the following terms:

EDIT.   Earnings before depreciation, interest, and taxes.

EBIT.   Earnings before interest and taxes

EBT.   Earnings before taxes

EBDT.   Earnings before depreciation and taxes

Net Income. Earnings after interest, depreciation, and taxes.

APPENDIX

E

Comprehensive List of Common Terms and Definitions Used by Business Appraisers

Business valuation professionals use various terms that a lawyer handling a family law case should understand. The following list provides the terms most commonly used by business valuators and provides their definitions. These terms have been obtained from a variety of sources including: The Appraisal Foundation, the American Society of Appraisers, The Appraisal Institute, and other recognized appraisal publications.

Acquisition Premium

A premium, over and above the standard control premium, associated with a unique buyer and a unique seller that would relate to a unique set of beneficial synergies or circumstances between the buyer and seller. This premium would not be considered when the objective is to determine the fair market value of a business.

Adjusted Book Value

The value which results after one or more asset or liability amounts are added, deleted, or changed from the respective amounts reported on the company's financial statements.

Appraisal

The act or process of estimating value. It is synonymous with valuation. Also, an appraisal is the stated result of valuing a property, making a cost estimate, forecasting earnings, or any combination of two or more of these stated results.

Appraisal Approach

A general way of determining value using one or more specific valuation methods (See Asset-Based Approach, Income Approach, and Market Approach).

Appraisal Method

Within approaches, a specific way to determine value.

Appraisal Procedure

The act, manner, and technique of performing the steps of a valuation method.

Asset-Based Approach

A general way of determining a value indication of the business's assets and/or equity interest using one or more methods based directly on the value of the assets of the business, less its liabilities.

Beta

A factor used in the Capital Asset Pricing Model to measure a certain type of risk. Beta is a function of the relationship between the return of an individual security and the return on the market as measured by the return on a broad market index, such as the S&P 500.

Book Value

With respect to assets, the capitalized cost of an asset less accumulated depreciation, depletion, or amortization as it appears on the books of account of the enterprise. With respect to a business enterprise, the difference between total assets (net of depreciation, depletion, and amortization) and total liabilities of an enterprise as they appear on the balance sheet.

Business Equity

The interests, benefits, and rights inherent in the ownership of the business enterprise, or a part thereof, in any form (including but not limited to capital stock, partnership interests, cooperatives, sole proprietorships, options, and warrants).

Capital Asset Pricing Model

The capital asset pricing model (CAPM) is a theory which shows how market rates of return for various assets are related to their systematic risks. This model provides a basis for one of the most common methods used by analysts to estimate the appropriate present value discount rate for use in the discounted cash flow valuation method.

Capital Structure

The composition of the invested capital of a business entity.

Capitalization

This term has three meanings: (1) The conversion of income into value, or (2) the capital structure of a business enterprise, or (3) the recognition of an expenditure as a capital asset rather than a period expense.

Capitalization Factor

Any multiple or divisor used to convert income into value.

Capitalization Rate

Any divisor (usually expressed as a percentage) that is used to convert income into value.

Cash Flow Analysis

A study of anticipated movement of cash into or out of an investment.

Common Size Statements

Statements in which each line is expressed as a percentage of the total (percentage of total assets on a balance sheet, or a percentage of sales on an income statement). This is usually the first step in ratio analysis of financial statements.

Control

The power to direct the management and policies of an enterprise.

Control Premium

The additional value inherent in the control interest of an enterprise, as contrasted to a minority interest, that reflects its power of control.

Cost of Capital

The amount of expected return that is required to attract investment. It depends on the general level of interest rates and the amount of premium for risk that the market demands, as well as the risks attributable to the subject business.

Discount Rate

A rate of return used to convert a monetary sum, payable or receivable in the future, into present value.

EBIT

Earnings before interest and taxes.

EBDIT

Earnings before depreciation (and other noncash charges), interest, and taxes.

Earnings Forecast

An estimate or forecast of, a measure of, the future net monetary return, or returns, derivable from something owned, or considered as being owned.

Economic Income

Any measure of income inflow into the subject being valued which can be converted into value through either discounting or capitalization at appropriate rates. This could include net revenues, net operating income, net cash flow, and so on.

Effective Date

The date on which the appraiser's opinion of value applies. Also referred to as the Appraisal Date or Valuation Date.

Enterprise Goodwill

That portion of the goodwill of a business not based on the ongoing personal efforts of the business-owning spouse but on the other intangible value of the enterprise. Enterprise goodwill will transfer upon the sale of the business and will outlast the divorcing spouse's involvement with the business enterprise.

Equity

The owner's interest in property after deduction of all liabilities. As an accounting convention the owner's equity equals assets minus liabilities.

Equity Risk Premium

Rate in excess of a risk-free rate to compensate and otherwise persuade an investor to invest in instruments with a higher degree of probable incurred risk.

Excess Earnings

That level of economic income above and beyond the fair rate of return on the net asset base used to generate that economic income. Also called Excess Economic Income.

Fair Market Value

The amount at which property would change hands between a willing seller and a willing buyer when neither is acting under a compulsion and when both have reasonable knowledge of the relevant facts.

Going Concern Value

The value of a business based on the premise that the business will continue to operate consistently with its intended business purpose as opposed to being liquidated. It also means the intangible elements of value in a business enterprise resulting from factors such as having a trained workforce, an operational plant, and the necessary licenses, systems, and procedures in place.

Goodwill

That intangible asset which arises as a result of name, reputation, customer patronage, location, products, and similar factors that have not been separately identified and/or valued but which generate economic benefits. According to Illinois case law, enterprise goodwill must be distinguished from personal goodwill.

Income Approach

A general way of determining a value indication of a business or equity interest using one or more methods wherein a value is determined by converting anticipated benefits.

Intangible Property/Assets

Nonphysical assets, including but not limited to franchises, trademarks, patents, copyrights, goodwill, equities, mineral rights, securities, and contracts, as distinguished from physical assets such as property and equipment.

Invested Capital

The sum of the debt and equity in an enterprise on a long-term basis.

Investment Value

Value to a particular investor based on individual investment requirements, as distinguished from the concept of market value, which is impersonal and detached. Also known as synergistic value.

Letter Stock (Restricted Stock)

Stock identical to a freely traded stock of a public company except for the fact that it is restricted from trading on the open market for a certain period of time. The duration of the restriction varies from one situation to another.

Liquidation Value

The net amount that can be realized if the business is terminated and the assets are sold piecemeal. Liquidation can either be orderly or forced.

Majority

An ownership position greater than 50% of the voting interest in the enterprise.

Majority Control

The degree of control provided by a majority position.

Market Approach

A general way of determining a value indication of a business or equity interest using one or more methods that compare the subject to similar businesses, business ownership interests, or investments that have been sold.

Marketability

The ability to convert an asset to cash very quickly, at a minimal cost, and with a high degree of certainty of realizing the expected amount of proceeds.

Marketability Discount

An amount or percentage deducted from an equity interest to reflect the lack of marketability.

Minority Interest

An ownership position less than 50% of the voting interest in an enterprise.

Minority Discount

An amount or percentage deducted from the pro rata share of the value of the entire business, which reflects the absence of some or all the powers of control.

Net Assets

Total assets less total liabilities.

Net Income

Revenues less expenses, including income taxes at the entity level.

Net Working Capital

The amount by which current assets exceed current liabilities.

Normalized Financial Information

Financial information adjusted for items not representative of the present going concern status of the business or items which distort the financial results of a business for other than economic reasons.

Pass-Through Entities

Businesses that pass through earning to their owners, generally subject only to federal taxation at the owner's personal income tax rate. Such entities include S corporations and LLCs.

Personal Goodwill

That component of the goodwill of the business which is dependent upon the ongoing personal efforts of the business-owning spouse. Personal goodwill will not transfer upon the sale of the business and will cease when the business-owning spouse is no longer involved with the business. However, in some cases, it is even possible to transfer this goodwill.

Premise of Value

An assumption regarding the most likely set of transactional circumstances that may be applicable to the subject valuation. Premises of value include fair market value in continued use and orderly liquidation value. The normal premise of value in divorce cases is fair market value in continued use.

Rate of Return

An amount of income and/or change in value realized or expected on an investment, expressed as a percentage of that investment.

Replacement Cost New

The current cost of a similar new item having the nearest equivalent utility as the item being appraised.

Report

Any communication, written or oral, of an appraisal, review, or consulting service that is transmitted to the client upon completion of an assignment.

Report Date

The date of the valuation report. Generally, the report date will differ from the appraisal date.

Reproduction New Cost

The current cost of an identical new item.

Risk

The degree of uncertainty as to the realization of expected future returns.

Risk-Free Rate

Rate of return available on financial instruments, which are considered to have virtually no possibility of default (e.g., U.S. Treasury Bills and Notes).

Rule of Thumb

A mathematical relationship between or among a number of variables based on experience, observation, hearsay, or a combination of these, usually applicable to a specific industry.

Standard of Value

The definition of the type of value being sought. It can be legally mandated or may be a function of the wishes of the parties involved. It usually reflects an assumption as to who will be the buyer and who will be the seller. It addresses the question: "Value to whom?"

Strategic Acquisition

A purchase by a buyer who expects to benefit from synergies with the purchased company such as: horizontal and vertical integration; elimination of redundant overhead; or better prices through reduced competition.

Subject Company

The company being valued.

Valuation Ratio/Multiple

A factor wherein a value or price serves as the numerator and financial, operating, or physical data serve as the denominator (for example, price/earnings ratio).

Weighted Average Cost of Capital (WACC)

The weighted average of the cost of each component in the structure of a company, each weighted based on the market value of that capital component, such as, the weighted average of the costs of all financing sources on the company's capital structure.

Index

Default judgment, 52
Defendant, 52
Defined benefit plans, 9, 52, 90
Defined contribution plans, 9, 52, 90
Dependency deduction, 113–116
Depositions, 18, 53
Depreciation schedules, 36
Designation rule (alimony), 67–68
Direct examination, 53
Discounts, 191–203
 blockage discounts, 198
 key-person discounts, 197–198
 lack of voting rights, discount for, 197
 marketability discounts, 193–197, 265
 minority discounts, 192–193, 266
 personal goodwill discounts, 199–203
Discounted future earnings method, 171, 173–174
Discount rate, 178, 262
Discovery, 16–28, 53
Discovery process, 156–157
Discretionary earnings method, 185–186
Dissipation, 44–46
Dissolution of marriage, 53, 231–234
Divorce decree, 53
Divorce lawyer, finding, 4–8
Documentation (in net worth analysis), 34–35
Due diligence, 243

Earnings forecast, 263
EBDIT, 262
EBIT, 185, 262
EBITDA, 171, 185
EBT, 185
Economic Growth and Tax Relief Reconciliation Act of 2001, 142
Economic income, 263
Effective date, 263
Emancipation, 53
Employees, former, 35
Employee Stock Option Plans (ESOPs), 9

Employee stock purchase plans, 222–223, 225
Employer(s):
 economic benefits received from, 35–38
 obtaining information from spouse's, 25, 27
Employment contracts, 20
Enterprise goodwill, 263
Entertainment and travel, 38
Equitable distribution, 53
Equitable division of property, 29
Equity, 261, 263
Equity risk premium, 175, 263
Escrow accounts, 8
ESOPs (Employee Stock Option Plans), 9
Estate documents, 22
Estate of Andrews v. Commissioner, 220
Estate of Bright v. United States, 220
Estate of Klauss v. Commissioner, 177
Estate of Lee v. Commissioner, 220
Estate of Woodbury G. Andrews, 197
Estimated tax payments, allocation of, 129–130
Evidence, 53
Excess earnings, 263
Excess earnings method, 189–190
Exercise (stock options), 224
Ex parte, 53
Experts:
 failure to hire qualified, 207
 hiring, 147–150
Expiration date (of stock option), 224
Extraordinary assumptions, 244

Fair market value, 162, 264
Filing status, 107–116
 and allocation of income in separate return, 110–112
 and assignment of income doctrine, 112–113
 and dependency exemptions, 113–116
 head of household, 109–110

and IRA deduction, 113
Financial Accounting Standards No. 123 (FAS 123), 228
Financial disclosure statement, 40–44
Financial expert, selecting a, 16–18
Financial statements, 253
 normalization of, 166–168
 in notice to produce, 20
Financial statement ratios, 257–258
Forensic accountant, 16
Forfeiture, risk of, 223–224
Form 2441, 136–138
Form 4506, 26
Form 8332, 114–116, 139
Form 8839, 141
Form 8857, 134, 135
Form W-2, 25, 140
401 (k) plans, 9, 90
Frye v. United States, 152

Gambling expenses, 45
Gifts from third parties, 29
Going concern value, 264
Goodwill, 199, 264
 enterprise, 263
 personal, 266
Grabowski, Roger, 176
Granting (of stock option), 224
Grounds for divorce, 53
Guardian ad litem, 53
Guideline company method, 182–184

Head of household, filing as, 109–110
Health insurance, 21
Hearing, 53
Hold harmless, 53
Home, see Personal residence
Homeowner's insurance, 8, 28
House accounts, 36–37
Households, separation of, 63
Hypothetical conditions, 244

IBA, see Institute for Business Appraisers
Ibbotson Associates, 175–176
Illinois, 31–32
Incentive stock options (ISOs), 222, 225